The American Enlightenment, 1750–1820

The American Enlightenment
1750–1820

Robert A. Ferguson

HARVARD UNIVERSITY PRESS

Cambridge, Massachusetts
London, England
1997

PRINTED IN CANADA

First Harvard University Press paperback edition, 1997

Library of Congress Cataloging-in-Publication Data

Ferguson, Robert A., 1942–
    The American enlightenment, 1750–1820 / Robert A. Ferguson. — 1st Harvard University
Press pbk. ed.
        p.   cm.
    Originally appeared in The Cambridge history of American literature, vol. 1, 1590–1820,
published by Cambridge University Press in 1994.
    Includes bibliographical references (p.   ) and index.
    ISBN 0-674-02322-6 (paper)
    1. American literature—Colonial period, ca. 1600–1775—History and criticism.
    2. American literature—Revolutionary period, 1775–1783—History and criticism.
    3. United States—History—Revolution, 1775–1783—Literature and the revolution.
    4. Politics and literature—United States—History—18th century.   5. Politics and
literature—United States—History—19th century.   6. Revolutionary literature,
American—History and criticism.   7. American Literature—1783–1850—History and criticism.   8. United States—Intellectual life—18th century.   9. United States—Intellectual
life—1783–1865.   10. Enlightenment—United States.
I. Title.
PS193.F47   1997   96-46816
810.9'002—DC21   CIP

For
John Paul Russo

CONTENTS

PREFACE

When I was asked in 1984 to write a short literary history of the American Enlightenment for a new *Cambridge History of American Literature,* it was with the understanding that I would limit myself to intellectual texts written between 1750 and 1820. The subject certainly seemed large enough for a 60,000-word monograph that would be linked with related contributions in a general volume on early American literature. Thirteen years later, half again as long as planned, and standing alone as a separate publication for the first time, *The American Enlightenment, 1750–1820* should be read with two elementary warnings in mind. First, the convenient organizational separation between political writings and more formally imaginative works should not be taken as an analytical divide in regarding fact and fiction in the period. Hannah Foster's epistolary novel *The Coquette,* like many sermons of the late 1790s, speaks directly to the decline of the clergy and to the vexed debate over prosperity and virtue in republican culture. The many voices of Charles Brockden Brown's Gothic romance *Wieland, or the Transformation* touch on the acrimony between Federalists and Republicans as surely as any political pamphlet at the turn of the century. If the scholarship of the last twenty years has taught us anything, it is that the relation between literary and historical studies must be seen as an intrinsic one.

My second caveat has to do with the writing of literary history as an enterprise. I found the assignment much harder to complete than I had imagined it would be. Growing skepticism about the accuracy and representativeness of dominant views, new questions about canonicity and about the artifice in any narrative perspective, the rejection of overly simplistic constructs of periodicity and of national identity are healthy initiatives in current literary interpretation, but they all compound the problems of the literary historian who must still tell a story. If *The American Enlightenment, 1750–1820* is longer and more complicated as a narrative than originally planned, it is because I have tried to incorporate "the telling of history" from different directions.

Those directions are manifold. The complicated nexus of religious and secular voices in the early republic cannot be recorded once and for all; it must, instead, be assembled in different ways with several bearings in mind. In a similar vein, the available texts and more tenuous voices of the day must be taken and seen in juncture, one with the other, if we are to come to grips with the unprecedented and often bizarre nature of an emerging democratic culture in eighteenth-century America. Finding the voices within the texts requires a careful sense of validations. The texts, though all-important, are the artifacts of an earlier but still shadowing presence, the voices of conflict in an age of revolution. There is, as well, a strange tonal juxtaposition to be identified and worked through from both ends in many of these writings. The expression of the loftiest reason, a benchmark of literary attainment in eighteenth-century writing, is often found cheek by jowl with a consuming rage and anger over particulars, so much so as to constitute the beginning of a permanent style in American politics—a style that brings out the best and the worst in users and receivers who inflate the variables of hope and dread.

Unmasking and understanding the originating juxtaposition of reason and rage in American political rhetoric are important goals of this study. We tend to forget that anger as well as optimism formed the original United States of America and that one result has been a series of contradictory notions of the citizen in new world republicanism. Most famously, we have J. Hector St. John de Crèvecoeur's response to his own question "What Is an American?" when, in *Letters from an American Farmer*, he claimed that "the American is a new man, who acts upon new principles; he must therefore entertain new ideas, and form new opinions." This wildly expansive aspect of American identity depends on the aspiration and presumed spread of knowledge, but there is another side of Enlightenment ideology, one based on the priorities of prudence, mechanism, design, and arrangement. Several years before Crèvecoeur, "the Pennsylvania Farmer" John Dickinson had already given voice to this alternative when he observed, "It will be impossible to determine whether an *American's* character is most distinguishable, for his loyalty to his Sovereign, his duty to his mother country, his love of freedom, or his affection for his native soil."

How should Americans aspire and expand together while maintaining the delicate balances of nation, region, locality, and individualism that were central to the colonial experience and quickly became even more central to the federated experiment? There has never been a simple answer to this question, and the conflations that have allowed partial responses have also stimulated never-ending charges and countercharges of conspiracy and betrayal. Nor are these responses surprising. Enlightenment thought assumed a unified answer to central problems or an unforeseen solution somewhere in the long view; it could never encompass the prospect of ultimate disagreement. Most Americans, in consequence, have had just two rhetorical recourses in conflict: *either* you misunderstand *or* you have turned your back on the truth for malicious reasons. Where mere misunderstanding ends, the politics of anger begins, and American leaders have always known how to manipulate the dividing line by playing on the separating aspects of their constituencies. To understand this process in its origins, we must look beyond the analogies that have made the citizen a projection of union and think more of American identity as a jumble of available characteristics shaped into useful combinations.

For all of these reasons, the literary historian of today must ask the reader to work harder than heretofore. In writing this history in the present tense, I urge you to enter into a particular awareness of history as subject and as enterprise. "Presentism" is a term that historians often use to denigrate a misleading application of contemporary standards to the past, and the warning has considerable merit; the dangers of inappropriate application always remain with us. My own use, however, reaches for another reality. Whatever the dangers, the imposition of the present on the past is unavoidable—so unavoidable that it is well for writer and reader to recall and maintain that limitation together.

Contemporary appropriations of the American Revolution occur in every era. That is what it means, at least in part, to have a legacy. But if the Revolution has changed with each succeeding generation, acknowledgment of this fact does not release the historian—even the historian as literary critic—into a realm of unbounded speculation. Instead, the hazards of an inevitable ahistoricism should force writer and reader back upon the joined integrity and volatility of primary materials. In this sense, use of the present tense signifies both the slippage in any ordering of the past and the sometimes contradictory impulse to recover history in the making.

Literary history in particular welcomes the present. It dwells upon extant texts, and I try to use that analytical convention to reach for more of the original excitement that Revolutionary writings provoked. Not fixed accomplishment but the messiness of ongoing event and the related immediacies of thought and act drive the often hesitant language of the period. The now arcane genres of sermon, pamphlet, and public document—not to mention the forgotten placards of ritualized protests—are fluid forms evolving under immense cultural pressure, not rigid categories in a static discourse.

What do we really know about the Revolution? First and foremost, we have the writings, the related texts, and other fabrications of those figures who participated in and witnessed events. Second, we have the so-called facts gathered about those events, then and later. Third, we have the contested ground of the history of interpretation regarding the period and its thought; and fourth, we have what might be called more generally the history of ideas. Like every scholar, I seek to combine the four elements in effective and graceful ways, and I try to do so with the many previous approaches to this cumulative record in mind. (The bibliography to this volume supplies a partial record of my own indebtedness.) At the same time, and in a competing goal, I mean to remind you of simplifications in the combinations themselves. The past is always more complicated than we can know. The most basic primary text is a gloss on some underlying incident, and each new layer of writing contributes to the studied appearance of history.

I try to entertain these difficulties within several recognitions. Current awareness of cultural diversity makes this a good moment for re-examining national origins. Then, too, the writings and speeches of the period are in themselves more rhetorically complex and more fully available to critical consciousness than many have realized. I believe that we are still learning how to read the basic texts of the Revolution and that the need for scrutiny now is all the more engaging because of a growing intellectual awareness of the dialectics in Enlightenment thought. This scrutiny, in turn, benefits from a singular piece of national good fortune: the federal union began in a moment when its citizens took ideas seriously—not always the case in American history. If this study opens any of these ideas to fresh inquiry for others, it will have served its most important purpose.

In the community of scholars, six have been more than communal during the course of this project. Ann Douglas and Richard Posner read and commented with care on parts of the manuscript. The general editor of the Cambridge history, Sacvan Bercovitch, and one immediate collaborator, Michael T. Gilmore, made important suggestions throughout. John Paul Russo and Priscilla Parkhurst Ferguson tested every word more than once. Separate but together, these figures made as fine a "committee of correspondence" as one could hope for.

I have been helped, as well, by the chance to place some rudimentary thoughts for this project in print, where other scholars have been able to comment and improve upon them. These items, for which I thank the editors and publishers, include: "'We Hold These Truths': Strategies of Control in the Literature of the Founders," *Reconstructing American Literary History,* ed. Sacvan Bercovitch (Cambridge, Mass.: Harvard University Press, 1986), pp. 1–29; "Ideology and the Framing of the Constitution," *Early American Literature* 22 (Fall 1987), 157–165; "'We Do Ordain and Establish': The Constitution as Literary Text," *William and Mary Law Review* 29 (Fall 1987), 3–25; and "'What Is Enlightenment?' Some American Answers," *American Literary History* 1 (Summer 1989), 245–272.

The American Enlightenment, 1750–1820

I

❦

FINDING THE REVOLUTION

I

Understanding the American Revolution is a literary pursuit, and John Adams assumes as much in his own famous summary of the event. "The Revolution," Adams insists in 1818, "was in the minds and hearts of the people," and those who would seek it must collect and search "all the records, pamphlets, newspapers, and even handbills, which in any way contributed to change the temper and views of the people." By concentrating on this change in ideas, Adams makes *"the real American Revolution,"* as he calls it, the central event of the American Enlightenment, and he turns comprehension of it into a permanent test of cultural well-being. In urging this understanding upon "young men of letters in all of the States," he also warns them against superficial explanations that stress "the gloriole of individual gentlemen." The transformations in thought that bind Americans together in 1776 and after take place beneath the surface of events. Only by a diligent search can one hope to find the deeper truth of *"radical change in the principles, opinions, sentiments, and affections of the people."*

This challenge, already problematic in 1818, remains the challenge of today. The task is to recover as much as possible of the Revolution, itself the greatest literary achievement of eighteenth-century America, while keeping in mind the gaps between surviving word and original thought, text and lost context, assertion and expectation, story and event. If *"the real American Revolution"* resists a narrative of heroics to reside elsewhere – in the minds and hearts of the people – how does one reach that level through extant writings? The primacy of textual evidence must be balanced against the incomplete and equivocal nature of that evidence. The relation of writer to text to audience must be treated as a variable and not as a fixed sequence.

Some of the difficulties over interpretation are already clear at the time that Adams writes. In 1815, Adams and Thomas Jefferson concur that "the most essential documents, the debates and deliberations in Congress from 1774 to 1783 were all in secret, and are now lost forever." They agree further that those few speeches that have found their way into print appear "very different" from the original performances that they themselves heard. "Who shall write the history of the American revolution?" Adams asks. "Who can write it? Who will ever be able to write it?" Jefferson's response is blunt and to the point: "Who can write it? And who ever will be able to write it? Nobody; except merely its external facts." Of course, the very awareness of difficulty also stimulates a battle over approximations in interpretation.

Adams and Jefferson fully understand that the Revolution *will* be told, and they compete with each other in the knowledge that their own tellings will control subsequent thought. This process, too, is part of the literature of the Revolution – part of the later movement of ideas in the minds and hearts of the people. Adams, in particular, fears the story already being told. "The history of our Revolution," he complains to Benjamin Rush in 1790, "will be that Dr. Franklin's electric rod smote the earth and out sprung General Washington. That Franklin electrised him with his rod, and thence-forward these two conducted all the policy, negotiations, legislatures, and war." Splenetic and self-righteous, Adams nonetheless has seized upon an important truth. The electric wand in his comic fable, a fusion of science and magic, conveys the fact and the means of an enduring popular perception. Americans use this device and others like it to personify the Enlightenment in a myth of national origins, one that leads to just the kind of "gloriole of individual gentlemen" that Adams warned against.

These exchanges indicate the problems in any literary recovery of the Revolution. Whereas the intellectual historian must rediscover and contextualize ephemeral documents and forgotten speeches, the critic must assign a relative importance to each. Both attempts must qualify or at least situate the mythologies that Adams has rejected. Meanwhile, the simplest questions become difficult when answers involve the underlying change in ideas.

When did the Revolution begin? How did it begin? As early as 1743, Samuel Adams, then twenty-one, took the affirmative in a Harvard Commencement Day *Quaestio:* "Is it Lawful to resist the Supreme Magistrate, if the Commonwealth cannot otherwise be preserved?" His words, a schoolboy's exercise, were an excellent personal preparation for rebellion, but the colony, not the schoolboy, set that exercise. The theme of lawful resistance was an early preoccupation of English subjects on both sides of the Atlantic. No wonder John Adams and Jefferson concluded that the Revolution began with "the first plantation of the country." No wonder, as well, that in assigning a proximate cause a Loyalist historian like Peter Oliver could waver between the vast generality of the Reformation ("Since the emerging so suddenly from worse than Ægyptian Darkness, the human Mind was not strong enough to bear so sudden a Flash of Light") and the specificity of a single incident in 1761 (the feud between James Otis, a rising young lawyer, and Thomas Hutchinson, then lieutenant governor in Massachusetts, over the latter's appointment to the Massachusetts court). Hutchinson wrestles with the same incident and, hence, with the same problem of scale, in his own history of the times. "From so small a spark a great fire seems to have been kindled," Hutchinson marvels in retrospect. Where should the emphasis lie between the abstraction in ideas and the narrower but deeper trauma of parochial episode? Does the emphasis shift when episodes in themselves take on a larger symbolic importance in revolutionary ideology?

Questions about the influence of ideas raise another difficulty. Do the writings of revolutionary leaders transform the thought of colonial Americans, or does popular pressure dictate the pace and tenor of those writings? The catalyst of change that John Adams emphasizes, does it come from top or bottom? Answers to such questions are unavoidably provisional, but they must be kept in mind. No one, for example, would deny that Alexander Hamilton's ideas control large elements of *The Federalist* when its eighty-five numbers appear serially in 1787 and 1788, but Hamilton's essays, a distinct majority in *The Federalist*, bear little resemblance to the political preferences he expresses so passionately in Philadelphia just a few months before. Hamilton's extravagant admiration for the British Constitution on the floor of the Federal Convention is nowhere in Publius, and the reasons for the shift are in his own letters. "If a Convention is called," Hamilton writes in 1780, "the minds of all the states and the people ought to be prepared to receive its determinations by sensible and popular writings, which should conform to the views of Congress." This language of conformity, preparation, popularity, common sense, and reception reminds us that even the rigid, aristocratic-minded Hamilton engages in a flexible, consensual literature where political leadership, individual expression, and the will of the people meet.

John Adams's warnings about re-drafted writings, about the inflated roles of Washington and Franklin, and about too much emphasis on individual heroics suggest another level of concern. The success of national formation quickly clouds critical perception. The revolutionary founders are apotheosized within their own lifetimes, and many of them live long enough to gloss their own accomplishments in retrospective accounts. The combination distorts the meaning and the context of original contributions that are already difficult to interpret. The writings of the Revolution cope with issues and take aesthetic forms that have no place in modern literature, and the best of them have become the sacral objects of a national observance — icons that are more and, therefore, less than the written texts that they once were. They are, in consequence, peculiarly the property of American civilization, but Americans do not read them now as they were written or were meant to be read.

Against the difficulties in viewing the Revolution as a literary phenomenon – the product of its public records, pamphlets, newspapers, and hand-bills – are two crucial complementary strengths. From below, the Revolution takes place in one of the most generally literate cultures that ever existed, and, from above, the elite's conscious sense of itself in the act of writing is one of its few forgotten virtues. Revolutionary Americans read voraciously, and their leaders write easily and often, leaving rich, varied materials both in print and in manuscript. No generation, whether in reading or in writing, has looked more carefully to the printed word as the basis of its identity, and this reliance is all the more remarkable in a society still on the border between oral and print forms of literary and intellectual transmission.

In eighteenth-century culture, the accomplished figure demonstrates a worthiness for place and preferment by writing about the world at hand. The young Jefferson becomes a prominent Anglo-American personage overnight with one essay, *A Summary View of the Rights of British America,* in 1774. The same can be said of Thomas Paine two years later with *Common Sense.* Alexander Hamilton, James Madison, and John Adams also prosper, in part through their works on government and the Constitution. One need only compare the more limited scope of their compatriots who leave no comparable bodies of work, John Hancock and Patrick Henry, for instance. Early on, Benjamin Franklin makes a fortune as well as his reputation from printing and author-ship. Even George Washington looms larger for his writings – his circular on leaving the army in 1783 and his presidential farewell in 1796.

The primacy of writing appears in crucial moments of self-assertion. John Adams, amidst the worldly tensions of 1777, distinguishes between "Kinds of Ambition," reserving for himself only those forms that are "Literary and Professional." His subsequent production in official documents, essays, trea-tises, letters, and diary entries more than justifies the way he gives first priority to a literary career. Jefferson's inscription for his tombstone begins "here was buried Thomas Jefferson, Author." All three sources of identifica-tion that follow – the Declaration of Independence, the Statute of Virginia for Religious Freedom, and the University of Virginia – celebrate this au-thor's sense of creativity and immediate service. Franklin's own famous epi-taph turns its subject into a work of literature with the promise that though this "old Book" itself decay, "the Work shall not be lost; For it will, (as he believ'd) appear once more, In a new and more elegant Edition." "Prose writing," Franklin confirms in his autobiography, "has been of great use to me in the course of my life, and was a principal means of my advancement."

Authorship controls identity because the leaders of the Revolution expect so much from what they write. Their major works invariably allude to their own importance as both text and historical event. Paine's *Common Sense* begins not with tales of British oppression but with a recital of the grave errors that previous writers have foisted upon the world. By correcting these errors, his own pamphlet will change history. *Common Sense* promises to turn the reader into another Noah, one who possesses the "power to begin the world over again." *The Federalist* claims to be the best discussion of the most important question of the age. In turn, Franklin's autobiography assumes for itself the praise of posterity, the attention of all future notables, and a literary niche somewhere above the contributions of Caesar and Tacitus. All three works share an important premise about writing: anything is possible when the right word receives the proper emphasis and reception. And although this presumed power of the word is biblical in its original conception, it flourishes anew as part of the timely spread of knowledge in Enlightenment thought, one of many dynamic conflations of religious and secular understanding found in eighteenth-century literary circles.

Revolutionary Americans use their faith in writing to stabilize the uncertain world in which they live. Either they accentuate perceived anxieties, problems, and unknowns on the page, to be subsumed in the substances of print, proof, style, and form, or they rigorously exclude them from what still pretends to be a "comprehensive" treatment of the subject. Jefferson's debate with the Continental Congress over the rhetorical use of slavery in the Declaration of Independence offers a clear case in point. The alternatives are either to make the horror of slavery a central theme in the document and then to make it a major grievance against the king of England *or* to remove all mention of slavery, which is done in the final draft. In a more positive variation of the same ploy, *The Federalist* responds to early republican fears of the continental wilderness by bringing all of nature under the lens of political order. "It has often given me pleasure to observe," writes Publius in *Federalist No. 2,*

that independent America was not composed of detached and distant territories, but that one connected, fertile, wide-spreading country was the portion of our western sons of liberty. . . . A succession of navigable waters forms a kind of chain round its borders, as if to bind it together; while the most noble rivers in the world, running at convenient distances, present them with highways for the easy communication of friendly aids.

The fantasy of geographical connection embodies political unity against the recurring early republican nightmare of chaos and dissension.

These devices — devices of contextualization within a theory of comprehensiveness — are conscious fabrications in the writer's search for a higher truth, and they betray a willingness, even an eagerness, to reshape and gild the cruder facts with which they must contend. As devices, they are also the counterparts of far more subtle stratagems in the literature of republican idealism. The overall tactic marks a major tendency of writing in the period. Removing a controversial subject like slavery and positing a superficially compliant natural world are attempts to forge artificial unities amidst a contentious, far-flung populace. Revolutionary writers face a deeply divided people across the 1770s and 1780s. Their assumed task is to extract consensus at all costs, and they write with a paradoxical brand of creativity in mind – a creativity of agreement.

Jefferson's account in 1825 of how he wrote the Declaration of Independence reveals the form of this aesthetic:

Not to find out new principles, or new arguments never before thought of, not merely to say things which had never been said before; but to place before mankind the common sense of the subject, in terms so plain and firm as to command their assent. . . . Neither aiming at originality of principle or sentiment, nor yet copied from any particular and previous writing. It was intended to be an expression of the American mind.

The pronunciamiento in the statement, the Declaration as an expression of the American mind, has controlled commentary to the virtual exclusion of the many negatives that Jefferson registers here. These negatives – "Not to find out new principles . . . not merely to say things which had never been said. . . . Neither aiming at originality . . . nor yet copied" – reveal a lost distilling process and its frustrations. Where agreement dominates in literature, authorial intent and creativity willingly define themselves through the limitations of consensus.

The deft business of securing assent through language must be understood against a frequent despair in the attempt. Franklin, for one, comes to accept division as the inescapable norm of human affairs. "[Men] are generally more easily provok'd then reconcil'd," he tells Joseph Priestley in 1782, "more disposed to do Mischief to each other than to make Reparation, much more easily deceiv'd than undeceiv'd, and having more Pride and even Pleasure in killing than in begetting one another." John Adams agrees. "[N]either Philosophy, nor Religion, nor Morality, nor Wisdom, nor Interest," he warns Jefferson in 1787, "will ever govern nations or Parties against their Vanity, their Pride, their Resentment or Revenge, or their Avarice or Ambition." Ironically, the triumph of the Revolution is accompanied by a grim awareness of human limitation and continuing acrimony among those who struggle to fulfill its continuing promise.

Agreement in such a world clearly requires a manipulation beyond mere understanding. The truth may be self-evident, but those who find it must be coaxed into agreement over its meaning. "I am a sincere inquirer after truth," Adams explains in 1790, "but I find very few who discover the same truths."

The basis of this pessimism is Adams's own experience in the making of governments. "The difficulty of bringing millions to agree in any measures, to act by any rule," he observes, "can never be conceived by him who has not tried it." This comment may sound strange coming from one of the presumed architects of national formation, but the success of Adams and his generation on just this score has blunted later perception of their concern at the time. To read the works of the early Republic as they were written is to recognize that the tone, scope, meaning, and shape of those writings were forged decisively in "the difficulty of bringing millions to agree."

This consensual literature does not lend itself to a simple evolving chronology even when chronology interweaves texts with events. Chronological narratives bring their own impulses to the presumed meaning of the Revolution. British actions – from the Revenue Act, or Sugar Act, of 1764, to the Stamp Act and the Troop Quartering Act of 1765, to the Townshend Revenue Acts of 1767, to the Tea Act of 1773, to the Intolerable Acts, including the bill closing Boston Harbor, in 1774 – do indeed elicit a series of American reactions (colonial protests and pamphleteering of all kinds, nonimportation and nonconsumption agreements, the Stamp Act Congress and, later, the Continental Congress, the formation of the Sons of Liberty and of the later Committees of Correspondence, the Boston Tea Party, and so on). But this catalogue, however true and however frequently rendered, conveys too much certainty in the patterns of measure and response.

Conventional documentaries of the period assume a gradual American exasperation with British policy, one that builds from slow objection and reluctant protest to outrage and, only then, to retaliation and rupture. Yet, for all of that, violent anger, mob behavior, broad civil disobedience, and clashes between colonials and British troops are part of the Revolution from at least 1766. The Sons of Liberty, adopting their name from Isaac Barré's speech in Parliament against the Stamp Act in 1765, formed immediately and widely in that year. A break with England might have come before 1776 but for the timely repeal of parliamentary measures (the Stamp Act in 1766 and the Townshend Acts in 1770). By the same token, the conception of a slowly evolving opposition misses the spontaneity and original power of early protest writings.

American exasperation explodes into rage from the first parliamentary designs on revenue in 1764. Moreover, that rage feeds upon a spirit of opposition that long predates the shift in British monetary policies. The squabbles of colonial assemblies and their royal governors go back for generations in the volatile tradition of Anglo–American politics. Jonathan Mayhew, the liberal pastor of West Church in Boston from 1747, already sees the radical possibilities in that tradition fifteen years before the first new revenue schemes and ten before George III's succession to the British throne. Mayhew's *A Discourse Concerning Unlimited Submission and Non-Resistance to the Higher Powers* (1750) inserts in colonial dissent a curious dialectic about how Americans must "learn to be *free* and to be *loyal*." "[A] warning to all corrupt *counselors* and *ministers* not to go too far in advising arbitrary, despotic measures," this most famous of prerevolutionary sermons celebrates the 101st anniversary of the execution of Charles I and redefines the Puritan Revolution in the process; the latter is no longer a rebellion but "a most righteous and glorious stand made in defense of the natural and legal rights of the people against the unnatural and illegal encroachments of arbitrary power."

Here are most of the rhetorical tools that Americans will use to justify later rebellion. *A Discourse Concerning Unlimited Submission* remains a touchstone, a permanent literary resource against which Adams and others can test their own spirits. Thus even though Mayhew dies in 1766, well before the war between England and America, Adams, in 1818, still extols the "transcendent genius" and "great fame" that made Mayhew a "great influence in the commencement of the Revolution." *A Discourse Concerning Unlimited Submission* is read and reread into the lexicon of protest across that half century. Long after its original publication, Adams finds the Mayhew sermon to be "seasoned with wit and satire superior to any in Swift or Franklin." "It was read by everybody," he concludes, "celebrated by friends, and abused by enemies." There is a lost distinction in these comments. Mayhew's sermon is remembered within the continuum of the Revolution, but it is first written as the deepest expression of a given moment in colonial life. We need to recover the powerful initial appeal in such writings and the assumption, now bizarre, of "transcendent genius" in them.

II

Two texts can illustrate the way in which works of the moment enter into the aesthetic of a consensual literature. Although they are both minor pieces, each dramatizes major implications in revolutionary writings. The first example, an article from the *Boston-Gazette and Country Journal* for February 26, 1770, describes the death in Boston of one Christopher Seider. Seider is an eleven-year-old street urchin who, while demonstrating in favor of the colonial nonimportation agreement, is killed by a Loyalist. Indeed, Seider was so obscure in life that the *Boston-Gazette* eulogizes him as Snider. Even so, the Sons of Liberty manage to turn the occasion of his death into the largest funeral ever seen in the New World. Their success gives credence to forgotten Loyalist charges, like the one made by Peter Oliver, who writes that "Government was in the Hands of the Mob, both in Form & Substance" from the late

1760s. The elaborate orchestration of the event also shows how colonists learn from each other in their dangerous transition from English subjects to American patriots.

If this first text springs up from the grass roots of the Revolution, the second reaches down from its loftiest branches. Thomas Jefferson, in 1818, relying upon a story within a story, re-tells a Franklin anecdote from 1776 concerning Jefferson's draft of the Declaration of Independence. Together, newspaper article and anecdote span the period (from 1770 to 1818) as well as the range of revolutionary action (from mob violence to the highest political deliberation). They also share a vital awareness of spectacle and display as parts of the forgotten ritual of the Revolution. Above all, both writings deal with an unruly present, one in which spectacle, display, and ritual contend with confusion and acrimony. As such, they represent the irreducible artifacts that challenge received history.

Christopher Seider would be remembered today as the first martyr of his country were it not for Crispus Attucks, Samuel Maverick, James Caldwell, Samuel Gray, and Patrick Carr, who die more dramatically two weeks later at the hands of British soldiers when a similar mob scene becomes the Boston Massacre. In many ways, however, the death of Seider is the more instructive tragedy because so much is made at the time of its more limited political potential. In all, twenty-five hundred mourners join the Seider funeral procession, held in the coldest weather, and most of Boston's fifteen thousand residents turn out to watch. "My Eyes never beheld such a funeral," writes John Adams. Notably, Adams also draws the conclusion that the Sons of Liberty had hoped for in staging the event: "This Shewes, there are many more Lives to spend if wanted in the Service of their Country."

Benjamin Edes and John Gill, the radical editors of the *Boston-Gazette,* set the tone of the funeral as political event:

This innocent Lad is the first, whose LIFE has been a Victim, to the Cruelty and Rage of *Oppressors!* Young as he was, he died in his Country's Cause, by the Hand of an execrable Villain, directed by others, who could not bear to see the Enemies of America made the *Ridicule of Boys.* The untimely Death of this amiable Youth will be a standing Monument to Futurity, that the Time has been where *Innocence itself was not safe!*

The controlling influence of the *Boston-Gazette* appears in a detail. The motto at the end of this Edes and Gill passage, in Latin — *Innocentia ausquam tuta* — adorns Seider's coffin in its procession from the Liberty Tree on Essex Street to the Old Granary Burying Ground on the edge of Boston Common.

The actual circumstances behind the rhetoric of Edes and Gill are more complicated. On February 22, 1770, market day, always a school holiday, young Seider is part of a mob of several hundred boys who gather around the North End shop of Theophilus Lillie to protest his continuing sale of British goods. Their rallying symbols are a carved head upon a pole and a painted sign with a pointing hand and the word "importer" inscribed beneath it, and they harass anyone who enters the shop while sympathetic adults, some armed with sticks, encourage and protect them. There are accompanying acts of petty vandalism: throughout the city importers' windows are broken and their houses and shop signs smeared with filth. Lillie's shop is a target because its owner has been listed in the *Boston-Gazette* among "the Names of *those* who AUDACIOUSLY continue to counteract the UNITED SENTI-MENTS of the BODY of Merchants thro'out NORTH-AMERICA" by prefer-ring "their own little private Advantage to the Welfare of America." In noting the precise location of a dozen shops, the *Boston-Gazette* invites direct action against them. According to the newspaper, the merchants identified have "sordidly detached themselves from the public Interest" and must be treated as "Enemies to their Country, by all who are well-wishers to it."

Although the politics may seem singular, they arise out of common circum-stance and conventional social behavior in ways that help to determine Chris-topher Seider's symbolic power in eighteenth-century America. Market day, with its idle crowds, provides frequent occasion for popular disturbance in colonial cities, and it has been a particular resort of the Sons of Liberty in their campaign against importers in the months preceding Seider's death. Organized bands of boys have been the first line of intimidation against unpopular individuals since the Stamp Act crisis five years before. And the intimidation can be extreme. Mob action is an accepted communal tactic of the times, one used regularly in New England against those who deviate from social and political norms. Everything about the extraordinary event of Febru-ary 22 is ordinary for the times except for its tragic conclusion.

The pattern of familiar practice extends to the particulars. The boys' procession, their effigies, and the signs they raise in front of Lillie's store come from the insurrectionary symbols and ceremonies that neighborhood gangs have employed for generations in New England Pope Day celebrations. These colonial adaptations of the English Guy Fawkes Day celebrations will grow into regular rituals of the Revolution, with the parading of liberty poles and other totems. The Sons of Liberty are using them in 1770 to routinize defiance of authority and to articulate the scene for rioting. Of course, the virulent identification of "otherness" in Pope Day anti-Catholicism translates easily to other possibilities, in this case to Tory sympathizers.

When Ebenezer Richardson, just such a sympathizer, tries to strike down the effigies in front of Lillie's shop, his behavior parallels that of rival gangs in traditional Pope Day celebrations. The result is also the same, a riot in the streets. Followed to his house by the angry mob, Richardson eventually fires wildly from a window, killing Seider, but not before the windows and the front door of his house have been broken in. Uppermost in Richardson's mind in 1770 would have been the wanton destruction of the houses of leading citizens like Thomas Hutchinson and Andrew Oliver in the Stamp Act riots of 1765 and the near fatal mob attack on John Mein, another friend of importers, in King Street just four months before. Richardson also knows that he cannot expect help from local authorities. It is typical of the times and the situation that Sheriff Stephen Greenleaf, the responsible official, refuses a direct order from Lieutenant Governor Hutchinson to disperse the mob around Richardson's house; "he did not think it safe to attempt," Hutchinson reports.

Edes and Gill channel the anger and ambiguity of these events into the clarity and order of further ritual. They first reduce Ebenezer Richardson to stock knavery. The Richardson of the *Boston-Gazette* is a hireling and an informer, a conspirator "directed by others," and a deliberate villain who provokes the incident through inflammatory and blasphemous language and physical hostility. Biblically, he is Cain covered with "the Blood of righteous *Abel.*" According to Edes and Gill, speedy vengeance, divine and otherwise, awaits this murderer and his *"Accomplices."*

The contrasting characterization of Christopher Seider, "little Hero and first Martyr to the noble Cause," is more complicated. Seider's double role of martyr and hero goes straight to the heart of a patriotic identity problem. How can the boy represent both complete innocence *and* justifiable opposition? In response, the *Boston-Gazette* carefully balances Seider's pious humility and steadfastness in death against the prospect of his *"martial Genius."* Among "the several heroic Pieces found in his Pocket" is a book entitled *Wolfe's Summit of Human Glory.* The reference is to the greatest military champion that America then knows. Seider belongs in the tradition of General James Wolfe, who, in a single embrace of victory and death at the Battle of Quebec (1759), frees the colonies from French influence, Indian attack, and Catholic corruption.

The moral contrast between Richardson and Seider does more than simplify choice. It dictates action. On the one hand, the tragedy of Seider's presumed innocence and early death is supposed to frighten and anger every American. "[W]e are fallen into the most unhappy Times," warns the *Boston-Gazette,* "when even *innocence itself is no where safe!*" On the other hand, Seider's more ambiguous "martial genius" signals the active patriotism of the bands of boys run by the Sons of Liberty. The reference is cleverly mediated through the English figure of Wolfe, but the overall meaning is clearly a radical one. Those Americans who *are* frightened and angry will be on the side of the Sons of Liberty, and the *Boston-Gazette* moves quickly to make the connection a controlling premise. Predicting that the Seider funeral "will be attended by as *numerous* a Train as was ever known here," Edes and Gill announce that only the Friends of Liberty should march in the procession. "Then," they conclude, "*all* will be hearty Mourners."

Marching in the funeral procession is necessarily a radicalizing act, and both sides of the controversy understand its political importance in this way. Like Edes and Gill, Thomas Hutchinson instantly draws the correlation to a similar funeral organized by English radicals during the John Wilkes riots of 1768. Hutchinson also comes closest to gauging the overall impact of the Seider funeral on the Boston community. Jotting in his diary, he glumly notes:

when the boy was killed by Richardson, the sons of liberty in Boston, if it had been in their power to have brought him to life again, would not have done it but would have chosen the grand funeral, which brought many thousands together; and the solemn procession from Liberty Tree, near which the boy's father lived, to the Town House and back to the burying ground made an inconceivable impression.

But why, precisely, should the Seider funeral have made "an inconceivable impression"?

The answer requires one more level of explanation. Americans of the period, as Americans, have a very limited sense of identity. Every colony looks naturally to England rather than to its immediate neighbors, and the one visible manifestation of intercolonial consensus of the moment, the nonimportation agreement of radical merchants, is particularly uncertain in the winter of 1769–70. Although rudimentary nonimportation resolutions begin in Boston in 1764, they fail to achieve the concerted agreement of the major colonial ports until 1768, and they do so then only with a cut-off date of January 1, 1770. Renewal of the nonimportation agreements in the fall of 1769 meets with less success, and the conservative *Boston Chronicle* smugly reports the widespread breakdown in the boycotts. When the radical leadership in Boston responds by putting nonimportation on a more coercive footing, the whole question of a free and united colonial spirit becomes inextricably involved.

The tragedy of February 22, 1770, partakes of this larger battle over American identity and direction. It converts a negation (nonimportation) into a positive assertion (the patriotic recognition of heroic sacrifice). Put another way, Seider's fate ennobles nonimportation, turning it from good policy into the stuff of legend and communal glory. Phillis Wheatley seems to have grasped these implications almost as quickly as did the editors of the *Boston-Gazette*. Obviously based on Edes and Gill's newspaper account,

Wheatley's occasional poem on the death of Seider is written within days of the event, and it dwells on just how "the first martyr of the common good" brings the community together into one "Illustrious retinue" against "fair freedom's foes."

The Seider funeral enables an inventive act in communal recognition. The ritual and reportage of the event are part of a precarious search for identity. Seider dies not only as a Boston boy but, more importantly, "in his Country's Cause." The preoccupation of Edes and Gill with signs and symbols of unity, their related concern with the pageantry of events, and their shrill insistence on the combined sentiments and actions of the people all hint at the primal needs involved. The radical editors' account stresses two dimensions of the funeral: the fact of the conflict and the placards − or symbolic writings − displayed in the procession (six in all) that interpret this conflict. Distinguishing "a very numerous Train of Citizens" from "a *few*, only excepted, who have long shewn themselves to be void of the Feelings of Humanity," the *Boston-Gazette* uses participation in the funeral to create a striking numerical imbalance in the conflict at hand. The article then carefully translates the Latin inscriptions on the Seider coffin and supplies the relevant biblical quotations posted on the Liberty Tree. As the inscriptions announce Seider's struggle and innocent martyrdom, so the quotations cry for a united, social act of vengeance in the trial and punishment of Ebenezer Richardson. These sentiments, concludes the *Boston-Gazette*, "cannot easily be misapply'd."

The emphasis upon communal reading is one more symptom of the importance of ritual. In supposing signs that cannot be misapplied, Edes and Gill infer a general application and interest; to this end, they repeat each placard in print, in English as well as in Latin. The painstaking double and sometimes triple renditions insure total availability, but they also uphold the different levels of experience and education involved in each repetition. The procedure includes every possible level of participation, from the presence of the lowest urban dweller at the ceremony to the educated gentleman's private Latin reading in his study. And, underlying everything is a basic faith in universal literacy.

The funeral of Christopher Seider, in sum, is itself a text to be mastered by a community reading in unison. The *Boston-Gazette* creates a world in which the sympathetic many have to join with each other and act against the tyrannical and unfeeling few. The participants in the Seider funeral discover their identity in this collective act of understanding. Next, however, they must demonstrate their solidarity, the root of group identity, by finding and punishing the few who have acted against them. That search will be an easy one; the unjust and unfeeling few can be detected in their opposition to the people or, more concretely, in their indifference to patriotic ritual. Here, in the momentum and the calculated promise of future events, is the continuum of the Revolution.

III

Six years after Christopher Seider's death, in 1776, the writers of the Revolution understand that the problem of conflict cannot be resolved in the simple polarities of British tyranny and American rights, self-interest and popular virtue. They have begun to accept the fact of acrimony *within* the American cause and the need to impose a truth upon it. These realizations come to life in an aside between Jefferson and Franklin over the Declaration of Independence. When Jefferson complains against "depredations" and "mutilations" during congressional revision of his draft, Franklin captures the essence of a writer's dilemma:

I have made it a rule, said [Franklin], whenever in my power, to avoid becoming the draughtsman of papers to be reviewed by a public body. I took my lesson from an incident which I will relate to you. When I was a journeyman printer, one of my companions, an apprentice hatter, having served out his time, was about to open shop for himself. His first concern was to have a handsome signboard, with a proper inscription. He composed it in these words, "*John Thompson, Hatter, makes and sells hats for ready money,*" with a figure of a hat subjoined; but he thought he would submit it to his friends for their amendments. The first he showed it to thought the word "*Hatter*" tautologous, because followed by the words "makes hats," which show he was a hatter. It was struck out. The next observed that the word "*makes*" might as well be omitted, because his customers would not care who made the hats. . . . He struck it out. A third said he thought the words "*for ready money*" were useless, as it was not the custom of the place to sell on credit. . . . the inscription now stood, "John Thompson sells hats." "*Sells hats!*" says his next friend. "Why nobody will expect you to give them away, what then is the use of that word?" It was stricken out, and "*hats*" followed it, the rather as there was one painted on the board. So the inscription was reduced ultimately to "John Thompson" with the figure of a hat subjoined.

The parallels to the founding of a nation are deliberate and amusingly apt. The apprentice who opens his shop is like the colonies that declare their independence. Both have embarked on a risky enterprise that may fail. The success of a step already taken now depends upon how others respond to the signification of that event. Whether a signboard or the Declaration of Independence, the written representation is a mixed symbol of celebration and vulnerability. This is where the opinion of others enters into the success or failure of the enterprise. The hatter will lose his shop if his friends do not act upon his representation. The Revolution will be for naught without a united front behind the claim for independence. Humor flows from the thankless role of the writer or sign-maker, who must stoop to the lowest common denominator to find agreement.

Franklin's anecdote supplies four alternatives for making a text in a consensual setting. Foremost, from the perspective of modern authorship, the beleaguered writer can impose a private text on a public audience. The hatter can hang his sign without consulting anyone, hoping for acceptance of the fait accompli. This is the strategy of Jefferson's *A Summary View of the Rights of British America* (1774) and of Paine's *Common Sense,* both of which captivate in their daring. But the risk of discord from unilaterial assertion is great, particularly for eighteenth-century intellectuals with a paramount sense of community. Second, a writer can draw up a text in the marketplace of debate, as the founders are doing with the Declaration of Independence in the moment of Franklin's anecdote. This background debate in Congress actually touches a creative norm of the times. In making a finished text, the gentleman of letters distributes private drafts to a circle of equals for advice before publication – a practice that explains something of the skill and co-operation demonstrated by committees in the Continental Congress and later at the Constitutional Convention. But what of the hatter's comic inability to please his friends? What happens when agreement proves impossible?

A third alternative appears in Franklin's punch line. The writer reduces the public text into an article of faith or an icon. The sign becomes an incontestable fact when it is just a name subjoined to the figure of a hat. Many of the important writings of the Revolution have this figural quality. They have been drafted to be posted and read in public places. Of newspaper-page length, they also seek substantiating form at every turn. The founders mean the Declaration of Independence to be read aloud in every town meeting in America. They keep the document short, and they couch their language in the familiar frame of legal pleading, the *declaration* or *count* that initiates an action in common law and that is also read aloud. *The Federalist,* cut into eighty-five parts, never violates its originating form in the newspaper essay or occasional paper. Everywhere in the literature of the Revolution, from handbill to formal document, the numerology of articles, sections, and papers provides a structure to be seen to go with the words that are read.

Naming is part of this iconography, the "John Thompson" on the sign. Franklin's hatter can accept any change that leaves him in place, and the writers of the Revolution also show considerable ingenuity in this respect. The signers of the Declaration of Independence and Constitution are themselves literalized on the signboards in question. The hieroglyphic significance of those signatures is a central aspect of acceptance and ratification. Gaining agreement means engraving the separate authority of the author on the text wherever possible – a policy that easily carries beyond name, signature, and even verifiable fact. When John Dickinson writes *Letters from a Farmer in Pennsylvania* (1768), he is neither a farmer nor, strictly speaking, a Pennsylvanian but a wealthy lawyer and rising politician from tiny Delaware. The created figure on the page, strategically sequestered on a small farm in a large middle colony, does a better job of convincing British Americans that he writes for all of them. Indeed, this whole question of the crafted persona in revolutionary writings deserves more careful attention. The writer's need for posting informs a much larger quest for entitlement in the designation of founder.

Thus far, the strategies of a consensual literature are easily traced in writings that have been imposed, negotiated, reduced, and figuralized, but a fourth possibility in the anecdote is much harder to grasp. Franklin reserves that fourth alternative for himself in his imputed silence, his strategy of avoidance. "I have made it a rule," he tells Jefferson, "whenever in my power, to avoid becoming the draughtsman of papers to be reviewed by a public body." This comment frames the anecdote, creating a strange inversion. In Franklin's *telling*, sound justifies silence, verbiage praises reticence, language explains its own absence. The man behind the anecdote thrives on such ironies: *"many Words won't fill a Bushel,"* says Father Abraham at the beginning of his long speech in "The Way to Wealth" (1758). But Franklin is also serious about his larger claim. Agreement often requires the second of the thirteen virtues enumerated in his autobiography: silence.

The major source of evil in Franklin's autobiography is disputation. Because words breed only words, and then anger, Franklin the boy must learn to use them sparingly. His proper creed also comes early, from Pope's *An Essay on Criticism:*

> Men must be *taught* as if you taught them *not;*
> And Things *unknown* propos'd as Things *forgot.*

Each assumed persona in the Franklin memoirs – the printer's apprentice, the town organizer, the philosopher, the leading politician, and the renowned scientist – proves, in turn, that silence is the best policy in a dispute. Franklin's first pseudonym, Silence Dogood, proclaims the point, and so does the worst moment in the diplomat's distinguished career. Hauled before the Privy Council of Parliament as colonial agent in 1774, Franklin stands motionless, enduring the invective of the king's ministers for two hours without change of expression or reply.

Where agreement is the goal, refutation feeds what it fights. This is Franklin's assumption and is Jefferson's too, when, in his own brief autobiography, he contrasts the reserve of Franklin and Washington to "the morbid rage of debate" and "singular disposition of men to quarrel" around them. "I never heard either of them speak ten minutes at a time," observes Jefferson, explaining why he in emulation "could sit in silence" during "wordy debate." John Adams summarizes the phenomenon in his diary: "The Examples of Washington, Franklin and Jefferson are enough to shew that Silence and reserve in public are more Efficacious than Argumentation or Oratory."

Silence is the vital interstice in a consensual literature; what is spoken or written is peculiarly a function of what *cannot* be spoken or written *there*. Many Americans, to take the clearest example, object to the notion of a national federal republic in 1787, so the Constitution, in creating one, never mentions the words "national," "federal," or "republic." The language that remains communicates the possibility in less controversial terms. The radical innovations of the document are also shielded by the innovators' public silence. The fifty-five delegates of the Federal Convention agree that "nothing spoken in the House be printed, or otherwise published or communicated without leave." Despite enormous pressures to break their silence, they stick to their "rule of secrecy" from May to September. They can do so because they have come to understand the value of silence. Adams traces the mastery of this lesson to the success of 1776. The Continental Congress, he reminds Jefferson in 1815, "compared Notes, engaged in discussions and debates and formed Results by one Vote and by two Votes, which went out to the World as unanimous."

The purpose of silence is to minimize and control difference. If properly restrained, private debate can be subsumed in a public language of shared meanings. The whole thrust of such writing is to mask uglier actualities and to keep dangerous passions below the combustion point. The corresponding task of the later critic is to decipher the realities of difference that are masked by such language. Every consensual text contains distinct utterances that work against as well as with each other. There are, in consequence, two kinds of implication at work in a narrative of levels. The separate voices that author the consensual text also compete in the hierarchical process of creation. The Franklin anecdote illustrates the difference perfectly. Franklin, Jefferson, and those modifying Jefferson's draft on the floor of Congress cooperate in producing the Declaration of Independence, and their acknowledged success glosses every difference. Even so, the voices in the anecdote also work at cross-purposes. The controlling theme of Franklin's anecdote is conflict, and this conflict spills beyond the surface of the narrative in important ways.

A simple historical fact shows how conflict informs the consensual text in this case. The modern reader needs to know that the typical eighteenth-century shop sign resembles that in Franklin's anecdote; it attaches a name to an identifying shape, whether of pipe for tobacconist, boot for shoemaker, key for locksmith, or hat for hatter. But if " 'John Thompson' with the figure of a hat subjoined" supplies the correct sign, then the mutilators of Jefferson's draft appear in a different light. They become the conscientious enforcers of regular form and acceptability. Simultaneously, the amiable exchange of Franklin and Jefferson turns into a contrast. Franklin, the leather apron man, a shopkeeper himself, knows better than anyone what kind of language the people will need in order to declare their independence to themselves and to the world, and he gently admonishes his aristocratic young friend from rural Virginia about the ways of the world. In Franklin's corrective, the practicality of a nation of shopkeepers supplants the wordy idealism of the agrarian ideal.

The ultimate story, however, belongs not to Franklin in 1776 but to Jefferson in 1818, and Jefferson's retelling of it through the Philadelphia journalist Robert Walsh, and then through James Madison, should give pause. Why should the author of the Declaration of Independence want to publicize this story against himself? In effect, Jefferson's act of appropriation is part of the general refashioning of revolutionary achievement that complicates every literary and historical analysis of the period. More than forty years after the event, he suddenly needs the surfaces of the anecdote; the retelling in 1818 identifies exclusive authorship of the Declaration of Independence at exactly the moment when that authorship is being questioned. Franklin as speaker disclaims any authorship for Franklin himself, and his humor automatically separates the committee member who supports language from the drafter who creates it. The older man appears as the guiding voice in support of young Jefferson's achievement, and his benevolent tones attach every reader to Jefferson's accomplishment; they also relegate dissent to the margins of those distant and unidentified congressional voices in the background. One of those distanced voices belongs to John Adams, and therein lies another story.

Jefferson's appropriation of Franklin's anecdote is part of a remarkable debate that turns on the changing nature of literary creativity in American culture. Across the first quarter of the nineteenth century, Jefferson and Adams spar over the terms and meaning of their achievement in the Declaration of Independence. Jefferson writes the document. Adams directs its progress in congressional debate; he is, in Jefferson's phrase, "our Colossus on the floor." Early on, Adams tells Benjamin Rush that Jefferson has managed to "steal" the fame of 1776. He also claims that his own personal declaration predates Jefferson's version by at least twenty-one years. "The Declaration of Independence I always considered a theatrical show," he adds in 1811, "Jefferson ran away with all the stage effect of that . . . and all the glory of it."

By 1817 Jefferson is feeling the need to correct attacks upon an authorship "that alone was mine." When, in 1822, Adams pointedly raises the committee structure behind the Declaration and dismisses the document itself ("there is not an idea in it but what had been hackneyed in Congress for two years before"), Jefferson responds with a long letter to James Madison in formal defense of his exclusive authorship. Clearly writing for posterity, he minimizes the committee's role ("they unanimously pressed on myself alone to undertake the draught") and discounts the language changes of Adams and Franklin ("their alterations were two or three only, and merely verbal"). And once again, Jefferson gives Franklin's anecdote as conclusive external evidence for his own claim.

The striking thing about this debate is that Adams and Jefferson are both correct. Adams's stress upon the committee structure that produces the Declaration and his insistence upon the community of language behind it presuppose the consensual nature of authorship that dominates the literature of public documents in the period. Nothing could have been accomplished in 1776 and 1787 if personal pride in individual authorship had been a material consideration. Still, Jefferson's claims of authorship are substantially accurate. His colleagues do indeed choose him for the task because of his acknowledged literary capabilities. "Writings of his," Adams admitted of Jefferson in 1776, "were handed about, remarkable for the peculiar felicity of expression."

Adams finds many voices authoring a common text. Jefferson, reaching instead for hierarchical placement within the creative process, sees only the one hand in composition. Together, they dramatize the vital tension at work in a consensual literature. But those tensions suffer a distortion in time. Jefferson's claims loom larger than they should in the emerging hagiography of the founders and in the more general magnification of authorial role in the nineteenth century. As the Declaration itself becomes an icon of national culture, so its individual creator becomes a separate source of interest. Obviously, the tensions as well as the assertions in a consensual literature must be held firmly in mind. Jefferson claims no more than his due, but he must not be understood without Adams on the same subject.

IV

The comedy and tensions in Franklin and Jefferson's colloquy over the Declaration of Independence should not disguise a last overarching affinity between the two figures. Their mutual distrust of the talk around them and their concentration on the hatter's signboard are symptomatic of their larger control of and faith in the new print culture in which they live. We find them here in the very act of mastering their crafts as the most accomplished writers of the American Enlightenment. Each leaves a timeless masterpiece in a vital genre of the period (Franklin's memoirs in autobiography and Jefferson's draft of the Declaration in the literature of public documents). Both command a full range of the literary forms available to them: the political pamphlet, the epistle, the newspaper article, the scientific essay, and the broadside. Each demonstrates a peculiar capacity in still other literary forms (Franklin in the almanac and the humorous sketch or bagatelle; Jefferson in the political oration and legal document). Both leave probing analyses of the still mysterious New World, in Franklin's *Observations Concerning the Increase of Mankind, Peopling Countries, Etc.* (1751) and his *Information To Those Who Would Remove to America* (1784) and in Jefferson's *Notes on the State of Virginia* (1784–5). Finally, both write early and late, leaving prodigious outputs for scholars to decipher in ongoing but still incomplete modern editions of their works.

Yet, and this amounts to a final difficulty in studying the literature of the period, Franklin and Jefferson themselves seem to remain mysteriously aloof from or somehow outside of their writings. Neither their productivity nor their life-long fame nor the immense record of their output in relevant archives quite reveals the writers behind the works to those who now read them. Modern scholarship, as a result, is obsessed with a search for "the real Franklin" and "the real Jefferson," sometimes to the point of positing a pervasive hypocrisy or even the absence of a meaningful self at the root of their authorial writings. It helps to recognize that the elusiveness of these writings is part of their inherent literary integrity. The game of levels they so openly engaged in is part of their intention and a source of their power.

As the creators of a consensual literature for a diverse and divided citizenry, the leaders of the Revolution write to reconcile and, thereby, to control. They seek to encompass difference within a consciously communal perspective. This search for agreement makes their writing thematically simple but rhetorically complex. Their language deliberately entertains several planes of implication at a time, and it is most successful when the same utterance performs many functions. The greater appeal of mixed intellectual modes is the goal of such language, but its craft lies in bringing modes together through style, tone, symbol, and form.

Many of these characteristics apply to political language in general. The difference in the Revolution lies in a special intensity. The urgencies of rebellion and national formation bring immeasurable weight to the problems and strategies of reaching for political agreement. Anger and doubt compound the primal goal of consensus. In response, the representative texts of the period distort the nature of conflict to create order and clarity in the name of authorial calm. Order and clarity, in turn, rely upon a figural emphasis in language that attaches to the ritual and ceremony of revolutionary practice. The founders struggle to make their signs, symbols, and literary personae at once familiar, dominating, and inclusive. Agreement, after all, means agreement within the trappings of a new order. But what order? Whose order? Everywhere in their denial of British rule, the leaders of the Revolution are aware of the need for a new ruler. They express that need awkwardly and anxiously in an abstraction, "the will of the people."

It follows that effective language in the early Republic requires a basic act of mutual recognition between leaders and led. The vigor in a slogan like *E Pluribus Unum*, the motto that Franklin, Adams, and Jefferson select for the Continental Congress, consists in its simultaneous appeal above and below. Taken from the Latin of Horace, the congressional motto confirms an agenda in the separate language of a self-conscious elite. It helps a governing group to realize that it is, in fact, governing. But taken also from the epigraph of *The Gentleman's Magazine*, the same slogan reaches toward the popular and becomes a cry to the people. "From many one" represents an act of communal incorporation. It instills the consciousness in its followers of belonging to a movement – *from* many *to* one – in which their act of solidarity has created a new society.

The manner of the early republican text is about this complete interpenetration of language, belief, power, and points of view. "We hold these truths to be self evident," announce the founders in 1776. The same words that describe permanent truths everywhere in the world also introduce and impose an explicit political group, the new holders of truth in North America, the "we" of the document. Truth and its holders share self-evidence and, hence, a common security from challenge. Belief in the former implies acceptance of the latter. They appear as one: truth invested in a unified leadership. The *manner* of the literature has to do with this turning of idea and belief into a language of political assertion. Its *content*, the substance of idea and belief, are the subjects of the following chapters.

Two frameworks of belief in particular dominate eighteenth-century American thought: the Enlightenment and Protestant Reform Christianity. Chapter 2 explores the meaning and central role of the Enlightenment in America, and chapter 3 analyzes religious thought as a controlling impulse in the Revolution and in the formation of the early Republic. These frameworks come together in an American civil religion, the central expression of New World republicanism. They also compete in the making of a distinctly American mind – a mind already caught in the opposing forces of secularization and revivalism, reason and faith, knowledge and belief, individuality and community.

2

❧

WHAT IS ENLIGHTENMENT? SOME AMERICAN ANSWERS

I

The Enlightenment in America is sometimes conveyed in a single phrase, the political right of self-determination realized. The reduction is possible because self-determination as a philosophical principle incorporates the basic eighteenth-century tenets of Enlightenment thought: the primacy of reason, the reliability of human understanding, the value of individual freedom, trust in method, faith in education, belief in progress, and a corresponding disregard for tradition, constituted authority, and received dogma. At the same time, the realization of self-determination in national ideology has tended to equate philosophical principle with political practice. Since the Revolution claims government by consent of the governed as the irreducible source of its achievement, self-determination becomes the sign and symptom of the Enlightenment at work in each succeeding generation. This is the legacy of the Revolution in daily life.

Not coincidentally, the Enlightenment has been a partisan concept in American historiography, one in which subsidiary notions of liberalism, progress, and rationality have shaped the character of historical reconstructions. Because the idea of an American Enlightenment coincides with national formation and a developmental sense of country, its proponents tend to dwell on the emerging prospect. They see and make use of the original aspiration of human freedom but lose all sense of the Enlightenment as a historical process with its own patterns of constraint. The result is a peculiar one-sidedness or intellectual vulnerability in critical inquiries about the subject.

The first task, then, is to put the Enlightenment into broader historical perspective, and one means to this end is the very different view of European thinkers. When Jürgen Habermas in *The Philosophical Discourse of Modernity* (1987) announces that "the permanent sign of enlightenment is domination over an objectified external nature and a repressed internal nature," he summarizes a tradition of European thought that scholars of the American Enlightenment have avoided. The differences are historically as well as philosophically based. European nations do not begin in the hope of the Enlightenment, and their modern circumstance, the direct experience of world wars and totalitarianism, has interrupted eighteenth-century legacies more obviously and decisively than in America. Continental intellectuals in particular have these devastations in mind and look less to an advance of freedom than to the threat of new kinds of institutional repression. They acknowledge scientific inquiry but emphasize the domination in scientific technologies. They think less of rational progressions and more of a reign of instrumental reason and the separation of thought from belief. For the European scholar, even self-determination can appear to be a social control as much as it is a political right, a methodology that has structured individuals into isolated monads and objects of manipulation.

The point is not to choose between American and European approaches but to use both to gain a more complete understanding. A glance at three different writings from the literature of the Enlightenment can demonstrate the need for both perspectives. First, take Thomas Jefferson's moving peroration on self-determination, written in 1826 in the last month of a long and brilliant life:

All eyes are opened, or opening, to the rights of man. The general spread of the light of science has already laid open to every view the palpable truth, that the mass of mankind has not been born with saddles on their backs, nor a favored few booted and spurred, ready to ride them legitimately, by the grace of God. These are grounds of hope for others.

Twentieth-century readers still welcome Jefferson's hope, but they see less openness all around. The light of science appears less general, the truth less palpable, the view infinitely more particularistic. Technology, the product of science, occasionally keeps "a favored few booted and spurred" in ways that Jefferson never dreamed of. Jefferson's actual language flows from another Enlightenment source, Algernon Sidney's *Discourses Concerning Government* (1698), a work that John Adams, writing to Jefferson in 1823, admires for demonstrating "the slow progress of moral, philosophical, and political illumination in the world." Neither the progress of illumination, however slow, nor the easy conjunction of moral, philosophical, and political disciplines would be such intellectual givens in describing the world today.

In effect, the results of the Enlightenment have cut across its original tenets. Enlightenment now appears as a function of what it has become and not as a philosophical frame for the advance of history. A second literary example suggests another level of problems that would have been either invisible or immaterial to eighteenth-century observers. When Samuel Johnson in 1778 expresses disdain for Benjamin Franklin's definition of a man as "a tool-making animal," readers of *The Life of Johnson*, now as then, enter into the exchange of wit at Boswell's expense. But Johnson also instinctively rejects what today would be called the instrumentalization of identity, or the reduction of thought to commodity, or, more simply, the subsuming, aggressive spirit of technologism.

A similar awareness might inform twentieth-century readings of a third example, Alexander Hamilton's brilliant *Report on Manufactures* (1791). In a remarkably prescient document, Washington's secretary of the treasury employs Enlightenment norms to sketch not just the first realistic projection of a national economy but also the first full-blown justification of child labor in American factories. The two manifestly go together. Hamilton predicts that "artificial force brought in aid of the natural force of man" together with "the genius of the people of this country, a peculiar aptitude for mechanic improvements" will bring disparate groups of workers together in a harmonious triumvirate of "cultivators, artificers, and merchants." Women and children, weak and unskilled labor, find their appropriate places in this triumvirate in the lowest levels of artificers – that is, as workers in factories. Noting the salutary example of the British cotton mills, where more than half of the labor force falls into these two categories ("many of them of a very tender age"), Hamilton proves that "women and Children are rendered more useful and the latter more early useful by manufacturing establishments, than they would otherwise be." Child labor and other forms of exploitation of factory workers follow so naturally and continue in force for so long in the American economy because they fit within a seamless or hegemonic rationale of early national identity.

Such writings make it clear that the Enlightenment must be understood in dialectical form. Reason, the original calling card, resides in both the liberation that it promises and the kinds of domination that it provokes – in both Hamiltonian prosperity and the child labor that prosperity assumes. Moreover, the original context of the Enlightenment allows for these tensions. Immanuel Kant shows his understanding of and illustrates the problem in a seminal essay, *An Answer to the Question: "What is Enlightenment?"* (1784). His treatment deserves attention because it recomplicates the original basis of Enlightenment thought and because the parallels between Kant and early republicans in America precede later cross-cultural differences on the subject. Indeed, the example of Kant offers something more. The Janus-face of enlightenment can be a means of interpretation, of joining European and American understandings together.

What is enlightenment? When Kant asks the question in 1784, the European Enlightenment already has spread over the course of the century, and its American counterpart, from its later beginnings in the 1750s, has itself just reached obvious heights with the new nation's victory in the Treaty of Paris. In other words, Kant can justifiably conceive of his answer as a description of contemporary life. That answer, perhaps in consequence, mixes negative experience with hope for change. *"Enlightenment is man's emergence from his self-incurred immaturity."* Kant thinks of it as overcoming "the inability to use one's own understanding without the guidance of another." Commentators generally avoid the clumsiness and qualifications of these constructions by leaping directly to Kant's famous motto of enlightenment (taken from Horace) – *"Sapere aude!* Have courage to use your *own* understanding!"* – but in so doing they lose sight of the philosopher's essential point. The Enlightenment may trade in ringing affirmations, but its deepest meanings lie in the uncertain struggle of light against darkness. Kant underlines that struggle in a reminder to his contemporaries: you live in an age of enlightenment, he tells them, not an enlightened age. Enlightenment means process, not result.

II

Kant's idea of enlightenment as struggle and process takes on special meaning in understanding the conflict between England and America. Born in the Enlightenment, the new republic is also ripped from a previous and clearly functional context, that of colony in the Anglo-American empire. Linear notions of the Enlightenment tend to obscure the fact of disruption in metaphors of progression from colony to province to state and then to union. The notion of process, to the contrary, allows for the blood, agony, and confusion of the Revolution – an event that brought anxiety to all, extraordinary social upheaval to most, and disaster to many. And while the recognition of a dialectic instead of a linear progression does not discount the tones of measured calm and of political inevitability that dominate a work like the Declaration of Independence, it does take into account the underlying element of rupture in a Declaration that is, among other things, a declaration of war.

The Enlightenment in America is itself a manifestation of protracted conflict, and in the pressure of that conflict are the delineations of a specifically American expression. Americans receive European ideas, but they use them to express their own needs in the prolonged crisis of the Revolution and national formation. Since creativity takes place in this exchange from European models to American requisites, the important questions address the transmission of ideas, style, tone, and rhetorical emphasis. What is the appeal of the Enlightenment in American thought? What influences are paramount? Do Enlightenment ideas change in a changing American setting? What are the constitutive metaphors, and how do Americans use them? What are the dynamics of the Enlightenment text?

The import of transmission also depends on the nature of linguistic engagement. At the level of popular idiom, the Enlightenment responds to communal uncertainty. At the level of event, it supplies more complex strategies of comprehension or control. In the formalities of the intellectual text, it resituates America in a theory of history that further orders the understanding of word and event. A sustained illustration of each level of expression follows: first, in popular idiom, the mysterious appeal of the national anthem ("The Star-Spangled Banner" is an instantaneous success in 1814); next, in the volatility of event, the near revolt of the revolutionary army in 1783; and, finally, in textual assertion, the impact of General Washington's farewell address, again in 1783. At every level, these examples also explicate the turmoil of revolutionary and early republican times.

Self-recognition, the *assurance* of independence, comes only with victory in arms between 1781 and 1783, and Americans have found a primal sense of identity in acts of war ever since. The argument here is not one of an assumed militarism or special belligerence but rather of a far more intrinsic sense of definition in the possibility and outcome of military conflict. Manifestations abound in an American psyche keyed from the start to the common defense, the right to bear arms, the conquest of frontiers, and, later, to the inevitable spread and victory of republicanism. For textual evidence, however, one need look no further than the national anthem as a central artifact of violent beginnings. Written on the night of September 13–14, 1814, "The Star-Spangled Banner" presents early republican fears in the guise of a helpless prisoner, a civilian who is plunged suddenly into war and who watches the naval bombardment of Baltimore's Fort McHenry from the perspective of his captors in the invading British fleet:

> O! SAY can you see by the dawn's early light,
> What so proudly we hailed at the twilight's last gleaming,
> Whose broad stripes and bright stars through the perilous fight,
> O'er the ramparts we watch'd were so gallantly streaming?
> And the rockets' red glare, the bombs bursting in air,
> Gave proof through the night that our flag was still there.
> O! say does that star-spangled banner yet wave,
> O'er the land of the free, and the home of the brave?
>   On the shore dimly seen through the mists of the deep,
> Where the foe's haughty host in dread silence reposes,
> What is that which the breeze, o'er the towering steep,
> As it fitfully blows, half conceals, half discloses?
> Now it catches the gleam of the morning's first beam.
> In full glory reflected now shines in the stream.
> 'Tis the star-spangled banner, O! long may it wave
> O'er the land of the free, and the home of the brave.

And where is that band who so vauntingly swore
That the havoc of war and the battle's confusion,
A Home and a country, shall leave us no more?
Their blood has wash'd out their foul footsteps pollution;
No refuge could save the hireling and slave,
From the terror of flight, or the gloom of the grave;
And the star-spangled banner in triumph doth wave,
O'er the land of the free, and the home of the brave.
     O! thus be it ever when freemen shall stand,
Between their lov'd home, and the war's desolation,
Blest with vict'ry and peace, may the Heav'n rescued land,
Praise the Power that hath made and preserved us a nation!
Then conquer we must, when our cause it is just,
And this be our motto – "*In God is our Trust*";
And the star-spangled banner in triumph shall wave,
O'er the land of the free and the home of the brave.

To rescue the original meaning of Francis Scott Key's words is to recognize that the crucial first stanza opens and closes with questions of a consuming anxiety. The proud hailing of the symbol of American identity, the flag, has taken place in the last gleaming of a previous twilight, but that affirmation is now lost in the temporal moment of the stanza, the approach of another dawn. Key's embracing questions are "Can you see?" and "Does it wave?" The only sure identification takes the form of conflict itself. Casting all of his hopes in the past tense of the battle just fought, the poet consoles himself with the remembered glare of rockets and bombs bursting; they alone "gave proof through the night that our flag was still there." Subsequent stanzas confirm these hopes in the light of morning but only after hours of dreadful uncertainty in shadows half concealing, half disclosing "on the shore dimly seen."

Dangers faced through military prowess dominate the last three stanzas. The narrative of doubts quickly raised and slowly settled can be measured in the march of grammatical modes across Key's four refrains. The star-spangled banner appears first in the interrogative mood (does it wave?), next in the subjunctive (may it wave), and only after "in triumph" in the declarative (it doth wave) and imperative (it shall wave) of stanzas 3 and 4. Throughout, Key punctuates victory with the havoc of war. Unfolding, in proper sequence, are the battle's confusion, blood, pollution, lost refuge, the terror of flight, and, finally, the gloom of the grave. Meanwhile, the poet's theme, the reiterated point of the anthem, insists upon the vital relevance of a "home of the brave" in maintaining "the land of the free." True republicans stand armed and vigilant "between their lov'd home, and the war's desolation." When they conquer in a just cause, the star-spangled flag, symbol of triumph, both receives and reflects their achievement ("In fully glory reflected now shines in the stream").

Here and everywhere in the America of the early Republic, the transference from conflict to saving knowledge takes place in the constitutive metaphor of light. Benjamin Franklin, the living symbol of the American Enlightenment, typifies this dynamic with one of his analogies from everyday life. "By the Collision of different Sentiments," he explains in his essay "The Internal State of America" (1785), "Sparks of Truth are struck out, and political Light is obtained." Two things separate American writers from their European counterparts in their use of the conventional metaphor. First, Franklin and other Americans bring tremendous confidence and authority to the fusion of science, politics, and light in their explanation of a world in conflict. Second, and paradoxically, American writers experience many more problems than Europeans in the practical matter of discerning the object so enlightened. "O! SAY can you see?" asks the anthem, where saying is patently easier than seeing. Francis Scott Key's song in 1814 is a lively type in the difficulty of perceiving an experimental republic on the edge of a vast and unformed new world.

It is worth elaborating how metaphors of light respond so readily to early republican problems of perception. Metaphors, by definition, are tropes of transference in which an unknown or imperfectly known is clarified, defined, or described in terms of a known; when metaphor succeeds, the strange and the familiar save each other. Because American intellectuals of the formative era are obsessed with the half formed, the partially visible, light is the perfect metaphor for solving their problem. Light brings unknown space under the control of experience. Its presence renders the strange familiar and the familiar more exciting.

Light in this construct is the instrument of a larger epistemology. To see is to know in eighteenth-century thought. John Locke's *Essay Concerning Human Understanding* (1690) is only the most conspicuous of a series of philosophical texts to place the visual organization of knowledge over the other senses. Strictly speaking, an epistemology of sight has its beginnings in ancient analogies of spirituality, intellect, and light. The analogy itself has functioned in every culture, but it is the Enlightenment that secularizes the notion of illumination to make vision a purely human understanding. In Johnson's *Dictionary of the English Language* (1755), "to enlighten" means to illuminate, to supply with light, to instruct, to furnish with increase of knowledge, to cheer, to exhilarate, to gladden, to supply with sight, to quicken in the faculty of vision. The same secular frame of reference enables Locke to introduce his arguments about human psychology with "the Bounds between the enlightened and dark Parts of Things." The parallel for eighteenth-century Americans is an obvious one: light spreading across the dark (because unknown) New World. Either light will reveal an order previously unseen, or it will create its own order out of an unclear(ed) wilderness.

The creators of the early Republic often resort to conventional images of light in coping with problems of perception and order. With characteristic optimism, Thomas Jefferson in 1813 sees education as the passing of light from one taper to another, and, though that passage is fraught with obstacles and even with danger, Jefferson eagerly notes that "he who lights his taper at mine, receives light without darkening mine." His more pessimistic correspondent, John Adams, gives the same image a more negative twist. "Is the Nineteenth Century to be a Contrast to the Eighteenth?" he asks Jefferson two years later. "Is it to extinguish all the Lights of its Predecessor?" Of all the founders, Adams senses the greatest difficulty in seeing his country. As vice-president he tells Benjamin Rush that the continent is a vast whispering gallery in which "the people can agree upon nothing." "[O]n what," he asks, "do you found your hopes?" Adams's own hopes depend upon filling that whispering gallery with light. His *A Defence of the Constitutions* (1787) creates an *"American Boudoir,"* a room ringed in mirrors in which "our States may see themselves in it, in every possible light, attitude and movement."

None of these standard metaphors is particularly American, but they respond to American needs by reducing complex experience to a single, manageable problem in perception. Key's "bombs bursting in air" supply light without the related intrusion of sound or the disaster of contact. Jefferson's candle replaces inchoate ignorance with the point of knowledge. Adams's room of mirrors quells the discordant voices of his whispering gallery. War, political illiteracy, and faction – major anxieties in the early Republic – give way to visual certainties. The trick, in each case, is to create a unified calm out of a noisy situation, to let the primacy of vision allay confusion. Adams gives another instance in *Defence of the Constitutions* when, in comparing the future of America to the immensity of the universe, he first creates a safe and familiar point of view:

A prospect into futurity in America is like contemplating the heavens through the telescopes of Herschell. Objects stupendous in their magnitudes and motions strike us from all quarters, and fill us with amazement! . . . that mind must be hardened into stone that is not melted into the reverence and awe.

In this passage, science, nature, history, and religion are meant to cohere. Adams joins them to give form to the unfamiliar and to hold the unimaginable in one marvelous view.

The same passage illustrates how Enlightenment norms welcome a dominating perspective. Adams's telescope controls perception even as it enables sight. By accepting the restriction of the lens, a viewer sees farther and engages in the assumption of understanding better. The technical knowledge thus gained triggers the additional assumption of more light for all. Adams, in fact, follows an eighteenth-century convention best summarized in Alexander Pope's epitaph for Isaac Newton:

> Nature and Nature's Laws lay hid in Night;
> God said, *Let Newton be!* and all was *Light*.

The telescope is the perfect heuristic device for acting out faith in the Enlightenment. Adams's simile, "A prospect into futurity in America is like contemplating the heavens," ties that faith to a central rhetorical ploy. As in virtually every other major literary work of the early Republic, singleness of vision doggedly searches for and finds sublime order.

Benjamin Franklin is the greatest American writer of the age in part because he alone understands that the obsession with perspective might be used against itself for greater literary effect. He appreciates, as Jefferson and Adams do not, that point of view can generate as well as control interest. Most of his famous sketches or bagatelles recast a familiar point of view in a bizarre or uncomprehending context. "An Edict by the King of Prussia" (1773), "Rules by Which a Great Empire May be Reduced to a Small One" (1773), "The Sale of the Hessians" (1777), "The Ephemera" (1778), and "A Petition of the Left Hand" (1785) are all cases in point. In every one, Franklin plays a game of realization between levels of perception. Appropriately, the prolific inventor seems to have been proudest of his bifocals, the device that brings contrasting views together. When skeptics question his "double Spectacles," Franklin responds in 1785 with a drawing of his invention that projects his glasses onto the page and, from there, to the very nose of his reader. "I have only to move my Eyes up or down," he observes in a claim for universal application, "as I want to see distinctly far or near, the proper Glasses being always ready."

A similar lesson in optics may have saved the Revolution two years earlier at Newburgh, New York. Now forgotten, the incident epitomizes the new nation's first attempts to see itself and illustrates the specific dialectic of reason and domination at work in the American Enlightenment. In 1783 the Continental army in camp at Newburgh comes close to rebelling over the failure of Congress to honor promises of payment. Mutinous pamphlets are circulated, and a cabal of well-connected officers orchestrate a formal meeting with the express purpose of challenging the government. General Washington, supposedly elsewhere, suddenly appears in full-dress uniform before the conspirators and steps onto the raised dais of the officers' meeting hall. Even so, his speech for the occasion, one filled with the theoretical ideals of the

Enlightenment, fails to move these thoroughly disillusioned followers, and Washington turns, instead, to a separate text, a letter from a sympathetic member of Congress who offers to seek the necessary funding.

The unfolding scene depends upon an eighteenth-century regard for spectacle and for the power of sentiment. Washington, renowned for his impeccable grace and decorum, finds himself unable to read the fine script of his congressional correspondent and pauses awkwardly. Then, fumbling in his waistcoat, he pulls into view what only his intimates have seen before, a pair of glasses. His next words end all opposition and reduce his officers to tears: "gentlemen, you will permit me to put on my spectacles. For I have not only grown gray but almost blind in the service of my country." Assured of victory, Washington then reads the letter that no one would later remember, and, without another word, slowly withdraws while his officers watch him, first, as he makes his way out, in the hall, and then, through the windows.

Visual reversals control the scene. The absent leader materializes as if by magic to dominate the situation, a not infrequent motif for Washington in revolutionary lore. (Similar advents quash a riot amongst the soldiery in 1776 and prove decisive at the battles of Princeton and Monmouth in 1777 and 1778.) Although he sees farthest in the crisis, this leader appears blind. His spectacles enable him to see, but, in the view of others, they bespeak an affecting inability − a rare personal but all too human failing. Washington's opponents once more become his followers (learn to see again as he does) only when they themselves are blinded by tears. Their aroused feelings, in an eighteenth-century understanding of the role of sentiment, then compels a new intellectual and moral awareness and, through them, a visionary rededication. In departing, the vanishing Washington grows in stature. Every eye frames him in the windows of the building from which the officers first sought to exclude him. At the heart of these reversals is the dialectic of the Enlightenment. Reason, having failed in Washington's original speech, finds another way to dominate (reason and emotion exemplified in the commanding figure) in order to obtain the consent of the governed.

It is not too much to suggest that Washington *is* the country in this moment. What exactly do we see in the midst of so many compounded ironies? At the center stands the uniformed figure, already on a pedestal or dais and then framed in the window when the example is complete. This father of his country is first and foremost a military hero, the American Cincinnatus. In its republican aspect, the Roman model in the Enlightenment embodies liberty; in its military aspect, discipline. Washington combines liberty and discipline, reason and domination. Pedestal, uniform, and the life of discipline in the service of liberty bring him into focus as a figure to be obeyed. At the same time, the notion of Cincinnatus signifies patriotic sacrifice. Washington's minor handicap in aging – "I have not only grown gray but almost blind in the service of my country" – raises that theme. It humanizes the unapproachable leader just enough to remind everyone that a living person has achieved such greatness in confirmation of the secular ideals of the Enlightenment.

Of course, the dangers in what happens at Newburgh are great. Kant's directive to have courage to do one's own thinking has been reified in the courageous individual as communal exemplum. Washington, in this sense, operates as the first figure in a hagiography that identifies America to other Americans. By the 1820s Daniel Webster and other civic orators will have arranged these beacons of light into fixed and eternal constellations that guide the nation. As the leaders of the Revolution are tied to national institutions, their writings and lives become blueprints for the history of the period. And when their words prove insufficient, the knowledge of their sacrifices in the act of founding can always be called upon. As a group, they overcome the vagaries of place and association in the emerging republic. The hagiography of transcendent individuals creates an instantaneous set of traditions, an imaginary national landscape for controlling space and understanding the world.

III

This imaginary landscape involves crucial literary questions – questions about the relation of writer, leader, text, and audience in the goals of the American Enlightenment. In Kant's essay *An Answer to the Question: "What is Enlightenment?"* the enlightened leader is a guardian who teaches that it is the duty of all citizens to think for themselves, but that guardian must also allow for "the great unthinking mass," or everything will be lost. The ideal, in Kantian terms, is *"a man of learning addressing the entire reading public."* The more frequent reality, and Kant's own example, is someone like Frederick the Great, king of Prussia, who demands obedience as an exemplary leader. The knowledge of the teacher and the status of the ruler combine in the ambiguous position of guardian. The combination is essential because a people can only achieve enlightenment slowly. Kant is quite explicit on the problem: not even a revolution, he says, can reform thought fast enough for reason alone to lead in the figure of learning. Those citizens who have not learned to think for themselves must defer to authority. Hence, when Washington's words fail to convince his officers at Newburgh, he must find ways to invest the exemplary leader in either that text or another at hand.

Just as the Enlightenment text divides in its dual attempt to command and to reason, require and to educate, so the essence of literary skill in writing such a text involves the creation of unities out of divergent possibilities. This skill marks the central dynamic in American revolutionary and postrevolutionary writings; the easiest recourse, one that bolsters the hagiographical tradition, is to weave together the claims of reason with the claimants to leadership. Specifically, in literary practice, the attempt to reason insists upon its right to authority, while the attempt to command urges its own rectitude, an interplay that makes virtue in leadership the pervasive theme of the period.

Two related features also inform the nature and energy of the writings of the American Enlightenment. First, and to an unusual degree, the leaders of the Revolution believe in ideas as intrinsic repositories of meaning. Second, the source of these ideas depends heavily on the international context of the Enlightenment. Both points have often been overlooked even though they are essential to the vitality and original courage of writings that now seem timeworn and pedestrian.

Ideas are repositories of meaning in that they answer the problematics of the unknown and indeterminate in revolutionary America. The first dilemma in perception always consists in knowing where one stands. Ideas supply that knowledge of place for America's first national leaders. Thus, in 1789, Franklin expresses hope that "a thorough Knowledge of the Rights of Man, may pervade all the Nations of the Earth, so that a Philosopher may set his Foot anywhere on its Surface and say, 'This is my Country.' " In this formulation, the complexities, particularities, and frustrations of time, location, and custom give way to an easier equation in which a knowledge of rights becomes a knowledge of country.

The spread of ideas lifts the chaos of the present into the ordered spaces of the future, all of which the Enlightenment has promised. Even in the worst of times, 1799, Jefferson trusts not to politics, or to states, or to other institutions but, as he puts it in a letter to William Green Mumford, "to the American mind . . . opened." Once again, ideas are substitutes for the messiness of place. This is what the hope of the Enlightenment can mean for the architect of a new culture. In writing to Mumford, Jefferson believes, like the Marquis de Condorcet, that the human mind is formed for society and that it is "perfectible to a degree of which we cannot as yet form any conception." Jefferson's belief in human progress is a controlling lens much as is John Adams's telescope in *Defence of the Constitutions*.

The presumed advance of knowledge can reduce discord and turmoil to momentary distractions. Describing the troubled election of 1800, Jefferson writes Joseph Priestley that it has been a raging tempest in a new nation of great extent and sparse habitation. Nonetheless, all is well. The storm has broken, and "science and honesty are replaced on their high ground," proof for Jefferson that "this whole chapter in the history of man is new." The excitement in these words has to do with the power of ideas in transmission. In Europe the Enlightenment must overcome the wreckage of human history, or, as Jefferson tells Priestley, "the times of Vandalism, when ignorance put everything into the hands of power and priestcraft." Not so, in America. Freed from the tyranny of the past, ideas, even the same ideas, flourish in a different way "under the protection of those laws which were made for the wise and the good." Jefferson's convictions carry him beyond the canniness of immediate political understanding. The intellectual possibilities of the Enlightenment in America have changed the facts! Properly understood, they make history itself new.

This enthusiasm in the sophisticated politician needs to be taken at face value. Jefferson, the enlightened thinker as president in what he calls "the Revolution of 1800," seeks not so much the origins of ideas as their application in a place where ideas have the chance to be different things altogether. Historians are forgetting this orientation when they concentrate on the details of cross-cultural refraction. Does Jefferson in 1776 base the Declaration of Independence on his readings of John Locke, as some have argued, or on alternative readings of continental philosophers like Jean-Jacques Burlamaqui, or on the Scottish Enlightenment? Do the court-and-country debates of England or the Common Sense traditions of Scotland control revolutionary rhetoric in America? Can we resolve these polarities by thinking of the American Enlightenment as a progression from moderate origins in the English Enlightenment toward the radical implications of the French and then on to the conservative reaction of the Scottish? Such questions cannot be answered in the way that many historians ask them – with nationalistic orientations in mind.

The Enlightenment text as literature grows out of a commitment to the general relation and spread of ideas. Franklin runs with this theme when he associates "country" with wherever a philosopher can find "the Rights of Man." The true philosophe thinks in terms of a universal language, identifying less with nations than with the republic of letters, and revolutionary Americans are peculiarly susceptible to the international scope of these identifications. As republicans, they easily accept the republic of letters. As Americans, they reject the specific example of *every* European national history. As citizens of the New World, they are interested in the fresh application of ideas and not in the origins and details of systems of thought. Above all, as Enlightenment thinkers, they believe in the global sphere of connections and the promise of republicanism throughout the world.

These tendencies explain Jefferson's seemingly casual but actually profound faith in abstractions and in decontextualized thought as he writes the

Declaration of Independence. In the Declaration, as he tells Henry Lee in 1825, he is addressing the tribunal of the world, not from any particular and previous writing but from the harmonizing sentiments of the day as expressed "in conversation, in letters, printed essays, or in the elementary books of public right, as Aristotle, Cicero, Locke, Sidney, etc." Only in this manner can he hope to achieve what he intended: "an expression of the American mind." The creativity in this process has too often been ignored. Jefferson uproots and then harmonizes European ideas to make something specifically American out of them.

Put another way, the American Enlightenment thrives upon perceived affinities rather than on exclusive correlations. An eighteenth-century intellectual still believes in reading everything. The higher goal of that intellectual in America is to find and to apply those portions of a universal knowledge that will work best in the unprecedented setting of new world republicanism. These priorities should not be mistaken for either the rejection of intellectual traditions or utilitarianism or simple opportunism. The leaders of 1776 have better reasons than most to believe in the power of ideas, but they have come to understand ideas within the praxis of successful revolution. Their relation to an idea is one of change. Possibilities dominate their thinking. When Jefferson tells Priestley that "this whole chapter in the history of man is new," he means that ideas have succeeded in transforming the nature of revolutionary America.

Belief in a different American future qualifies the relevance of the European past. Jefferson, Adams, and Franklin, in particular, pick and choose among European frames of reference, and they do so while convinced of the limited bearing of each. They borrow ideas instead of accepting or rejecting them out of hand. Indeed, no other generation of American thinkers before the twentieth century, saving perhaps that of the first Puritans, feels and exercises such a sense of parity with its European counterparts, and the sources of this self-confidence should be clear. The success of the Revolution ratifies the independence of each additional American decision. So too, for Americans, the corresponding failure of republicanism in Europe limits the relevance of European thought and confirms the need for at least some areas of intellectual separation.

Just how widely and loosely eighteenth-century Americans select their ideas can be seen in the actual patterns that they borrow from the European Enlightenment. From the French Enlightenment of Voltaire, Montesquieu, and Buffon, they take the philosophe as international hero, a love of system, literary style within system, the uses of a philosophy of history in political science, a fascination with technology, a belief in a natural order, and a distrust of organized religion. From England comes empirical investigation in general, Newtonian science and Lockean psychology, the Whig theory of history, political oratory, and the rights of English subjects. The Continental legal philosophers (Grotius, von Pufendorf, Burlamaqui, Beccaria) contribute the primacy of natural law, the notion of a government formed in compact under law, and the essential analogy between a rule of law and the life of reason. The Scottish Enlightenment, in turn, furnishes a secular vocabulary that nevertheless keeps Providence safely in mind. It also encourages the primacy of public learning and educational institutions, the relation of economic growth to political freedom, and, not least, the justification for a colony's right of revolution.

Again, however, it is the interpenetration of these influences that counts in America. When in 1826 James Madison calls Jefferson "a 'walking Library,' " he is celebrating the capacity to apply any combination of ideas in the activity of American life. The great goal in this life of activity is to connect science (the regularity and knowability of the world) with morality (the politics of the good life) in social progress. The leaders of the Revolution, in another manifestation of the hagiography of heroes, themselves illustrate the combinations at work. Franklin can be the universal beacon for the path to be taken because he symbolizes the union of science and politics. In Turgot's phrase, "[H]e seized the lightning from the sky, and the sceptre from tyrants."

IV

The intellectual self-confidence, scope, and facility of revolutionary thought are a part of the ultimate paradox of the Enlightenment in America. For alongside these characteristics is a heightened uncertainty, leading to a strange juxtaposition of moods in representative texts of the periods. Even the most measured thought acquires an urgency in actual writings. Reason, no matter how reasonable, gives way to emotion in crucial moments. The conjunction of science and history, the spread of light, the belief in ideas all translate into a single imperative or tonal byword: "now."

Thomas Paine's *Common Sense* offers a case in point. "Now is the seed-time of continental union, faith and honor. The least fracture now will be like a name engraved with the point of a pin on the tender rind of a young oak," writes Paine. "It might be difficult, if not impossible," he adds, "to form the Continent into one government half a century hence." Delay of any kind is impossible: "the *time hath found us*"; "the *present time* is the *true time*. . . . that peculiar time, which never happens to a nation but once." Its special urgency notwithstanding, Paine's pamphlet is quite typical in its claim. The rhetoric of the Revolution reads in general like a race against time from first to last.

Stridency will dominate any revolutionary statement, but *Common Sense* achieves this tone with the deepest metaphor of the Enlightenment, and it did so in a way that suggests an American place in history. Deeper, more important than even the notion of light in the optimism of eighteenth-century thought is the concept of an approaching maturity. "Youth is the seed time of good habits, as well in nations as in individuals," Paine explains, right after claiming that "the heaviest achievements were always accomplished in the non-age of a nation." Remember that Kant defines enlightenment as humanity's emergence from a self-incurred immaturity. How are Americans to interpret this idea in a New World setting of national beginnings? How, in sum, are they to construe a condition of unavoidable cultural adolescence? Separation from the mother country can imply either a natural movement toward the control of one's own destiny or the untimely, irreparable loss of the orphan. The distinction depends not just on the worthiness of the English mother – a much debated issue in the 1770s – but also on assumptions about the maturation process in America. Only children can be orphans.

As Paine's words indicate, revolutionary writings trade constantly on the theme of youth in action as a mixture of vulnerability, necessity, and virtue. They also argue all sides of the question with considerable facility. While the newness of history in America is a favorite theme, so is the assumption that Americans have somehow outdistanced European peoples by a thousand years. The answer to this apparent contradiction lies in a new kind of maturity through education – an answer that Enlightenment norms encourage. On the other hand, the same answer increases every sense of historical urgency: the greater the presumed discrepancy between European and American peoples, the more immediate the peril of cross-cultural contamination through immigration.

The leaders of the American Revolution worry that education might not proceed fast enough to secure a virtuous republic of unified citizens. The very theme of virtue raises the danger of corruption; inevitably, foreign influence becomes every republican's first fear. Jefferson, in *Notes on the State of Virginia,* writes that immigration disturbs American principles and will reduce the populace to "a heterogeneous, incoherent, distracted mass." More pessimistic writers think it only a matter of time before ignorance and corruption from abroad overwhelm the Revolution.

The emphasis in *Common Sense* on youth in action also reduces history to a fleeting moment. Act now, says Paine over and over again, or lose the possibility forever, and the assumption is one that the leaders of the Revolution share with surprising unanimity. From their studies of the republican form of government in history, they conjecture that the people will become "careless" and "forget" their virtue. "It can never be too often repeated,"

Jefferson warns in *Notes on the State of Virginia,* "that the time for fixing every essential right on a legal basis is while our rulers are honest, and ourselves united. From the conclusion of this war we shall be going down hill." The concept of maturity translates easily into metaphors of national identity and growth, but the inevitable passage of youth translates just as easily into the rise and fall of nations. *Common Sense* is not the only paradigmatic text in 1776; the same year brings the first volume of Edward Gibbon's *The Decline and Fall of the Roman Empire.*

Their view of history also leads revolutionary writers to articulate the gravest dangers in failure. Education, exploration, and invention should unite in the general advance of humanity, but that possibility depends upon prompt action in the more immediate and unpredictable realm of politics. Progress, in other words, is not a predetermined evolution through fixed stages of history. The moment can yield permanent darkness as easily as additional light. These alternatives, in their starkness, define the fullest meaning of crisis in the eighteenth-century American mind. In the fresh dispensation of the new world, events are freighted with an extraordinary double capacity for either good or ill. The stakes are permanently high. Whatever revolutionary Americans do or do not do, they believe that their actions will change the direction of history — possibly forever.

The assumption of urgency denotes another difference between European and American Enlightenment. The conviction of a historical crisis comes late to the European Enlightenment and then only when the battle of ideas has assumed political dimensions. In America, by way of contrast, the Enlightenment *begins* in the political arena, where it unleashes the earliest recognitions of stress and disjuncture. The writers of the American Revolution always ask the same question: What should be done in the present moment? Answers aside, the strategy has its own appeal: it demands the possibility of meaningful action, and it fosters the belief, accepted by later generations of Americans, that social destiny and perhaps history itself can be controlled by recognizing and responding to crisis.

We see as much in George Washington's "Circular to the States" (1783), or, as it was then known, "Washington's Farewell to the Army." In his stoicism, Washington imparts the centrality of crisis in republican thought more convincingly than, say, the rabble-rousing Paine, or the anxious John Adams, or even Jefferson, the man of ideas. Washington's use of standard literary conventions also clarifies the impulses of the day in a way that more original writers might not. This conventionality, however, should not disguise a considerable skill. Washington's writings, as clearly as those of any other leader, make the American Revolution a literary phenomenon. "Circular to the States" is a representative text that we no longer know how to read.

Washington's "Farewell Address" as president in 1796 would rhetorically duplicate and overshadow this earlier effort, but in the 1780s there is no more important document in America except for the Constitution itself.

The four expressed goals in "Circular to the States" will dominate discussion four years later in Philadelphia. In fact, Washington's articulation of them in 1783 prefigures and, to a considerable extent, enables the agenda of 1787. The writer urges a stronger union, a sacred regard to public justice, a systematic attention to the public defense, and, lastly, a spirit of subordination and obedience to government in the sacrifice of local prejudices to the larger community. Each of these goals bespeaks the larger one of capping the Revolution by safely channeling the energies of rebellion. Not surprisingly, then, Washington's address raises a fear of potential chaos – a fear expressed variously as licentiousness, a state of nature, the extreme of anarchy, and the ruins of liberty.

Less conventional is Washington's astute resolution of the dichotomy between instruction and commandment in the Enlightenment text. Although major aspects of "Circular to the States" depend upon the writer's experience and station as General of the Army, the address rests within the reiteration of Washington's pending resignation and retreat to domestic life. His readers, as he tells them, are receiving his last official communication as a public character. It is a natural time for reflection, but Washington adds to the power of the moment by holding onto the unique relevance of his experience as commander in chief of the army. His "many anxious days and watchful nights" in that service give him a special perspective and entitle him to write "the more copiously on the subject of our mutual felicitation." Under the circumstances, he can also insist that "silence in me would be a crime." The last moment in office thus becomes the *most* public, the most assertive. The words that follow build into what Washington himself calls "the Legacy of One, who has ardently wished, on all occasions, to be useful to his Country." This conceit is well chosen. Legacies bestow, but they also stipulate and require.

The address proper opens with a paean to the Enlightenment in America: "The foundation of our Empire was not laid in the gloomy age of Ignorance and Superstition, but at an Epocha when the rights of mankind were better understood and more clearly defined, than at any former period." This prospect appears just as bountiful whether regarded from "a natural, a political or moral point of light." The metaphorical use of light typically joins different categories in a common focus or "point." Washington argues that "the free cultivation of Letters, the unbounded extension of Commerce, the progressive refinement of Manners, the growing liberality of sentiment, and above all, the pure and benign light of Revelation, have had a meliorating influence on mankind and increased the blessings of Society." These elements, taken together, have given Americans "a fairer opportunity for political happiness than any other Nation has ever been favored with" and have made them "the Actors on a most conspicuous Theatre."

The image of actors on a stage is a telling one. Theatricality is never far from either Washington's sense of persona or his prose. In this instance, his classical song of praise abruptly shifts toward eighteenth-century melodrama. Noting the many blessings that the United States enjoy, Washington warns that "if their Citizens should not be completely free and happy, the fault will be entirely their own." The conditional clause is a signal. It carries us over the edge of pleasing encomium toward sensational incident and emotional appeal. The prospect of perfect felicity raises the other possibility, of failure, and thought of the later is too awful to bear.

The swift downturn that follows represents a darker, more concrete version of what, in 1783, is only an abstract issue in European thought. Writing just a year before Kant's essay on enlightenment, Washington actually wrestles with the same subject. Both men worry most about the uncertain period between revolution and enlightenment. But where the European philosopher works out a positive solution to a perceived problem, the American soldier and man of action dwells far more on the immediate implications of failure. Practical responsibilities bring an anxiety that theory does not have. The readers of "Circular to the States" learn that "this is the time of their political probation . . . this is the moment to establish or ruin their national Character forever." Washington draws the conclusion that Kant would only hint at. "[I]t is yet to be decided," he writes, "whether the Revolution must ultimately be considered as a blessing or a curse: a blessing or a curse, not to the present age alone, for with our fate will the destiny of unborn Millions be involved."

Washington, the most phlegmatic of men, emphasizes "the importance of the Crisis, and the magnitude of the objects in discussion." Everything depends on whether or not "we have a disposition to seize the occasion and make it our own." Five times in a paragraph, Washington intones "this is the moment," either "favorable" or "ill-fated." The only options in this rhetoric of extremes are sudden victory or permanent defeat. There is no middle ground either in the moment or for the unborn millions to come. At issue is whether the United States "will stand or fall," "whether they will be respectable and prosperous, or contemptible and miserable as a Nation." Significantly, this balance in contrasting fates will appear more and more critical to Washington in retirement at Mount Vernon during the middle 1780s. Worries about "the present unsettled and deranged state of public affairs," which he expressed to Jonathan Trumbull in early 1784, soon become major anxieties; "from the high ground on which we stood," he writes James Warren by late 1785, "we are descending into the vale of confusion and darkness."

V

The American literature of the period thrives in the resonant space between the hope of blessing and the fear of curse. It defines itself in that crisis; this is where it holds its audiences. In so doing, early republican writings depend heavily upon the process of the Enlightenment. It is the struggle toward realization, not the celebration of knowledge, that creates meaning and interest. The Americans who fight for their independence on the edge of the British Empire cannot compete with European writers for centrality in any presentation of knowledge. Instead, they find their importance on the very different edge of the Enlightenment. In dramatic combinations – the hope of blessing and the fear of curse – they place themselves where light and darkness meet.

Skillful choreography of these processes epitomizes literary creativity. When Alexander Hamilton begins *Federalist No. 1* with the observation that the United States are "an empire, in many respects, the most interesting in the world," he means, first, that "the fate" of that empire hangs in the balance and, second, that American government is the greatest test of the Enlightenment ("it seems to have been reserved to the people of this country, by their conduct and example, to decide the important question, whether societies of men are really capable or not, of establishing good government from reflection and choice"). The fate of empire presents the possibility of failure; the experiment with good government establishes a context for thinking about success. In conflict, these factors, failure and success, constitute "the crisis, at which we are arrived," and a negative consequence will carry beyond the moment to "the general misfortune of mankind." Every reader has an investment in the uncertain struggle that Hamilton has sketched.

The difficulty, of course, is that the struggle remains uncertain; the outcome unclear. Process reaches only so far in the explanation of ends, and the human scale of the Enlightenment has a way of trapping every user somewhere in the broader reaches of history. Reason might clarify events, and the spread of knowledge might even make history new, but both remain entirely within the never-ending flux of circumstance – the rise and fall of nations. Time may be on the side of the Revolution, but for how long? The limits of reason and knowledge are clear even to the most optimistic early republicans when this question and others like it are asked.

In response, as well as by heritage, revolutionary writers often express their thought in spiritual terms. Washington's decision to filter the Revolution through "the pure and benign light of Revelation" and through the language of "blessing and curse" is symptomatic of a general reliance on religious forms and ideas. "Statesmen, my dear Sir, may plan and speculate for liberty," John Adams explains in 1776, writing to his cousin Zabdiel Adams, "but it is religion and morality alone which can establish the principles upon which freedom can securely stand." For most revolutionary Americans, history is still a safer subject with Providence in mind.

Providence, however, must not be misused. In his *Defence of the Constitutions of Government,* the same Adams will insist that American government has its beginnings in "the natural authority of the people alone, without a pretence of miracle or mystery," "without the monkery of priests." "It will never be pretended," he observes here, "that any persons employed in [the formation of the American governments] had interviews with the gods, or were in any degree under the inspiration of Heaven. . . . it will forever be acknowledged that these governments were contrived merely by the use of reason and the senses." In these words, Adams shares the general disdain of the Enlightenment for religious enthusiasm and superstition; yet he also knows that the natural authority of the people is a dangerous variable left to itself and that a government "merely contrived" will soon disappear in the immense scale of universal history.

It is part of Adams's American identity that he already has secured the coherence of a higher view. "The people in America," he begins *Defence of the Constitutions,* "have now the best opportunity and the greatest trust in their hands that Providence ever committed to so small a number since the transgression of the first pair; if they betray their trust, their guilt will merit even greater punishment than other nations have suffered, and the indignation of Heaven." Adams, no doubt, believes in this version of the covenant, but it is also an intellectual and political convenience, at once defining the people and placing external limits upon them. His easy mix of secular and religious explanation is everywhere in the period, and, writ large, it signifies a blend of belief and convenience that remains the single most elusive quality in the rhetoric of the times. Far from representing a loss or even a qualification in conviction, the intellectual facility of Adams and others seems to have fed upon itself. A potentially corrosive, separate faith in the Enlightenment actually explodes into fervor, and it does so precisely because it helped Americans bring their own peculiar brand of the Reformation to the Revolution.

The American Enlightenment does not quarrel with religious orthodoxies as its French counterpart does; it rests, instead, in the common or shared rhythms and patterns that the Enlightenment has taken from Christianity. The parallels in intellectual reference – salvation and progress, the health of the soul and the corresponding gauge of public interest, the regenerate

Christian and the virtuous citizen, exultation of the divine and celebration of design — are homologies in American thought rather than substitutes, one for the other, as in European philosophy. Moreover, although many eighteenth-century Americans seem to have been aware of the slippage between categories, they hold to their combinations.

The explanation lies in the still puzzling connection between Enlightenment thought and Reform Protestantism in the moment of revolutionary engagement. As the challenge of reason against mere authority supplies the broadest intellectual legitimacy and mutual recognition in American pamphleteering, so the divinely ordained mission of the primitive church motivates and justifies radical communal action. Never mind that the abstract projections of reason rob formal religion of its essential mysteries and of its retrogressive impulses toward purification! The enlightened spread of knowledge and the oppositional strategies in Congregationalism join in the idea of vigilance as patriotic virtue.

There is, in fact, no Revolution without the combination. When the Reverend Samuel Sherwood of Connecticut connects piety, public virtue, and love of country in *Scriptural Instructions to Civil Rulers and all Free-born Subjects* (1774), one of the most influential of all revolutionary sermons, he believes that only "fear of the lord" in a people "incessantly vigilant and watchful" can make a state free. A masterful conflation of divine sanctions and secular rights, *Scriptural Instructions to Civil Rulers* extols "the common cause, the public good, and general interest in the land" and seeks "to make up, unite, and gather into one common interest, all the good protestants in this land." Unmistakably, fear of the Lord and the people's vigilance over their rights do go together; a godly people, by definition, *will* discover and *will* act on the common cause. Sherwood and other ministers soon turn these stances into an involved typology of biblical text to American event. In *The Church's Flight into the Wilderness*, Sherwood's clerical counterpart to Paine's *Common Sense* in the same year, "the light of revelation" will also be "the path of the just." Here, in 1776, revelation and reason will fuse in the mission of national union.

3

RELIGIOUS VOICES

I

Religious voices speak first in the Revolution. At one level, this primacy merely restates the dominance of religious expression in early American culture. Until 1765, religious publications in the colonies outnumber all other intellectual writings combined, and they remain the single largest category of publication throughout the revolutionary era. But initial dominance only begins to explain the importance of religious expression in Anglo–American political debate. The relation between dissenting religious traditions and the growth of oppositional political discourse is a barometer of cultural modification and literary creativity throughout the era.

Steeped in the English revolutions of the seventeenth century, radical Protestants in eighteenth-century America know how to oppose a king. Jonathan Mayhew's approval of "the Resistance made to King Charles I" in *A Discourse Concerning Unlimited Submission* (1750) is shocking to his contemporaries not because it "takes the side of Liberty, the *BIBLE,* and Common Sense, in opposition to Tyranny, *PRIESTCRAFT,* and Nonsense" – standard dichotomies in eighteenth-century Protestant thought – but because, in rejecting "the slavish doctrine of passive obedience and nonresistance," it also advocates the right to judge and then act against a king as part of "the natural and legal rights of the people against the unnatural and illegal encroachments of arbitrary power."

Similar language could be heard in England, but it dominates debate in America in a different way altogether. Mayhew, after all, first preaches *Discourse Concerning Unlimited Submission* before his own congregation in the prestigious West Church of Boston. He and other American clergymen can take greater risks than their English counterparts when accused of "preaching politics instead of *CHRIST*" because they face a large and uniquely sympathetic audience for radical Protestant polemics. The single greatest factor in the evolution of a revolutionary dynamic is the religious distinctiveness of that audience. Maintained and encouraged from church congregation to church congregation across the denominational spread of reform Protestantism, this distinctiveness breeds a colossal presumption. Never mind that John Adams lives on the obscurest fringe of the British Empire in February 1765; he is also an attentive reader of Mayhew's sermons, and of countless others like them, when he writes "I always consider, the settlement of America with Reverence and Wonder — as the Opening of a grand scene and Design in Providence, for the Illumination of the Ignorant and the Emancipation of the slavish Part of Mankind all over the Earth." Some have stressed the conscious art in statements like this one, but there is no chance of understanding the early American scene, either of the colonies or of the early Republic, without assessing the interplay between religion and politics as a source of liberty.

The differences from England are instructive and somewhat startling against the continuities of religious origin and influence. In the eighteenth century, at least two of every three colonial Americans place themselves somewhere within the religious dissenting tradition. England, by way of contrast, lapses into a moderate Anglicanism after the exhausting religious wars of the preceding century; dissenters dwindle to a small minority, as low as 7 percent of the total English population. By 1775, in his *Resolutions for Conciliation with the Colonies,* Edmund Burke finds it necessary to spell out the difference for an uncomprehending Parliament. Religion in America, he warns, "is a refinement on the principle of resistance" and "of that kind which is most adverse to all implicit submission of mind and opinion." Long after the fact, the Loyalist leader and historian Peter Oliver will still blame the Revolution on the dissenting clergy, "the black regiment" of rebellion in America.

But if religious dissent is a pivotal issue in the ideological formation of the Revolution, the exact nature of its influence remains the most complex and vexing puzzle in the question of national origins. Taken together, the remarks of Burke and Oliver point to one area of confusion. Did the oppositional modes of religious dissent well up into politics from the radical spirit of a Protestant people, as Burke's parliamentary speech implies, or did an organized clergy push colonial yeomanry toward rebellion, as Oliver would have it? The possibilities here often depend on the methodology of the investigator; for each preaching moderate scorned by a combative congregation, there is a "fighting pastor" just a parish away. If the ministry does lead, do rational liberal clergymen show the way, or does that honor belong more appropriately to their radical and evangelical counterparts? Nothing less than the presumed meaning and direction of American culture has been at stake in answers to these queries.

The questions themselves have been compounded by further historical investigation. It is now clear that the completed Revolution marginalizes clergymen in the political and economic life of the new nation. Ministers lose more ground in the social upheavals of the time than do any other intellectual grouping, and their downward mobility must be read in the light of a continuing vitality, unappreciated until recently, in the religious life of the people. Beyond these complications lies another mystery. How do religious conviction and the rational ideals of the secular Enlightenment come together so uncannily for certain Americans at the center of revolutionary activity? Forgotten ideological affinities explain their success. Perhaps nowhere else have the sudden and profound changes of the Revolution so obscured later understanding.

The most articulate strand in an American dissenting tradition comes, of course, from Puritanism, the legacy of seventeenth-century Anglo-American Presbyterianism and Congregationalism. The intellectual foundations of Puritanism lend themselves to oppositional discourse in ways both large and small. Among the more crucial influences are primitivism, anti-institutionalism, antiauthoritarianism, separatism and other assertions of local autonomy, the legalism of covenant theology, and biblical exegesis as regular cultural practice. The duty of reading the Bible on one's own – the Bible as the supreme guide in communal life, as the only true source of the connection between divine and human history, as the personal property of every true believer in the pious act of interpretation – appears to have been especially crucial in the evolution of a language of dissent. Because Puritanism ritually exposes the sinful heart to public judgment in a conversion experience, it also contrasts good and evil and relates individual morality to communal prosperity in compulsive ways. We are never far from the capacity to identify and resist an unworthy leadership.

Resistance to authority is, in fact, a general trait in colonial religious expression. Although most colonies follow the European model of an established church, pressure against religious uniformity represents the broadest single trait in colonial religion. Open competition among proliferating denominations and active lay involvement in church government distinguish American religion from its European origins and promote a general resistance to hierarchy. Establishmentarianism suffers in every region. William Livingston of New York is expressing an American conception when, in *The Independent Reflector* (October 11, 1753), he observes, "I Believe, that if the whole Kingdom professed one Religion, it would be of no Religion; and that the Variety of Sects in the Nation, are a Guard against the Tyranny and Usurpation of one over another." The underlying premise, toleration through the widest variation, is made famous as part of J. Hector St. John de Crèvecoeur's answer to "What is an American?" in *Letters from an American Farmer* (1782); another permutation will guard against the power of factionalism in *The Federalist No. 10* (1787).

Even in Virginia, where Anglican dominance is never in doubt, colonial leaders resist high church forms and centralization of authority. Faith in the Church of England does not prevent local vestries from controlling their own religious institutions. Later, when difficulty over Virginia's state-wide church tax erupts in the Parson's Cause of 1758, Virginians are already well on their way to a rhetoric of taxation without representation. "And what must be done with those Harpies, those Beasts of Prey, the publick Collectors?" asks Richard Bland, Virginia planter and Anglican vestryman, in his *Letter to the Clergy of Virginia* (1760). "Must they be left to feed, without Controul, upon the Vitals of the People?" The clerical response, an action to enforce payment through the Virginia courts, gives the lawyer Patrick Henry his first platform as the defender of American liberty.

The true measure of religious antiauthoritarianism can be taken in colonial fears of an America bishop. Anxiety over the prospect fuels controversy throughout the eighteenth century and leads to a major intercolonial eruption against the Church of England between 1767 and 1770. Eventually, the issue absorbs more ink than the Stamp Act dispute does and becomes a staple of radical ideological dissent – so much so that John Adams in 1815 can tell Jedediah Morse that "apprehension of Episcopacy" contributed as much as any other cause to the Revolution. The depth of this concern must also be understood against its groundlessness in fact. Establishment of an Anglican bishop in America remains an unlikely prospect at every point in the colonial period.

This discrepancy between fear and reality actually develops out of more intrinsic urgencies in early American character. Ministers like Charles Chauncy in Massachusetts, the most vocal leader in the antiepiscopacy movement of the late 1760s, do worry about the spread of Anglicanism in the New World, and for evidence to support their claims they have the growth in Anglican congregations (from three hundred to four hundred and fifty in America between 1750 and 1776) and Anglican missionary zeal (the English Society for the Propagation of the Gospel proselytizes throughout New England and the middle colonies). Even so, Anglicanism does not grow faster than other denominations in the period, and the real cause of protest lies deeper.

Colonial Americans, in effect, use their diatribes against episcopacy to recognize each other across denominational affiliations. Chauncy's *A Letter to a Friend* in 1767 is just one of many efforts in this category. Responding to John Lord Bishop of Landaff, Chauncy remonstrates against attempts "to EPISCOPISE the Colonies," but he does so in order to remind Americans of "the ERRAND of our forefathers into this Country" and of their indoctrination "in the PRINCIPLES OF CHRISTIAN LIBERTY." An embattled figure in colonial religious disputes, Chauncy can expect general agreement, even applause, on this issue. Distaste for high church ritual and practice is part of the broadest communal identification; liberty and piety are renewed in the name of the forefathers' first errand.

Almost as important in growing colonial self-recognition is the ease with which Chauncy can identify a British enemy. Distinctions between American virtue and English corruption constitute an increasing element in colonial discourse, but American leaders quickly grasp that it is safer to express these distinctions in religious rather than in political terms. Ecclesiastical differences are acceptable under liberty of conscience; political disputes raise the unacceptable prospect of faction. Not heresy but treason is the fear of the eighteenth-century Anglo-American intellectual. Accordingly, Chauncy can refer without risk to "malignity" and "the abounding growth of iniquity" in England, to English "secret back-biters and revilers" who act "through bigotry, prejudice, malice, interest, or some other lust of the flesh or mind," and, most particularly, to "that yoke of bondage" that forces the first Americans to flee England in order to "enjoy the freedom of men and christians."

The contrast in *A Letter to a Friend* is between British manipulation ("if Bishops should be sent to the Colonies, the people would generally turn Church-men") and American piety ("true Christianity is not *more generally* better practised in any part of the world"). When corrupt colonists do appear, they can be conveniently excluded from the purity of the American past. "Those that are so," Chauncy notes, "came to us from abroad." The moral bifurcation in this geographical scheme is a volatile ideological tool for Chauncy and others. In context, and under the pressure of language and events, the contrast slips into a conspiracy of evil against good, and the performance of unmasking British corruption appears at once an exercise in bravura and prudence. As a minister addressing his own flock, Chauncy can reject British culture and still remain free of political charges, all the while rallying Americans around their own popular standards of meaning.

Religious thought brings its own dynamic to the deepening political crisis of the 1760s and 1770s. Christian polarities contribute less to an understanding of complex problems in diplomacy and more to explanations based on an absolute difference. The identification of England with malignity and of America with virtue raises obvious biblical and historical parallels in the wars of the Lord – parallels that soon become exact in scriptural readings. By 1776, the apocalyptic "image of the beast" (Revelation 13:14–15) signifies "the corrupt system of tyranny and oppression, that has of late been fabricated and adopted by the ministry and parliament of Great-Britain." Here, in *The Church's Flight into the Wilderness,* Samuel Sherwood uses biblical typology to make the case for rebellion. "[W]e have incontestible evidence," explains Sherwood, "that God Almighty, with all the powers of heaven, are on our side." Acceptance of the premise assures victory. It also renders all thought of compromise impossible; one does not negotiate with the Antichrist.

The American revolutionary spirit owes everything to such rhetoric. In the skilled hands of the radical clergy, faintheartedness means impiety. As Samuel Langdon, preaching before the third Provincial Congress of Massachusetts, and David Jones, preaching in Philadelphia on a day of continental fast, both put the matter in 1775, "If God be with us, who can be against us?" The refrain plays upon the biblical trope of the chosen people, but it also helps many colonial minds over a political hurdle. In their respective calls to arms, even Langdon and Jones stumble over the question of royal allegiance. Like most colonial English subjects in 1775, they find it hard to fight their king.

The answer, for many of those who seek independence, comes through God's presence in colonial politics: heavenly authority supersedes an earthly king. "We must keep our eyes fixed on the supreme government of the Eternal King, as directing all events, setting up or pulling down the kings of the earth," says Langdon. Or, in the more succinct motto of Enlightenment so frequently ascribed to figures like Franklin and Jefferson, "rebellion to tyrants is obedience to God." These words demonstrate the power of belief and the limits of mere reason in the Revolution if properly understood. Interestingly enough, their source is not the secular Enlightenment but the darker side of English Puritanism. Long before Jefferson toys with the notion as an epitaph or Franklin proposes it for the Great Seal of the United States, the phrase "rebellion to tyrants is obedience to God" is already on the lips of John Bradshaw, the regicide judge who, as president of the parliamentary tribunal in 1649, refuses Charles I the right to speak before he is sentenced. Bradshaw already knows what eighteenth-century American Whigs would learn: faith, not logic, carries a rebellion.

II

Revivalism is the religious phenomenon most closely associated with the Revolution — expressly, the series of revivals at midcentury known as the Great Awakening (1734–50). Recently, however, historians have come to differ greatly over the nature, range, impact, and overall meaning of the Great Awakening; the very designation has been questioned as an unwarranted assumption about the solidarity of scattered events. Granted by some, but at issue for others, are the intercolonial character of the Awakening, its importance to lower-class protest, its relation to radical politics, and its lasting impact on social and religious institutions. And yet certain facts and assumptions remain common to all interpretations: prerevolutionary revivals take on a regional character that distinguishes them from earlier, more local communal outpourings, and their expanded scope gives them a significance that dominates religious thought and writing in America into the 1760s.

The diffuse and eclectic aspects of midcentury revivalism should not be ignored but neither should the cohesive impact of singular, affecting preachers like Jonathan Edwards among New England Congregationalists in the 1730s and 1740s, Gilbert Tennent among the Presbyterians of the middle colonies in the same decades, Samuel Davies among the Presbyterians of Virginia in the 1750s, and, above all, the English Methodist itinerant George Whitefield, who tours the colonies seven times between 1740 and his death in 1770. Their appeal is unprecedented in colonial life. Edwards counts thirty-two towns caught up in the Connecticut River Valley revival of 1734–5. Whitefield preaches in 1740 to fifteen thousand people in Boston, the largest crowd ever assembled there. Moreover, the scope of these appeals, their ability to reach across all cultural boundaries, thrives upon each preacher's recognition of broad social disjuncture.

The common thread in all prerevolutionary revivalism is its insistence upon crisis. Revivalist preachers do not have to look far to arouse the vulnerabilities of their congregations. Invasion from the wilderness remains a realistic fear in the middle third of the eighteenth century, a fear realized in the French and Indian Wars (1754–60). "The arrows of death fly unseen at noon-day," runs a characteristic warning in Edwards's *Sinners in the Hands of an Angry God* (1741). The late 1730s and 1740s are also times of enormous demographic dislocation (the colonial population moves often and rises from under three hundred thousand in 1700 to more than two million by 1770), of severe economic recession (Americans fall to their lowest standard of living in the century in 1745), and of epidemiological disaster (the diphtheria outbreak of 1735–7 alone kills as many as twenty thousand Americans; epidemics of various kinds regularly destroy between 5 and 10 percent of the population). By the same token, metaphors of communal breakdown, of rampant materialism, and of sickness dominate revivalist narratives.

One consequence is that prerevolutionary Americans already accept crisis as their accustomed frame of experience. Psychologically, they also look toward the revivalist's remedy: a dramatic change in status or conversion that separates sin and corruption from virtue and purity. Samuel Finley, a follower of Gilbert Tennent in the middle colonies, shows the way in *Christ Triumphing and Satan Raging* (1741) when he teaches his adherents how to "discern the Signs of THESE TIMES." "Why do you not either make the Tree good, and its Fruit good; or else corrupt, and its Fruit corrupt?" he asks. The true

Christian must make a choice for purity on the spot. "I tell you further," exhorts Finley, "that *the Sin against the Holy Ghost shall never be forgiven*. And I verily fear, that many, both Ministers and People, in this Generation, will be guilty of it. . . . tho' you be exalted nearer Heaven, yet woe to you, for with a more dreadful Vengeance will you be plung'd deeper into Hell."

The struggling Christian has but one comfort in this moment of extremities, but it is one filled with later social and political implications. The necessity for an immediate choice between heaven and hell is suddenly communal in its stress upon the present moment. For unlike most earlier forms of Christian exhortation, revivalism provides the assurance that no decision need ever be made alone. Its thrust toward immediate conversion within the listening group is one more sign of the desirable possibilities in union and, beyond, of a far more glorious opportunity for all.

Admonition works because it represents possibilities in the sinner's predicament, and these possibilities are immense in the fullest understanding of crisis. Revivalist writings frequently make the point that critical times are the best evidence of God's presence and coming glory. "Man's Extremity is the Lord's Opportunity," writes Samuel Davies, giving most succinct expression to the concept in *The State of Religion among the Protestant Dissenters in Virginia* (1751). Or, to take Jonathan Edwards' more complete formulation: "When [God] is about to bestow some great blessing on his church, it is often his manner, in the first place, so to order things in his providence, as to show his church their great need of it, and to bring them into distress for want of it, and so put them upon crying earnestly to him for it."

Here, in the single most influential statement on the subject, *Some Thoughts Concerning the Present Revival of Religion in New England* (1742), Edwards displays how extremity and opportunity could cohere in an explicit vision of America. Revivalism is nothing less than "a strange revolution, an unexpected, surprising overturning of things, suddenly brought to pass." Surprise, in this sense, relates directly to the "innumerable difficulties" that bring "God's dear children into great distress." The presence of distress "gives more abundant reason to hope that what is now seen in America, and especially in New England, may prove the dawn of that glorious day." *Some Thoughts Concerning the Revival* depends upon an involved antipodal reading to prove that the millennium – "when the saints shall reign on earth" – must begin in America instead of in the Old World. "When God is about to turn the earth into a Paradise," Edwards reckons, "he does not begin his work where there is some good growth already, but in a wilderness. . . . he will begin in this utmost, meanest, youngest and weakest part of it, where the church of God has been planted last of all."

Millennialist optimism, the projections of Christ's thousand-year reign on earth, pushes revivalism inexorably toward the notion of harmony and union in this world and, for that purpose, toward the need for conviction and action by a united people. *Some Thoughts Concerning the Revival* calls for "an agreement of all God's people in *America . . .* to keep a day of fasting and prayer; wherein we should all unite on the same day." By making "the union and agreement of God's people in his worship the more visible," a united America encourages God to "bow the heavens and come down, and erect his glorious kingdom through the earth." Edwards is hardly alone in these hopes. From the beginning of the century to the end, rhetoric about the future of America is about how and when heaven and earth will come together.

Five years later, in *An Humble Attempt to Promote Explicit Agreement and Visible Union of God's People,* Edwards gives further scope to a philosophical conception of union that comes out of crisis. Of England, he observes, "it looks as though the nation could hardly continue in being, but must sink under the weight of its own corruption and wickedness." Only by reiterating that "the church's extremity has often been God's opportunity," can Edwards believe "a happy change is nigh." In particular, the "remarkable religious awakenings" beginning in New England and continuing elsewhere give Edwards hope for an *"explicit agreement,* to unite in such prayer as is proposed to us." The peroration that follows will resonate in the American psyche for decades to come: "Union is one of the most amiable things that pertains to human society; yea, it is one of the most beautiful and happy things on earth, which indeed makes earth most like heaven." This "strange revolution" of Edwardsian revivalism, happiness out of distress, will be familiar enough in the Revolution proper. Actual separation from England will depend heavily on a glorious kingdom, the visible union of a godly people.

The millennialist preoccupations of revivalism also answer a central dilemma in Protestant communal life. The intolerable discrepancy between God's elect and other souls, all destined for eternal damnation, disappears in postmillennial society. Joseph Bellamy, Jonathan Edwards's most influential student, illustrates the point perfectly in a sermon on the subject that achieves an immense and lasting popularity in late-eighteenth-century circles. *The Millennium* (1758) takes as its text Revelation 20:1–3, the Angel of Heaven chaining Satan in the bottomless pit for a thousand years. Its theme is how Christ's subsequent reign on earth will change the nature and meaning of history. Conceivably, since "the glorious day is coming on," history itself may already have begun to change!

All things are suddenly possible in 1758. The incredulous question from Isaiah 66:8 ("shall a nation be born at once?") becomes a glorious statement of fact in Bellamy's hands ("a nation shall be born in a day"). The technical portions of *The Millennium,* an exhaustive typological determination of the fall of Antichrist, build slowly toward Bellamy's joy in the new dispensation. And this joy includes the inference that "the greater part of mankind may be saved." *"Many are called and few are chosen;"* Bellamy agrees, "yet it does not hence follow, that this will be the case when *a nation shall be born in a day,* and *all the people shall be righteous. . . .* it shall be quite otherwise, when *satan is bound."* Psychologically irresistible, the prospect inspires elaborate description. *The Millennium* dwells longingly on the demographics of prosperity to come: "let that universal peace and prosperity take place, which indeed will naturally result from the sincere practice of pure christianity, and mankind will naturally increase, and spread, and fill all the earth."

One does not have to be a convert to respond to this brand of talk. Bellamy's faith in a different history does not sound that different from Jefferson's. Glory out of crisis, optimism from revolutionary change, corruption in Europe, deliverance through America, the value placed on union, the miracle of sudden nationality, and the saving rewards of natural prosperity – all of these concepts transpose easily to the political debates of the 1760s and 1770s. The shift in the whole circumstance of the articulation of ideas is one more proof of the separate vitality of language in transmission. Grounded in the hope of personal salvation, the rhetoric of revivalism flatters all Americans in its cohesive approach to that end, and large numbers of colonists seem to have taken the surface of that appeal into political notions of communal identity. Salvation, the original source of that rhetoric, thus enters into a sense of general well-being that all citizens share irrespective of their religious state of mind or preference. One outcome is the widest diffusion of a rhetorical emphasis arising from the specificity of religious anxiety. (Revivalism, it should be remembered, fills a dominant role in only half of the colonies, albeit in those most active early in the Revolution – Virginia, Rhode Island, Pennsylvania, New Jersey, Connecticut, and Massachusetts.)

Two literary circumstances further magnify the impact of revivalist thought. First, by the 1770s, the available writings of figures like Edwards, Tennent, Bellamy, Davies, and Finley are known to the intellectual elite of every colony. That in itself supplies a cultural setting in which appreciation and use carry beyond the originating conditions of belief. Second, these same writings stimulate their own controversies and contention in colonial life. In one of the consummate ironies of the period, the revivalist quest for awakening and union actually causes more acrimony and division than any other phenomenon of the times. Certain tensions are intrinsic. The inroads of itinerant preaching create inevitable problems for local ministers, and these problems become acute when the concept of awakening rejects the status quo ante. It is the zeal of revivalism that then exacerbates tensions by publicizing them in both pulpit and print.

Gilbert Tennent leads the attack, establishing himself as the unquestioned leader of revivalism in the middle colonies. In the most notorious sermon of the period, *The Danger of an Unconverted Ministry* (1740), he proposes that "an ungodly Ministry is a great Curse and Judgment." Those ministers who resist the revival are likened to the biblical Pharisees; "as it was of old, so it is now." They resemble each other "as one Crow's Egg does another." "Now, what Savour have Pharisee Ministers?" asks Tennent. "In Truth, a very stinking One, both in the Nostrils of God and good men." Among other things, "they have not the Courage, or Honesty to thrust the Nail of Terror into sleeping Souls." His condemnations lead Tennent to strike at the source of conventional ministerial learning, the existing seminaries, and he also challenges the authority of established ministers through their congregations. "Let all the Followers of the Lamb stand up and act for *GOD* against all Opposers," commands Tennent, and, he then asks, "Who is upon *GOD's* Side? Who?"

Such preaching – the established clergy responds in kind – divides congregations and entire communities. "New Side" and "Old Side" factions exist in the middle colonies by 1741; "Old Lights" and "New Lights" formally separate in New England a year after. At the highest level, conflict leads to impressive exchanges on theological issues, as in Jonathan Edwards's *Some Thoughts Concerning the Present Revival* (1742) against Charles Chauncy's *Seasonable Thoughts on the State of Religion in New England* (1743). At the lowest, it brings new extremes of vituperation to American religion and American life generally. Take, for instance, the conservative minister Timothy Cutler's description of Tennent touring Boston in early 1741: "people wallowed in the snow for the benefit of his beastly brayings."

Conflict over revivalism changes the whole nature of religious thought in eighteenth-century America. The actual terms of debate are quickly summarized: the philosophical basis of the conversion experience (with more specific questions about the respective roles of reason and the affections in achieving religious conviction), the status of itinerant preaching, and the education and role of the clergy. In the heat of exchange, each of these debates shifts attention from the holiness of God's strictures toward problems in individual and communal behavior and from the mystery of Providence to assertions about human capacity.

The result is a curious paradox in the history of ideas. For if revivalism recovers a vital piety, it simultaneously carries religious thought toward a more human dimension. As revitalization assures the continuing power of religion in American thought, so a growing humanism furnishes more and more common ground for the mix of theology and Enlightenment ideology. "Our people do not so much need to have their heads stored, as to have their hearts touched," writes Edwards of revitalization in *Some Thoughts Concerning the Present Revival*. Counters Chauncy in *Seasonable Thoughts on the State of Religion*. "[T]he plain Truth is, an *enlightened Mind*, and not *raised Affections*, ought always to be the Guide of those who call themselves Men; and this, in the Affairs of Religion, as well as other Things." Bridging these differences philosophically is difficult; making rhetorical use of every possibility is not. The debate over revivalism frees American writers to blend the rational and emotional appeals available to them in the mix of religion, politics, and communal life.

Elisha Williams establishes the political potency of combining these appeals as early as 1744. A tutor and the rector of Yale College and then a judge of the superior court of Connecticut, Williams writes *The Essential Rights and Liberties of Protestants* to oppose restrictions on itineracy during revivalism. His essay traces "the Rights of *Conscience and private Judgment* in Matters of *Religion*" through biblical, legal, and philosophical traditions, verifying that in each tradition these rights "are unalterably the same." Conflating civil and religious liberty, Williams ascertains that both are "inherent," "natural and unalienable." Nevertheless, "bigotted Clergy, and arbitrary weak or popish Princes" occasionally decide otherwise. *The Essential Rights and Liberties of Protestants* already asks the crucial question in 1744. What can be done about it? What should be the response when civil authority attempts to alienate a natural right?

The answer is a step in the articulation of colonial liberties. Since the English Enlightenment, by way of John Locke and the Glorious Revolution, has confirmed that "the Rights of *Magna Charta* depend not on the Will of the Prince, or the Will of the Legislature," the same must be true of religious liberty, "a Priviledge more valuable than the civil Rights of *Magna Charta*." Freedom of worship is, therefore, "without controul from human Laws," a right that "no Man can touch and be innocent." Conversely, to challenge religious liberty is to be absolutely guilty. There is room to blame even a king in this language.

Elisha Williams strengthens the cause of civil opposition by joining Enlightenment conceptions of law to a religious frame of reference. He does so in part because of his belief in the need for a stronger oppositional stance. Like so many other colonial writers, he fears "that Christian *Liberty*, as well as Civil, has been lost little by little." "So precious a *Jewel* is always to be watched with a careful eye; no People are likely to enjoy Liberty long," he concludes, "that are not zealous to preserve it." The mixed modes of Williams's conclusion – "a careful eye" and "zeal" in the name of liberty – develop into watchwords in later colonial discourse; they already express the tensions in revivalism. The same tensions help to make liberty an ever-pressing theme.

The religious contentions at midcentury recharge the antiauthoritarian-ism in American Protestantism. To fully comprehend the development one must recognize the changing role of the clergy. Colonial ministers are originally unrivaled cultural intermediaries in their villages and towns. They represent unquestioned leadership and hold social and political power far beyond their official functions. But at midcentury clerical factionalism over revivalism erodes that status and more. When Gilbert Tennant asks "Who is upon GOD's Side?" the question strikes at the authority of specific ministerial opponents, and it also raises a previously unthinkable presump-tion about communal leadership in general. Suddenly, answers are conceiv-able that place Providence in the mass rather than in the hierarchy of civil society.

That presumption feeds on the continuing acrimony over clerical author-ity. Somewhere between the extremes of the rationalist Jonathan Mayhew, arguing in 1748 for the ascendency of a trained clergy (*The Right and Duty of Private Judgment*), and the Baptist Isaac Backus, arguing in 1768 against "pretended knowledge" and for the right of the people to judge religious matters for themselves (*A Fish Caught in His Own Net*), Americans have entered a democratic continuum that will occupy them indefinitely through many a twist and turn. In the most significant of these transmutations, the people themselves become the unit of meaning in religious debate.

The changing balance between clerical authority and the people's right to choose for themselves is particularly momentous for the disenfranchised. Anne Hutchinson's desire to instruct her Massachusetts Bay neighbors in 1636 cannot rest on their need for that instruction. By 1767, in the revivals of Newport, Rhode Island, Sarah Osborn answers successfully with just this argument. "I am rather as a Servant that Has a Great work assigned Him," she writes the Reverend Joseph Fish on March 7, 1767, after he has criticized the prayer meetings in her home. Osborn, a housewife and schoolteacher, resists the authority of her minister by making herself a servant of both God *and* the people. The gatherings in her home are "a Sweet Sementing bond of union that Holds us together in this critical day." Against the accusation that she seeks "to fill a Larger sphere," Osborn even dares to pun on her minister's name: "Dont think me obstinate then Sir if I dont know How to Let Go these shoals of fish." Surrounding everything she writes is Osborn's excitement about the changing world that revivalism means: "O that the Lord of the Harvest may send forth Labourers into His Harvest and crown their Labours with success." The tone, so in keeping with the climate of the times and her own immediate needs, is one that no minister can safely reject.

A divided clergy, the people's growing capacity to resist both sides, the sheer variety of religious practice, and the ideological basis of evangelical impulses generate an assumption of freedom in religious affairs that will gradually configure similar feelings in politics. As the promise of heaven expands in millennialist thinking, so does a certain democratic right of people to be saved therein on their own terms. At the end of the century, Judith Sargent Murray will demonstrate the full ideological potential of this promise in her essay "On the Equality of the Sexes" (1790). "Is it reasonable," she asks, "that a candidate for immortality, for the joys of heaven, an intelligent being, who is to spend an eternity in contemplating the works of Deity, should . . . be allowed no other ideas, than those which are suggested by the mechanism of a pudding, or the sewing of the seams of a garnet?"

Revivalist controversies over ministerial education have consequences that are more immediate but just as unexpected by those in religious authority. New Lights found the College of New Jersey, soon to be Princeton University, in 1746. The Anglicans respond with King's College, later Columbia University, in 1754. In 1764 Baptists establish the beginnings of Brown University. Dutch New Light clergy erect Queen's College, later Rutgers University, in 1776. Eleazar Wheelock is a New Light minister when he begins the plans for Dartmouth College in 1769. But although the impetus for all of these colleges is a seminary that will educate a doctrinally appropriate ministry, the outcome is far different.

Religious enthusiasm sparks but it does not control these educational enterprises. Enforced religious toleration and the realities of institutional growth push each college beyond its sectarian base. Each, without losing sight of its religious origins, becomes a center of general Enlightenment thought. The transition is constitutive; to be a faculty member in the third quarter of the eighteenth century means to combine religious and Enlightenment thought for the instruction of a colonial elite. Pupils like James Madison, Aaron Burr, and Hugh Henry Brackenridge of the College of New Jersey or Alexander Hamilton of King's College prove expert in their own manipulations of the combination for political purposes.

The overall spirit and contentiousness of revivalism make it an intellectual catalyst of the age and continuing source of cultural formation. In political terms that are also literary, the notion of "awakening" establishes a recognizable rhetorical stance for expressing and maintaining vigilance. Prudence and fervor, distress before joy, fear next to hope, reason within enthusiasm are some of its mixed tones. Americans at midcentury accept the appropriateness of these swings in mood and wield them to articulate communal ambivalences and anxieties. Although they wish for the unified liberty that true awakening will bring and speak of it in providential terms, they counter the very prospect (and all centralization) with other individuating principles, namely, with liberty of conscience and purification through separatism. The denominational politics of the times are full of the frustration of agreeing to disagree within a sustaining vision of higher union.

The literary work that comes closest to expressing these tensions and frustrations is Ezra Stiles's *A Discourse on the Christian Union* (1760). There may be no more prescient document of colonial confederation. Notwithstanding his conservative background as an Old Light Congregational minister, Stiles talks the language of revivalism in his zeal for pure and undefiled religion, in his stress upon the errand into America, and, above all, in his desire for "universal protestant liberty and communion." Like the revivalists, he preaches that all will "harmoniously unite in carrying on and perfecting the one same great and noble work" and that "all-prevailing TRUTH will terminate the whole in universal harmony." But there is this difference: Stiles wants union as much as he wants orthodoxy, and he espouses expediency to get it. He acknowledges the difficulties in projected union mostly to minimize them. Yet, "it is the congregation in its parochial congregational capacity that the law considers." Yes, there are a variety of sects in temporary collision. Yes, everyone must protect the unalienable right of private judgment in religion. Still, union must be made to thrive within these distinctions. "If we have any public benevolence," pleads Stiles, "any tender affection for pure and undefiled religion – by the tender mercies of Jehovah! by the love of Jesus! – let us bury and lay aside our trifling differences."

The telling analogy in *A Discourse on the Christian Union* is to the colonies themselves. Just as American churches are "distinct, ecclesiastical sovereignties, in point of power and controul. . . . So the thirteen provinces on this continent subsist independent of one another as to jurisdiction and controul over one another – yet in harmony." Stiles posits the equality and independence of churches (and colonies) as "the essential basis of the general union and confederacy." The analogy holds because "the same principles may take place in confederating a multitude of lesser bodies, as in confederating larger bodies, such as provinces, cantons, kingdoms." Stiles wants nothing to hinder "the purpose of cementing us together into a respectable body," and, to insure as much, he carefully balances parts to whole in his theory of union. The ensuing plan – "one general confederacy and public union, reserving to each part its power, liberty and proportionate influence in the mighty whole" – epitomizes American thought from colony to early Republic.

Stiles can complete this vision only by bringing religious and Enlightenment frames of reference together. He is painfully aware that religion alone has not brought harmony in revivalist America. *A Discourse on the Christian Union* expresses the hope that recent changes "made among mankind by science and letters" will keep future conflicts from dividing sects and colonies. In this way, the disputes of well-meaning Christians will give way to the benevolence of truth, and "the spirit of alienation will more and more subside." Not just faith but faith in knowledge prevails in Stiles's version of the millennium. "Such is human nature, especially enlightened with the pure light of revelation and sciences."

Whatever their differences, revivalism and the Enlightenment do meet in the colonial intellectual's favorite metaphor of light brought out of darkness. The conjunction protects the American colonies in their typological significance as a chosen people (Deuteronomy 26–8). Stiles finishes *A Discourse on the Christian Union* by distinguishing America from "the ruin of the Hebrew republic" under the wisest of the Jewish kings, Solomon. "We may then reap great advantage in consulting and duly applying that history, which may be in some measure typical of our own." He trusts that the corruption in Solomon's court will not repeat in a more enlightened age, though a warning remains for English subjects on both sides of the Atlantic to heed – "so fatal is the ill example of princes."

The success of Ezra Stiles's immediate plan for American Congregationalism conveys the larger relevance of his ideas. His call for a confederacy of American dissenters leads to an intercolonial organization of Congregational and Presbyterian churches that meets annually, either in New Jersey or in Connecticut, between 1766 and 1775. In any given year, these so-called "congresses" have delegates from six or more of the colonies. They receive support from local Presbyterian "committees of correspondence," and their unifying theme is opposition to the spread of British episcopacy. Here are the prototypical organizational structures that will conduct many of the political acts of the Revolution. The movement from denominational politics to colonial resistance is less of a shift than it is an interaction.

Stiles, a moderate whig and president of Yale in the 1770s, writes better than he knows in 1760. The conciliatory tones of *A Discourse on the Christian Union* attest to a powerful colonial yearning for language that will at once individualize and unify, fulfill and purify. Stiles even lives to reformulate this paradoxical yearning in republican guise. In *The Future Glory of the United States,* written in 1783, the year the Treaty of Paris ratifies American independence, he reinvokes the millennial possibilities of "every man's reaping the fruits of his labor and feeling his share in the aggregate system of power." But, even as he is writing, the paradoxes deepen between reaping and sharing, between fulfillment and purification, between the Enlightenment and revivalism. "We are ardently pursuing this world's riches, honors, powers, pleasures"; observes Stiles in an amalgam of triumph and remonstrance, "[L]et us possess them, and then know that they are nothing, nothing, nothing."

Progress on these terms, living in the world with weaned affections, borrows from Puritanism and lives in revivalism, but it will not survive even Stiles's death in 1795. Nineteenth-century Americans will pursue "this world's riches" in the name of property, an unqualified possession. Prosperity will mean everything to them, in what has often been termed the Protestant Ethic, and Stiles will have shown them the way. By and large, the unknown cost of success will be more superficial success. The same appropriation of revivalism into Enlightenment thought that supplies a more amiable, inclusive theory of union necessarily qualifies reformist fervor. In the transformation of ideas, the procedural energy in "ardent pursuit" stays in "this world," and the new theory of union licenses a rampant materialism in modern American life.

III

The closer we get to the Revolution, the less satisfactory the printed text becomes as a barometer of thought, and never more so than in religious expression. As radical Protestantism privileges the spoken word, so the courage of revolutionary action depends upon the immediacy of speech. With both propensities at work in what is still an oral culture, speech dominates expression in a way that is now irreclaimable. In part, too, the problem is one of lost perception. The two controlling forms of religious expression in the Revolution, the congregational utterance and the sermon, each reflect a spontaneous emphasis in American religion; the decorums and reactive power of the independent or separate congregation meet the pivotal role of the preaching minister. Obviously, the revolutionary sermon survives in publication, though in fractional numbers and debased form. The congregational utterance, on the other hand, is a forgotten mode of expression. The most conventional and frequent sort of revolutionary participation, it survives only in the interstices of other comments; yet there is no true understanding of the sermon without it.

The congregational or communal utterance in America flows from the underlying idea of covenant. Leaders may interpret the covenant, but only God and a chosen people can make and sustain one. While God will agree to be bound, the people must give frequent voice to their understanding of divine purposes or the covenant is broken. One such moment arrives when a new congregation stands officially before God and vows to form a church. Another comes when a congregation accepts an individual convert's evidence for membership in the community of saints. Other moments include the sacraments and the declaration of creeds. Still others stipulate days to be set aside for the acknowledgment of God's mercy in a time of trial. Thanksgiving, election, and fast day observances all render public witness. Though they feature a minister's words, their purpose is to extract a collective confirmation of faith. The first duty of a people is acceptance of God's will; the second is constant vigilance in His name, protecting the covenant against transgression.

If these duties are stringent, they are also understood to be powerfully restorative; God can do much with and for a godly people. The assumption helps to reveal how the election sermon of Abraham Williams in Boston in 1762 could equate "the *Voice of the People*" with "the *Voice of God*," or how Jonathan Mayhew, a year later in *Observations on the Charter and Conduct of the Society for the Propagation of the Gospel,* could praise the American people as "philosophers and divines in comparison of the common people in England." The same assumption indicates why Charles Chauncy, celebrating repeal of the Stamp Act in a Thanksgiving sermon from 1766, could think of colonial opposition as divinely inspired: "it was under [God's] all-wise, overruling influence that a spirit was raised in all the colonies nobly to assert their freedom as men and English-born subjects." In a quieter vein, it also justifies Quaker insistence on progress through the people. "Christ knoweth the state of the people," writes John Wollman in *Essay on the Ministry* (1772), "and in the pure feeling of the gospel ministry their states are opened to His servants."

Out of such ascriptions comes a growing sense of empowerment in the people. Nathaniel Niles, preaching in Newburyport, Massachusetts, on June 5, 1774, declares that "we should all endeavour to turn the attention of our fellow members of the community on the conduct of our rulers." A student of Joseph Bellamy, he draws an instructive analogy between soul-searching in personal salvation and vigilance in politics. Members of a congregation do not depend upon their minister for redemption, why, then, should they trust political leaders for effective government? Niles expects his listeners to take "the standard of right and wrong" and apply it themselves, and he urges them to "excite others to do so likewise." "We should endeavour on every alarming occasion," he argues, "to collect the sentiments of the body, and vigorously pursue those measures that are thought the most salutary for the whole." By 1776, in Samuel West's election sermon, the people are deemed "the proper judges to determine when rulers are guilty of tyranny and oppression." They can be trusted because "by their conduct they have shown that they were regulated by the law of God written in their hearts."

Hearing the voice of the people is a more difficult proposition. There are echoes of congregational self-confidence in the local resolutions of mass meetings and instructions to legislators — not in the actual language so much as in the presumed right of the collectivity to give advice. Similar nuances emerge in political writings couched in the form of creeds. William Livingston's elaborate anticlerical parody of the Thirty-nine Articles of Religion, in *The*

Independent Reflector (October 11, 1753), creates notable controversy in New York when it glosses the convention of the Christian's "open Declaration of the Religion he professes." On the brink of Revolution in Boston, *The Massachusetts Spy* (January 19, 1775) issues "An English Patriot's" version of the Apostles' Creed. "I believe all political power to be derived originally from, and invested in the people," it reads, trusting in God to simultaneously advance His glory and the nation's welfare. Sympathetic readers would have imagined intonation in unison, a solemn justification of faith and inclination.

The religious voice enters revolutionary discourse by insisting that faith and liberty are inextricably intertwined. In possibly the most noteworthy rendition of the theme, *The Snare Broken* (1766), Jonathan Mayhew contrasts Slavery, "the deformed child of Satan," with Liberty, "celestial Maid, the daughter of God, and, excepting his Son, the first-born of Heaven." All distinction between faith and liberty disappears in this sermon. Mayhew's personal growth in liberty receives proper documentation through classical authors, but it is the scriptures that first teach him that " 'where the Spirit of the Lord is there is liberty.' " Mayhew's successor in the West Church of Boston, Simeon Howard, is one of many ministers to devote entire sermons to the idea that "loss of liberty is soon followed by the loss of all virtue and religion." *A Sermon Preached to the Ancient and Honorable Artillery Company in Boston* (1773) explicates a favorite biblical text of the Revolution in Galatians 5:1 ("Stand fast therefore in the liberty wherewith Christ hath made us free").

How the popular mind receives religious explanations of political liberty appears in the words of William Manning, a semiliterate Massachusetts farmer who sees "almost the first blood that was shed in Concord." Events – "scores of men dead, dying & wounded in the Cause of Libberty" – have forced Manning to evaluate "serious sencations" and to overcome a few doubts. His reminiscences, *The Key of Liberty* (c. 1794), catch the tenor and source of his ideas:

I have often thought it was imposable ever to seport a free Government, but firmly believing it to be the best sort & the ondly one approved off by heaven it was my unweryed study & prayers to the almighty for many years to find out the real cause & a remidy.

The recourse to heaven is a natural one. Manning is "not a man of Larning" and "no grate reader of antiant history," but he has listened to countless sermons on the subject when "highly taken up with Liberty & a free Government." The oral transmission in pulpit oratory rules thought and pen, overcoming the awkwardness in both.

As the primary literary vehicle of the times, the sermon forms a dialectic with the people's voice and prepares more Americans for rebellion than do books and pamphlets. If four hundred pamphlets are published in America during the revolutionary era, more than eighteen hundred sermons emerge in the same period from Massachusetts and Connecticut alone, and these numbers do not begin to impart the weekly dimension of actual sermons, religious talks, and prayer meetings held in local communities across America. The sermon is the bellwether of rebellion; it records the Revolution in the piety of response to daily trouble.

The occasional or weekday sermon deserves particular consideration in this regard. It exists elsewhere, but, as the sermonic subgenre that officially combines religion and politics, it takes on heightened status and scope as a dominant art form in instances of early American conflict. Delivered on fast days, election days, thanksgiving days, ordinations, dedications, and other holidays, the occasional sermon takes communal well-being rather than personal salvation as its province. The emphasis naturally shifts with each occasion, but all of these sermons revolve around the people's covenant, and the minister accepts an assignment replete with vested cultural anxieties.

The formal constrictions on the speaker are part of the assignment. In the occasional sermon, the health and direction of society dominate as immediate and unavoidable generic concerns. Thus, when Samuel Davies preaches on the death of George II in 1760, his subject is not the king's death but rather the "strange, untried period" and "anxious contingency" that this death brings to a system where "the least irregularity or defect in the minutest spring, may disorder and weaken the whole machine." Davies takes his text from 2 Samuel 1:19 ("how are the mighty fallen!") and uses it first to arouse a proper fear. "When *the mighty is fallen*, shall not the feeble tremble?" he asks. "If the father of the people must cease to live, shall not the people expect to die?" As in most evangelical preaching, understanding comes only out of crisis.

On the Death of His Late Majesty, King George II astonishes the reader today mostly in the extent to which its formulaic considerations already dictate the terms of future debate. To be sure, Davies discusses the loyalty due once and future kings. But George II receives homage as a servant of the people ("the monarch himself frowned upon the principles of arbitrary power; and was an advocate for the liberties of the people"), whereas George III provokes fear as an unknown quantity ("the best of kings . . . may have evil counsellors, and evil counsellors may have the most mischievous influence"). Loyalty, as a virtue, connotes neither "servile artifice" nor "mercenary cringing" nor "complaisance of flattery" but "a disinterested love to our country" and "public spirit." Prophetic words follow. "This you must do," urges Davies, in a claim of loyalty, "or turn rebels against your own hearts and consciences."

The occasional sermons of the 1760s and 1770s push the same terminology into a reversal of implications as rebellion and loyalty change places. By the time of his Boston election day sermon in 1776, Samuel West will have proven that only God deserves full submission and that, therefore, all unquestioned authority in this world is "slavish" and "proof of a very sordid and base mind." Now the previous metaphors for limiting authority begin to disestablish it. If magistrates are really "the servants of the people," then, "in the common affairs of life," they can be replaced or dismissed as a master would any servant. For Nathaniel Niles in *Two Discourses on Liberty* (1774), public spirit is still the source of political order and virtue, but, because the source of public spirit is liberty, it always distinguishes between government and tyranny. Accordingly, "he who infringes on liberty rebels against good government, and ought to be treated as a rebel." "It matters not what station he fills; he is a traitor" reasons Niles. Instead of conveying the presumption of obedience when there is turmoil, official position now suggests the possibility of crime compounded. "He that fills an elevated station is proportionably more criminal in the same rebellion, than those in a lower state."

These rhetorical shifts, multiplied a thousand times in other sermons, cast a different light on the blemish of rebellion. The Reverend John Cleaveland of Ipswich carries them to their logical conclusion when he consigns Thomas Gage, general of the British armies, straight to hell in the *Essex Gazette* (July 13, 1775). "An aggravated damnation" applies in this case even though, officially, General Gage represents the king. As Cleaveland puts the matter directly to Gage, "[Y]ou are not only a robber, a murderer, and usurper, but a wicked Rebel: a rebel against the authority of truth, law, equity, the English constitution of government, these colony states, and humanity itself." The British commander, in sum, qualifies as one of those evil counselors who mislead a king in Samuel Davies's original nightmare. Iconographically, Gage dons the mantle of disgrace that Americans cannot tolerate on themselves, that of rebel and traitor.

Inevitably, the occasional sermon spiritualizes the theme of loyalty and rebellion as one of its charges. The proclivities are everywhere apparent in these texts: Davies's conception of loyalty in 1760 "will qualify you for both worlds"; Niles, in 1774, joins civil and spiritual liberty as body to soul and makes both together "the loan of heaven"; West's combinations of scripture and right reason, revelation and common sense, clarify the duty of obedience in 1776. Under all of these elements is a link between the Christian's doubt and the rebel's uncertainty, one that allows for a powerful similitude in responses. Superficially, the parallel means that religious sources can easily enter into a political frame of reference. "If salvation has not come from our gracious sovereign King George, we cannot expect it from the hills," Niles observes wryly. "We must look still higher." West, in turn, makes St. Paul "a strong advocate for the just rights of mankind." The special power of the occasional sermon comes from the integrity that the form itself assigns to these parallels. God holds all of the answers and offers the history of redemption to those who would decipher the present, but responses in His name must also meet the immediacy of colonial unhappiness and bewilderment. The occasional sermon serves that purpose by filtering emotional dislocation through the context of event. Generically, it tells the people how to feel and what to do in the moment.

Two Discourses on Liberty illustrates the strategy perfectly. In a Massachusetts pulpit right after the British close the port of Boston, Nathaniel Niles does not hesitate to ask the questions on everyone's mind. "What shall we do? Shall we renounce the authority of our gracious sovereign? Shall we take up arms against his troops? What shall we do?" Reiteration captures something of the helplessness and uncertainty of colonial reactions in 1774 — feelings subsequently obscured by the brag and bounce of patriotic oratory. Of course, helplessness and uncertainty are familiar impulses among the unworthy supplicants of God's grace. Niles makes the connection, and the appropriate response is also the same. "Such is the kindness of our God," Niles explains, "that, humanly speaking, it is in the power of America to save both herself and Great-Britain. . . . let us remember, that the effectual fervent prayers of the righteous avail much." Exactly how Americans are to pray opens a path toward renewed efficacy: "let us all, like Daniel of old, piously pour out our hearts before God, acknowledging our own sins, and those of our people."

Although zeal against sinfulness dominates all radical Protestant sermonology, the occasional sermon sharpens that recourse by stressing the original purity in the social covenant. God will reward or punish a covenanted group; so much more is to be gained from collective piety or to be lost in communal sinfulness. As Samuel West expresses the idea: "our cause is so just and good that nothing can prevent our success but only our sins. Could I see a spirit of repentance and reformation prevail through the land, I should not have the least apprehension." Everywhere in the occasional sermon, fear and uncertainty signal an underlying sinfulness. Niles's own version of colonial difficulties compares American uneasiness to that of the prodigal son (Luke 5:16). Unfortunately, the prodigal's specific answer is fraught with a difficult ambiguity in the American crisis. "Let us return to our father's house," he advises. But which house and which father?

The story of the eighteenth-century occasional sermon is in part about this search for proper patriarchy. Do Americans find solace in colony and king?

"George was our Father, too," Samuel Davies reminds the British in 1760. Niles still values that veneration in 1774: "let the world see that their king is dearer to the Americans than their blood." Or do Americans rely instead on a parent closer to home? "Let us learn to live in the plain manner of our fore-fathers," Niles advises in almost the same breath, associating American ancestry with purity and liberty. Simeon Howard indicates the distance to be covered when he preaches before the Boston Artillery Company in 1773: "British America, especially the northern part of it, is by its situation calcu-lated to be a nursery of heroes."

Of the occasional sermons, the annual election day sermon is the most significant for revolutionary politics and is the least accessible today. Lost is all sense of its original reception. The colonial minister who delivers an election sermon speaks before the assembled magistrates of the province in a ritual of renewal and affirmation. He is God's chosen representative as well as the designed spokesman of the community, and his words are published for all to examine. The surviving record is itself an indication of assumed merit and general dissemination. Of the two hundred twenty-two election sermons delivered in Connecticut, Massachusetts, Vermont, and New Hampshire between 1750 and 1820, two hundred and eleven appear in print, a number in multiple editions.

Reading these sermons today, a twentieth-century eye sees derivative Whig theory garnished with biblical typology, but *listening* to them, with an ear for eighteenth-century expectations, reveals a striking creativity – especially in the election sermons delivered right before the Revolution. As God's represen-tation and as his community's spokesman, the election day minister of the 1770s occupies a unique position for testing both the nature of British rule and the resolve of an American people. Realizing their position also seems to have brought out the best in these preachers. We glimpse in them a disruptive power in speech that does not belong to print. The belief required for indepen-dence literally is born in these sermons.

Gad Hitchcock, pastor of Pembroke Church in Boston, is just such a figure as he delivers the Massachusetts election sermon for 1774. General Thomas Gage, the new military governor, recently arrived from England with shiploads of British troops, is Hitchcock's nominal host. Indeed, many of Gage's supporters walk out in the middle of Hitchcock's performance – enough for the Yankee minister to quip that he preached a moving sermon. What causes this degree of offense? On the surface, Hitchcock's sermon is the usual explanation of constitutional theory in government with appropriate injunctions to colonial rulers as the trustees of society. Where Hitchcock deviates is in his creative use of the rhythms, prerogatives, and expectations of the genre. The election sermon conventionally seeks renewal and social affirmation, but Hitchcock breaks the form. He steadfastly refuses to rise above the sorrows of his people.

The biblical text of Hitchcock's sermon immediately ranges the people both for and against authority: "When the righteous are in authority, the people rejoice: but when the wicked beareth rule, the people mourn" (Proverbs 29:2). The standard triadic plan of the sermon – doctrine, reason, uses (text, explication, application) – then dramatizes the contrasting possibilities in biblical times and in the American present. Gage and his retinue could not have liked Hitchcock's opening description of "Hebrew polity," a disintegration into monarchy under the sons of Samuel with "prevailing wickedness, and corruption among some in high station." The rhetorical foreshadowing of ills in America would have been clear without Hitchcock's direct claim of parallelism; "we need not pass the limits of our own nation for sad instances of this." The tone of sadness is crucial in understanding the speaker's performance. Just as Hitchcock's opponents cannot quarrel with scripture, so they find themselves disarmed by the melancholy premise of the people mourning under evil leaders. Claims of evil are not made by Hitchcock in 1774, but he does insist over and over again on the corollary. "It is, however, certain that the people mourn!" Would they not rejoice if authority were righteous?

The goal of righteousness enhances the election day opportunity. Invited to give "counsel of God in respect to the great affairs of this anniversary, and the general conduct of government," Hitchcock uses this leverage to confront the executive officers before him. "Our danger is not visionary, but real – Our contention is not about trifles, but about liberty and property." For those who would scoff, he adds "if I am mistaken in supposing plans are formed . . . incompatible with every idea of liberty, all America is mistaken with me." Alluding next to America's "well known loyalty," Hitchcock respectfully but firmly demands "a redress of our grievances." A truly righteous authority will respond sympathetically. "Suffer me to remind you," Hitchcock admonishes Gage and the assembled officers of state, "that you act for God, and under his inspection . . . you must one day give an account to Him whose eyes are as a flame of fire, of the motives of your conduct."

The minister expresses hope for reconciliation but prepares for conflict, and his sermon raises the theoretical prospect – perhaps the necessity – of formal opposition. Only by responding to resistance, Hitchcock speculates, will the worst leaders "learn to do that out of interest, which the best constantly do out of a good principle and true love to their subjects." Certainly, the alternative, "public misery and slavery," embodies "a state of affairs infinitely worse than that of public disturbance." Once again, the theoretical and ceremonial frames of the sermon allow a clergyman to say more to British authority, face-to-face, than a mere political figure ever could.

Gad Hitchcock stretches that license to the limit in the uses of his sermon. Asking the assembled rulers "to apply the subject," he announces that "the united voice of America, with the solemnity of thunder and with accents piercing as the lightning awakes your attention, and demands fidelity." This united voice, all America, takes the first-person, plural pronominal form in Hitchcock's peroration, and it sends a final challenge to General Gage, the British governor who carries orders for disciplining the colonies. Gage must recognize the inevitable limits of colonial cooperation. While Americans revere civil government and love peace and order, they will not part with their rights and privileges. "The soil we tread on is our own, the heritage of our Fathers." An encompassing benediction will soften the exclusivity and independence of this assertion, but not before both tendencies are under-scored. "We have therefore an exclusive right to it," Hitchock warns the threatening interloper.

Ministers accurately take the pulse of American anxieties in the 1770s, and, as those anxieties grow, the clergy effectively removes middle ground by reminding the faithful that God will hold everyone to a strict accounting. "If the foundations be destroyed," asks Hitchcock, "what can the righteous do?" The force of that question leads inexorably to another. If the choice be between tyranny and resistance, what then? In Hitchcock's words, "which of the two shall we chuse, for the sake of the happy effects and consequences of it?" The dynamics of the election sermon force the preacher and his followers to face these unpalatable questions squarely. Philosophically and temperamen-tally, the minister assumes the task of crafting answers consonant with belief. If those answers stress prudence, they are nonetheless increasingly blunt. "With respect therefore to rulers of evil dispositions," Hitchcock declares in 1774, "nothing is more necessary than that they should believe resistance, in some cases to be lawful."

Two things must happen for most Americans to choose resistance: they must believe in their solidarity, and they must believe in the rectitude of their stance in opposition. To a remarkable extent, these difficulties are questions of literary expression in the hands of the clergy. Ministers define the parameters of belief in early America, and performances like Hitchcock's incorporate "the united voice of America" and "the doctrine of resistance." Radical Whigs will need little more than British intransigence to turn these beliefs into revolutionary actions. Arguably, the clergy instills revolutionary conviction too quickly and thoroughly for its own good. Thomas Paine orchestrates "a new method of thinking" in 1776, one in which rebellion comprises "the glorious union of all things." These appropriations of evangelical language, while obvious, are already divorced from their original context. Paine insists upon it. The second edition of *Common Sense* ends with the wish that "mingling religion with politics, *may be disavowed and reprobated by every inhabitant of* AMERICA."

IV

Something vital disappears from revolutionary sermonizing once battle lines have been drawn, though it is not easy to identify the strict nature of the loss. The conviction of the people and ministerial zeal remain in place. If anything, these elements increase through the activity and success of the Revolution. They double again in the rampant revivalism of the early Republic, when, amidst broad social dislocation, evangelical preaching dominates the culture as never before. Does religious expression lose its communal thrust? Not really. Historians have demonstrated the central role of evangelical activity as a building block in emerging communities and, more generally, as one of the unifying elements in early national life. In the 1790s and after, the Second Great Awakening will turn much of America into a revivalist society. What does vanish, and very quickly, is the ministry's proprietary hold over a national covenant.

Independence reduces the occasional sermon as a major intellectual event. The preacher's most dramatic literary tool, the use of biblical typology in formulating the hypothetical case for resistance, also loses its exclusive edge. Rather than adroit rhetorical foreshadowing, the new states now need straightforward political confirmations, skills more attuned to secular oratory and governmental office. Ironically, war with England also removes the ministerial elite from the front lines; firsthand confrontation no longer colors the possibilities in the election day ceremony. Where a minister's performance once took shape in the crucible of conflict (a royal governor and his often recalcitrant legislature as one audience), it now enters upon a broad field of ideological consensus. The pressure on language is simply not the same. Finally, the doctrine of separation of church and state enters a radical new phase in 1776: where it previously signifies toleration and the discouragement of any denomination as the religion of state, the doctrine now separates all religious and governmental action. Ministers cannot assume the role of community representative on as many political topics.

The formula of the election sermon remains intact under these new handicaps; the psychological exigencies do not. A designated minister still counsels newly elected magistrates on the nature of human happiness and on the duties of rulers in achieving that goal, and he still voices alarm over a sinful people. Gone from the language, however, is the excitement of a unique burden – a minister, not selecting but selected, rising alone to articulate the needs of a culture in crisis. Others now share that burden and will soon assume it as their exclusive right.

Documenting the diminished literary power of the political sermon is a thankless task. Phillips Payson, a Chelsea pastor who leads troops from his parish in combat, delivers a Massachusetts election sermon in 1778 that is not without appeal. Yet Payson intuitively sees that his words have missed an essential balance. "I must not forget to mention religion, both in rulers and people," he reminds himself halfway through. Railleries against the British induce another cautionary note: "it is difficult to keep the passions or the tongue within the bounds of Christian moderation." If Providence has brought Americans within sight of the promised land ("We stand this day upon Pisgah's top"), Payson submits a prosaic gauge of that prospect. "We should take mankind as they are," he tells the gathered leaders of Massachusetts, "and not as they ought to be. . . . So in our searches for truth and knowledge, and in our labors for improvement, we should keep within the ken or compass of the human mind." There is good Yankee acumen in these sentiments, but Payson's election day predecessors and their audiences would have expected more.

Success and certainty make for a less interesting story than struggle and doubt. Four years after Payson, Zabdiel Adams's election sermon of 1782 dwells heavily on what he and others dub "the rising glory of America." The Reverend Adams belongs too much to the strain of his cousin John Adams to ignore dangers, but he finds himself, like Payson, "in sight of the promised land." The outcome is another version of God's glory through worldly prosperity:

Behold her seas whitened with commerce; her capitals filled with inhabitants, and resounding with the din of industry. See her rising to independence and glory. Contemplate the respectable figure that she will one day make among the nations of the earth; behold her venerable for wisdom, for counsel and for might; flourishing in science, in agriculture and navigation, and in all the arts of peace. Figure to yourself that this your native country will ere long become the permanent seat of Liberty, the retreat of philosophers, the asylum of the oppressed, the umpire of contending nations, and, we would hope, the *glory of Christ,* by a strict attachment to his gospel, and divine institutions.

In this paean to national prosperity, religion melts into the other elements of cultural well-being as one of many strengths. The passage itself could have come from any early republican intellectual; nothing about it suggests God's designated representative.

Whether converging or clashing, the optimisms of millennialism and national prosperity do not prevent election sermons from remaining good indicators of cultural anxiety. Phillips Payson, Zabdiel Adams, and Simeon Howard, who delivers an election sermon of his own in 1780, all worry about the successful completion of the Revolution. Howard also frets over the constitutional crisis in Massachusetts as he watches the state reject one constitution and debate another. The standard formula obtains. A litany of ills (covetousness, luxury, dissipation, infidelity) produces the usual consequence ("God often brings distress and ruin upon a sinful people") and the predictable solution ("Would we but reform our evil ways . . . we might then, putting our trust in God, humbly hope that our public calamities would be soon at an end"). The arrangement, though in debased form, is still that of the Puritan jeremiad.

Originality lies in the adjustment of the formula to the pressure of events. For his part, Simeon Howard turns the jeremiad into an outline for governmental reform. The dangers of "impious, immoral men at the head of government," of "weak and illiterate men," of "double-minded men," of "indecision in council," of "ineffectual exertions," and of "doubting and wavering in the supreme authority" all loom in his appeal for a stronger constitution. So does the presumed connection between religious faith and American glory. But Howard, in a move that will become reflexive in later election sermons, now worries more about the presumed connection between personal salvation and national prosperity. There is just a touch of a new fear: secular nationalism. Heaven conspicuously "owns" the Revolution, "not merely for our own families, friends, and posterity, but for the rights of humanity, for the civil and religious privileges of mankind." Still, the "eye of Heaven" will almost certainly be elsewhere on Judgment Day. Howard wants Americans to remember that national identities are ephemeral things, a "baseless fabric" in the end.

Could it be that revolutionary zeal actually encroaches on Christian piety? Any response to this question embarrasses the American clergy in 1780. Promoting patriotism takes from the chief end of glorifying God; resisting it puts the ministry against the people in a time of war. The answer of a previous time, an uncompromising injunction against the things of this world, seems somehow less appropriate in all of the excitement about republican nationalism. The equivocation in Howard's voice is an indication of changing times and lost certainties. "Whatever others may do, and however it may fare with our country," he advises, "it shall surely be well with the righteous." The focus remains on piety, but the subjunctive mode of Howard's words – "whatever others may do," "however it may fare" – allow for an audience that does not have to choose quite so directly between salvation and worldly happiness; the commitment of revolutionary ideology is to success in both worlds.

In but not *of* the world, *in* but *no longer leading* the Revolution, ministers instinctively reach for language that will bolster their flagging intellectual ascendancy in the culture at large. Their obvious resort is to the increasingly popular terminology and thought of the Enlightenment. As the Republic flourishes, so do the propensities of ministers to speak in Enlightenment terms – particularly before prestigious election day audiences. Eighty election sermons are published in America in the last quarter of the eighteenth century, and there is no better register of the link that grows between religion and the Enlightenment. But these sermons also suggest a price to be paid. Secularization has weakened original parallels between religious and civil liberty, purification and virtue, sinfulness and civic corruption. Gone as well is the initial excitement of placing Enlightenment thought in religious discourse by pre-revolutionary intellectuals like Elisha Williams and Ezra Stiles.

The Revolution itself forces more and more attention on this world over the next. When, for instance, John Tucker's election sermon of 1771 turns the voice of reason into the voice of God, orthodoxy requires that he carefully distinguish between civil and ecclesiastical arrangements. Samuel West's own election sermon in 1776 can rely on the same wording; here, too, the voice of reason is the voice of God, but West, facing the new primacy of common sense and the immediate exigency of Revolution, blurs distinctions. Right reason and revelation seem much closer together: "whatever right reason requires as necessary to be done is as much the will and law of God as though it were enjoined us by an immediate revelation from heaven, or commanded in the sacred Scriptures." And yet no eighteenth-century minister in the mainstream can really claim that reason *is* revelation. Where in these differences does God's inscrutable will end and common sense in the world begin?

There is never a straight contest over authority in these sermons. Providence conveniently supports common sense, right reason, and natural law in all of them. Samuel Langdon's election sermon in 1775 asks "the Father of Lights" to "irradiate" the minds of colonial leaders, who, as "happy instruments," will then dispel the current gloom of events. Phillips Payson decides more conventionally in 1778 that "nature has given us the claim [of independence], and the God of nature appears to be helping us to assert and maintain it." But where exactly is God in these presentations? Metaphorically, a "Father of Lights" is somehow less imminent in human affairs then the biblical flashing eye of Judgment Day. Does God now speak mainly through the design of nature? What then of scripture?

The problem with Enlightenment thought is that it invariably leaves the formulating minister somewhere on the sidelines. The history of redemption and scripture call explicitly and peculiarly on the minister's expertise; nature, science, reason, and even common sense do not. It may be that the dictates of common sense and reason are, in Samuel West's understanding, "abundantly confirmed by the sacred Scriptures," but confirmation still leaves the believer a little too firmly in this world. The already embattled minister faces an exasperating trade-off. Using the language of fashion simultaneously attracts a wider audience and undermines the speaker's authority. Dimly down the road are other difficulties. Sooner or later, the Enlightenment fixes on perfectibilities in human history and places them over a concern for salvation. Universal meanings give way to notions of empirical completeness. The autonomy of reason controls human action. The individual becomes less a soul and more a link between generations. All of these transformations work against clergymen, the first keepers of the religious voice. Significantly, each transformation also indulges a new secular leadership in the creation of an American civil religion.

V

The problems of the clergy are the solutions of the new political elite. The leaders of the Revolution immediately use separation of church and state to exclude the ministry from active roles in the republican experiment. Between 1776 and 1796, the constitutions of seven states prohibit ministers from assuming public office (Delaware, Georgia, Kentucky, New York, North Carolina, South Carolina, and Tennessee). The general aim, as Jefferson describes it in a letter to the Danbury Baptist Association in 1802, consists in "building a wall of separation between Church and State," a goal that the architects of the Republic adhere to with single-minded purpose and resolve.

The success of the doctrine of separation only intensifies secular vigilance against the clergy. For Jefferson it amounts to an obsession. He is president in 1801 when his letter to Moses Robinson inveighs against "the dominion of the clergy, who had got a smell of union between Church and State." "My opinion is that there would never have been an infidel, if there had never been a priest," he assures Mrs. Samuel Smith in 1816. A year later, as Connecticut finally abandons its state-supported church, he applauds John Adams on one more victory against "Monkish darkness, bigotry, and abhorrence": "I join you therefore in sincere congratulations that this den of the priesthood is at length broken up, and that a protestant popedom is no longer to disgrace the American history and character." Adams responds in kind. "Do you know," he warns Jefferson, "that The General of the Jesuits and consequently all his Host have their Eyes on this Country?" This vehemence, the invective of the Enlightenment, is difficult to comprehend as a question of belief or even of religious liberty. The real contest takes place over the control of civic expression on religious subjects.

Many changes in the Revolution mandate a re-articulation of values, and the role of religion in republican life is one such change. The issue is joined in the assumption, broadly shared, that republican virtue depends on religious principle. No significant secular leader would have disagreed with Jefferson's comment in *Notes on the State of Virginia* (1784–5) that national liberties depend on "a conviction in the minds of the people that these liberties are the gift of God." In fact, the standard eighteenth-century expression of the idea comes in Washington's presidential farewell (1796). For Washington and other early republicans, religion and morality are the twin pillars of human happiness and the indispensable supports of political prosperity. Clearly, religious commentary belongs in the civic realm. But who rightfully should assume responsibility for that commentary in educating a republican citizenry, and what ends should communication have in mind? If the place of religious thought in republican foundations is assured, even crucial, the context of explanation and use is not.

The ensuing battle over the proper role and expression of religion in a virtuous republic is often shrill. Secular revolutionary leaders find their enemy not in the clergy, as such, but in the political power of revivalism. They fear religious enthusiasm at least as much as they do economic inflation and factionalism, and the surge in evangelical outpourings after the Revolution increases their apprehension. Revivalism, after all, mounts a direct and formidable challenge to a conservative intellectual elite trying to cap the Revolution. Closer to the raw power of protest and closer to communal stirrings in the western territories, it offers the clearest alternative explanation to Enlightenment discourse in postrevolutionary culture.

As a result, the fear of revivalism cuts across party lines. Adams, for one, associates "Awakenings" directly with political upheaval. He draws the link for Benjamin Waterhouse in 1815: "mankind must have a crusade, a war of reformation, a French Revolution, or Anti-Revolution to amuse them and preserve them from Ennui." Jefferson also sees the danger. "The atmosphere of our country is unquestionably charged with a threatening cloud of fanaticism," he writes Dr. Thomas Cooper in 1822, "lighter in some parts, denser in others, but too heavy in all." A second comparison is to disease. Instruction "will be the remote remedy to this fever of fanaticism." Long before, Benjamin Franklin has outlined the form that instruction must take. As he tells Mary Stevenson in 1769, "[T]hose who have Reason to regulate their Actions, have no Occasion for Enthusiasm."

The political elite assigns itself the task of directing religious expression into safe channels. The underlying struggle in this enterprise is hard to see because it also takes place between conflicting and shifting genres and on unequal terms. Spontaneity, emotionalism, and personalism suit the speech in the form of revivalist sermons, but these oral performances, by definition, do not survive their own time; the cooler, abstract, universalizing rhetoric of Enlightenment discourse conforms instead to the published work. Secular leaders make their way by following the objectifying combinations of such liberal religious figures as Ezra Stiles, but their ascendancy in the public sphere is also the technical outcome of print culture over oral culture, itself another victory of the Enlightenment.

In secular postrevolutionary discourse, as in the election sermon of the period, the voice of reason is the voice of God but with a difference. Reason does not so much join revelation in the language of the political elite; it becomes revelation. These writers can make the complete, logical transition in ways that an orthodox clergy cannot. Where ministers stumble over the Enlightenment in their efforts to sustain religious dogma, the secular leaders of the Republic easily objectify both frameworks in a language of universals. They assume that religious commentary and Enlightenment discourse come together – always the goal – but that they need not come together everywhere or in every form. Delicacy of placement is the issue and a discerning test of literary skill. Two characteristic examples, both well-known, can be used to demonstrate the complexities involved: the first, from Franklin's *Autobiography,* or memoirs, the second, from Jefferson's first inaugural address.

These efforts cannot be read as simple confrontations between frames of reference; their conscious sense of their own success depends upon a conflation of alternatives. Hence, it is still possible to argue over the question of whether Franklin borrows from Congregationalist ideas or succumbs to them. His "bold and arduous project of arriving at moral perfection" has been read as both an adaptation of the Puritan objective of sanctity and a mockery of it. Franklin seems to have welcomed every possibility. In the organization of the memoirs, he carefully locates the project of moral perfection right after a claim of solitary daily worship, "a little liturgy or form of prayer for my own private use." Even so, the overall tones of this and every other section fit the calming, encompassing, and rationalizing rhetoric of the Enlightenment.

Franklin's memoirs, the first part written in 1771, tell the story of a man who succeeds despite his mistakes. The constitutive metaphor for these mistakes is the erratum, or printer's error; the narrator corrects errors in life after they happen, much as a printer would replace a defective font of type. This device deliberately contradicts the fundamental form of autobiography in Franklin's day – that of the religious conversion narrative, which moves from feelings of inadequacy in sin and helplessness toward a single dramatic transformation or influx of divine grace. There comes a moment, however, when Franklin's anticonversion narrative rises above its tactical view of error to address the larger problem. As the narrative switches from private experience toward the public figure, Franklin pauses to summarize "the then State of my Mind," and in this summary he traces his youthful mistakes to "Want of Religion." Since this defect entails an absence within the self, it requires a different corrective agency, something beyond the removal of defective fonts from experience. What, the narrator asks at this juncture, has protected me from myself?

Franklin's answer turns upon a vital triptych in Enlightenment thought: reason, Providence, and nature. Citing first his mastery of the utilitarian forms of reason, he writes that "this Persuasion, with the kind hand of Providence, or some guardian Angel, or accidental favourable Circumstances and Situations, or all together, preserved me." The interesting aspects of the passage – the things that make it so characteristic in the rhetoric of the secular elite – are the parallelism that makes the triptych possible and the stylistic ingenuity that carries it off. Reason, Providence, and nature exist on the same plane of importance in Franklin's explanation: *either* Franklin's utilitarian reason, *or* Providence, *or* circumstances and situations in the natural world, *or* "all" have preserved him. Each category exists separately, but the implied connections, the tone, and the last inclusive repetition of the conditional conjunction hold "all together" in a loose union of equal considerations.

The difficulty in the triptych is, of course, Providence. Franklin quietly brings the Ruler of the Universe down to scale, and his joined phrases, "the kind hand of Providence, or some guardian Angel," accomplish this purpose smoothly. Deity is connoted rather than named. The adjective "kind" gently dismisses the angry God of Calvinist lore, and the additional, slightly vulgar metonym for Providence, "guardian Angel," slips the concept into the less controversial world of social parlance. The point of the language is to diminish and coordinate without offending, to retain the idea of divinity while removing all particulars of dogma. No one can disagree. Franklin writes a language for everyone to believe in.

The diminishing impulse and moderating tones of this rhetoric have been misread. It is inaccurate to regard early republican leaders as detached figures who manipulate theological issues entirely for social purposes. Mere manipulation does not explain their persistent personal interest in religious questions. Most of these leaders profess their faith and engage in the tenets of Bible study. Washington and Adams are stolid but lifelong churchgoers, and the latter makes religion his primary source of investigation in his later years. Franklin and Jefferson's various theological inquiries illustrate that religion is an intellectual duty as well as a civic freedom. Franklin's "Preface to an

Abridgement of the Book of Common Prayer" (1779), his proposed new version of the Bible (1779), and his revised account of the Lord's Prayer (1779), and Jefferson's two detailed compilations from the New Testament – "The Philosophy of Jesus" (1804) and "The Life and Morals of Jesus" (1819–20) – are tangible commitments to the religious life around them.

A belief based on reason that utterly subsumes revelation may be especially hard for a modern mind to comprehend and appreciate. Jefferson can be a sincere Christian in a letter of 1803 to Benjamin Rush and then can dismiss the virgin birth, the divinity of Christ, original sin, blood atonement, and the Trinity as delirious fabrications, when writing to William Short in 1819. The uncompromising vigor of both stances has to do with Jefferson's total self-confidence in reason, his fear of revivalist excesses, and his correspondingly sharp rejection of biblical revelation ("merely the ravings of a Maniac," he tells Alexander Smyth in 1825).

In the fullest explanation of his belief, appearing in a letter to Adams from 1823, Jefferson answers some of these apparent contradictions in himself and for the culture at large. As organized Christianity is "a system of fancy absolutely incomprehensible," so there are "evident proofs of the necessity of a superintending power to maintain the Universe." Jefferson, the Enlightenment figure, rests in the appearance of order and the system of design. "I hold (without appeal to revelation) that when we take a view of the Universe, in its parts general or particular, it is impossible for the human mind not to perceive and feel a conviction of design, consummate skill, and indefinite power in every atom of its composition." The interesting aspect of this thinking in context is that it carries Jefferson back into a Christian orientation rather than away from it. His letter to Adams concludes not just with faith in "a fabricator of all things" but with acceptance of Jesus as "the most venerated reformer of human errors." The combination is a powerful one in a moment in time. Jefferson belongs to the first generation of the Enlightenment in America and therefore holds to an absolutist faith in reason, but he also belongs to a Bible culture of extraordinary vitality.

Because of that vitality, the idea of Providence always surfaces at critical times in American politics, often when other sources of explanation remain unavailable or have failed. Paine raising the millennium in the bold new hope of a continental republic, Adams summoning "rays of ravishing light and glory" in the difficult moment of independence, Jefferson warning of God's anger over slavery, Franklin asking for prayer amidst the acrimony of the Constitutional Convention – all couch their hardest problems in religious terminology. Convenience but also necessity and sometimes faith are at work in the contrivance. All three impulses encourage the instantiation of religious forms in the rituals of political life.

Because the early Republic is still a Bible culture, God appears therein as the best available symbol of order and purpose against chaos and confusion. George Washington employs traditional aspects of that symbol when he begins his first inaugural address with "fervent supplications to that Almighty Being who rules over the universe." Although stripped of teleological tensions and all thought of biblical revelation in Washington's construct, "the great Author of every public and private good" still expects "some return of pious gratitude." Notably, the benefits of order and purpose initiate a duty of worship. "No people can be bound to acknowledge and adore the invisible hand which conducts the affairs of men, more than the people of the United States," Washington intones. "Every step by which they have advanced to the character of an independent nation seems to have been distinguished by some token of providential agency."

The passage should sound familiar. Washington's first official moment as president appropriates the minister's idea of a national covenant. If Washington dilutes that covenant in abstraction and tonal quiescence, in keeping with Enlightenment discourse, he also renders it possible for every citizen to "adore the invisible hand." In the process, the doctrine separating church and state yields and then protects a distinct religious dimension within the political realm. Through such language we gain just a glimpse of what will become an elaborate, institutionalized civil religion in America. From a literary perspective, three levels of implication are at work: the writer's engagement in religious thought, the writer's tactical use of religious terminology in secular explanation, and the writer's strategic awareness of the role of religious discourse in the life of the nation.

No practitioner of this interaction (the measure of belief, the mechanics of literary skill, and the exercise of ideological awareness combined) proves cannier than Thomas Jefferson or uses it more productively in supplanting the clergy in political life. Jefferson's opposition to the clergy leaves him acutely aware of their power through ritual. In yet another diatribe against "the priests of the different religious sects" and their "holy inquisition," he fastens on that source. "We have most unwisely committed to the hierophants of our particular superstition, the direction of public opinion, that lord of the Universe," he writes to William Short in 1820. "We have given them stated and privileged days to collect and catechise us, opportunities of delivering their oracles to the people in mass, and of moulding their minds as wax in the hollow of their hands." This rejection of the occasional sermon is no more than earlier policy has dictated. In 1801, President Jefferson abruptly ends the practice previously accepted by Washington and Adams of national fast day observances, and his prohibition is followed automatically in the presidencies of his Virginia followers, James Madison and James

Monroe. By then, 1825, all formal ceremonial observances of national purpose and identity have passed from pulpit to podium.

The primary architect of the separation of church and state, Jefferson is also first to ply the language of civil religion with complete effectiveness. He supplants the clergy by succeeding them in his own inaugural address. As the new president, he consolidates "an age of revolution and reformation," outlines "the creed of our political faith," and closes with a benediction to "that Infinite Power which rules the destinies of the universe." Along the way, he enumerates the justifications for thinking of America as "a chosen country," and prominent among them is a proper sense of religion. The people are

enlightened by a benign religion, professed, indeed, and practiced in various forms, yet all of them including honesty, truth, temperance, gratitude, and the love of man; acknowledging and adoring an overruling Providence, which by all dispensations proves that it delights in the happiness of man here and his greater happiness hereafter.

These words are profoundly nonsectarian in tenor even as they sustain scriptural interpretation. They do not rule out the biblical God of history; providence still presides over the world. They also evoke a human realm of obligation to further God's will (happiness here and hereafter). At the same time, the chiefly secular virtues of "a benign religion" (honesty, truth, temperance, gratitude, and love of humanity) drain judgment of its edge and convert Jefferson's passive verb ("enlightened") into an overarching theme. By the end of the passage, an enlightened people have become the Enlightenment. More than anything, the passage is calculatedly inclusive and participatory. It inspires without requiring specific acts of faith.

Jefferson's genius as both a writer and a leader of government guide him toward a notable political truth: cohesion and well-being rather than mystery and salvation attract and drive civil worship. The inaugural address of 1801 invites Americans to bask together in providential favor as they enjoy the "dispensations" of a promised land. Future American leaders will adopt the same strategies. Occasion, language, and ritual merge in the citizen's sense of belonging to a proper celebration of republican identity. Behind such exercises, though, and essential to them, is an unspecified modicum of belief. The language holds because it once compelled, and the capacity to wield that language owes everything to earlier ceremonies. Although he does not acknowledge the fact, Jefferson fully comprehends the nature and power of the election sermon, those occasions when the clergy offer "their oracles to the people in mass." Elected, Jefferson delivers his own lay sermon. The measure of his awareness is in his language to the people in democratic union.

4

❦

WRITING THE REVOLUTION

I

First to study the Revolution, the historian David Ramsay also first proclaims the utter centrality of its writings. "In establishing American independence," he observes in *The History of the American Revolution* (1789),
"the pen and the press had merit equal to that of the sword." Writings can
equal events because events, small in themselves, often take their primary
significance from the symbolism that language gives them. Five people die
in the Boston Massacre; just eight, in the battle of Lexington. Clearly, it
is not size and scale that shake the old order but something else. The
international hue and cry of the Intolerable Acts in 1774 take place over
342 chests of tea dumped in Boston Harbor. In the war, General Washington's Continental army sometimes dwindles to fewer than four thousand
soldiers, and that army's arduous retreat to Valley Forge in the winter of
1777 takes it only twenty miles from the British army in Philadelphia.
Numbers are even smaller in the South. The battles of King's Mountain
and Cowpens, major American victories in 1780 and 1781, engage fewer
than three thousand at a time. Important in themselves, such incidents
take their fullest significance from revolutionary ideology or from the way
they contribute to a familiar sense of story and to an understanding of
occurrence. Either way, the prime value of a revolutionary event is often in
the telling.

At another and prior level, the pen enables the sword. Americans write
about the idea of revolution long before they can conceive of the act in
realistic terms. Writing the thought inscribes the conception, which, in
time, blurs the line of distinction between thought and act. Somewhere, a
legitimate rhetoric of opposition grows into the outrageous possibility of
revolution. Where, for example, should one place Jeremiah Dummer's *A
Defence of the New England Charters* (1721) on this continuum? Dummer
rejects all thought of colonial revolt as "ludicrous" in his "short digression"
on the subject, and yet John Adams can properly call this pamphlet the
handbook of the Revolution. As Adams tells William Tudor in 1818,

" '[T]he feelings, the manners and principles which produced the Revolution,' appear in as vast abundance in this work as in any that I have read."

How can Dummer and Adams both be right about *A Defence of the New England Charters?* Dummer, colonial agent for Massachusetts and Connecticut and an American lawyer in London, raises the idea of revolution only to dismiss it: "it would not be more absurd to place two of his Majesty's Beef-Eaters to watch an infant in the Cradle, that it don't rise and cuts its Father's Throat, than to guard these weak infant Colonies, to prevent their shaking off the *British* Yoke." Nevertheless, the double languages of the American and the Englishman, of the native pamphleteer and the imperial agent, do render the absurd sensible. In *A Defence of the New England Charters,* Dummer worries repeatedly about the "arbitrary" power of the Crown, the "unnatural insult" to colonial rights, and the "oppression" of royal governors. The dangers he cites are real and growing: "Oppression rushes in like a Tide, and bears down every Thing before it." To the extent that British rule appears as a burden, literally as a "yoke," it welcomes the thought of being thrown off. Dummer's metaphors belie their surface meanings. An infant cannot commit patricide, but, later and often enough, children do revolt against their parents.

The pressure that Dummer places on his own predicament shows that he grasps the uses to which his language might be put. He knows that *A Defence of the New England Charters* raises more questions than it answers. Admitting that Parliament has the *power* to revoke the colonial charters, he insists that it has no *right* to do so. To think otherwise would be "abhorrent from all Reason, Equity, and Justice." To limit Parliament, however, means that anything can happen, and, in a telling allusion, Dummer turns himself into the son of the legendary Lydian King Croesus in the *Histories* of Herodotus. The conceit plays upon a figure who, mute from birth, learns to speak only in an emergency, as invading Persians destroy both king and country. Whatever the inconsistencies in his position, Dummer writes because he believes he can hesitate no longer. Extremity has given voice to the rashest implications: "for how little so ever one is able to write, yet when the Liberties of one's Country are threaten'd, it's still more difficult to be silent."

Here, in the span between dumb silence and bold statement, is the voice of the Revolution, one that is half-English, half-American, and, in its stuttering progressions, often less than half of itself. No figure demonstrates the dynamic involved better than Patrick Henry, who seeks to embody this voice. Indeed, the great orator would later claim the Revolution for himself through his speech in the Virginia House of Burgesses against the Stamp Act in 1765:

All the colonies, either through fear, or want of opportunity to form an opposition, or from influence of some kind or other, had remained silent. . . . I determined to venture, and alone, unadvised, and unassisted, on a blank leaf of an old law book, wrote the [seven resolutions against the Stamp Act]. Upon offering them to the House violent debates ensued. . . . The alarm spread throughout America. . . . The great point of resistance to British taxation was universally established in the colonies. This brought on the war which finally separated the two countries and gave independence to ours.

While Patrick Henry, as usual, is exaggerating for effect, his description catches the flavor of revolutionary discourse. The need for bold speech comes out of the prevailing silence of a paralyzing uncertainty. Reducing that uncertainty are a series of controlling rhetorical premises: the announced thematic resistance to taxation, the spread of alarm, the sudden universality of belief through exhortation, and the notion of action following from proper language. But if Henry can think of himself as "alone, unadvised, and unassisted," he also speaks within a familiar and frequently expressed Whig tradition of legal precedents. Four of his seven resolutions against the Stamp Act reiterate the rights of English subjects. Henry may write them on the "blank leaf of an old law book," but his language owes much to the printed pages of that law book and of others like it. He writes within a coherent and established English legal theory of opposition.

Henry's actual words before the Virginia legislature in 1765 dramatize the interstices between revolutionary thought and assertion. When he proclaims that "Caesar had his Brutus, Charles the First his Cromwell, and George the Third – " the sequence prompts interrupting cries of "Treason!" in the House. "And George the Third," counters Henry above the din, "may profit by their example – if this be treason, make the most of it." The words themselves may not be exact – Henry's recorded speeches all come from spellbound listeners writing after the event – but they are true to a spirit of the times in which *the exchange* of words dominates and symbolizes action.

That exchange, at least on Henry's part, is deliberately contrapuntal. The juxtaposition of perceived meanings (a cautionary note for his king versus a plan of revolt) increases the whole by "making the most" of opposition. Henry's stock parallels of tyrants and opponents carry from a familiar past toward an uncertain present and create, along the way, an unbearable hiatus in the speaker's moment of threatened liberties. His manipulation of the Whig theory of history forces every auditor to glimpse resistance. But how much resistance and what kinds? Henry's rhetoric flows from a continuum of oppositional stances, and the perception of ongoing conflict has rendered extreme action more and more conceivable.

At the same time, the shouts of "treason" shatter the continuum of legitimate opposition. Henry's words and the reaction to them in the House of Burgesses typify a struggle to think the unthinkable in eighteenth-century

America – a struggle already glimpsed in Dummer's *A Defence of the New England Charters*. To conceive of rebellion, the extreme in resistance, is to force a strategic reconception. Suddenly, the whole subject has to be recast. Well enough do Henry's opponents grasp the notion of opposition, and well enough do they accept even the examples of previous and successful rebellion against a king, but they accept with their English heritage firmly in mind. Opposition seeks an extension of English legal rights, not the desertion of them. For colonial Americans, it is one thing to defend constitutional rights against corruption, conspiracy, and betrayal as members of the British Empire; it is quite another to act so as to reject a place in that empire altogether.

How does one defend English rights if one is no longer professedly English? Every protesting colonial American voice stumbles over the implications. Jeremiah Dummer, in the first of many attempts to face the problem, tries to solve it by making American rights more English than those of the English. In *A Defence of the New England Charters*, he writes,

the *American* Charters are of a higher Nature, and stand on a better Foot, than the Corporations in *England*. For these latter were granted upon Improvements already made, and therefore were Acts of meer Grace and Favour in the Crown; whereas the former were given as Praemiums for Services to be perform'd, and therefore are to be considered as Grants upon a *valuable Consideration;* which adds Weight and Strength to the Title.

The difficulty in this formulation is that the writer's "better foot" still rests on English soil. Dummer can put American charters over English corporations only by resorting to the Anglo-Saxon notion of consideration on a contract. The very nature of his argument leaves him entrenched "from time out of memory" in the English common-law tradition.

Dummer typifies the ways in which British Americans recognize their situation without being able to expound it fully. Again and again, protest loses its power when challenged at the sticking point, and one reason is a curious bifurcation in the perception of problems. For although the conflict between Britain and the American colonies revolves around practical questions of finance, trade, and economic imbalance, the discourse of conflict comes almost entirely from the separate sphere of constitutional theory and legal argument.

The ensuing stammer in revolutionary writings is the most significant literary characteristic of those writings; overcoming it, the first indication of revolutionary success. We need to understand this process better. A great deal has been made of the facility of colonial political writers in the 1760s and 1770s and of the convenient availability to them of an English oppositional rhetoric. Disgruntled Americans like John Dickinson, Benjamin Franklin, and Thomas Jefferson prove a literary match for the best intellects of the age in London, and their ability is one of the first things that English readers notice at the time. Mutual recognition is possible because American eloquence makes powerful use of the rhetorical devices in English politics. Even the most inflexible British reader sees familiar parallels in colonial argumentation: the restraint on power through mixed forms of government, the condemnation of standing armies, the dangers of corruption in the constitution, the fear of conspiracies against liberty, and the emphasis upon public virtue.

It may be, though, that scholars have made too much of these parallels and of an oppositional, or "country," rhetoric as the basis of interpretation. Seventeenth-century commonwealth writers like James Harrington, Algernon Sidney, and John Milton are vital influences on radical thought in both England and America, and eighteenth-century popularizers like John Trenchard and Thomas Gordon then magnify their influence in such works as *The Independent Whig* and *Cato's Letters*. But these influences in themselves stress the enabling capacities rather than the hesitations in protest, and it is the hesitations that define the evolution of colonial protest. Until 1776, the dominant Anglo-American perspective remains *against* the thought of rupture between England and America. A more formidable writer than Trenchard or Gordon – or, for that matter, than Harrington and Sidney – dramatizes this perspective in the final moment of crisis.

The sharpest single argument against independence comes in Samuel Johnson's *Taxation No Tyranny; an Answer to the Resolutions and Address of the American Congress* (1775). Properly read, *Taxation No Tyranny* conveys better than any other document of the times the immense intellectual problems that eighteenth-century Americans are facing in the act of rebellion. Johnson, the leading writer in the English-speaking world, seizes upon every embarrassing inconsistency and half-way measure in colonial claims. His well-known jibe – "how is it that we hear the loudest yelps for liberty among the drivers of negroes?" – is only the most caustic rejoinder in a systematic exposure of American contradictions and hypocrisies. Juxtaposing the creation of the Continental Congress against colonial claims of loyalty to king and country, Johnson asks, "[S]ince the Americans have discovered that they can make a parliament, whence comes it that they do not think themselves equally empowered to make a king?" To any insistence upon "all the rights of Englishmen," he responds that rights bring legal obligations. As the assertion of the one requires accountability in the other, "it seems to follow by consequence not easily avoided, that [our colonies] are subject to English government, and chargeable by English taxation."

Johnson's eloquence turns colonial protest into seeming ignorance and intractability; the Americans are being merely obstinate when they are not being dangerous and unruly. In the equivocation that taxes might be possible but not in the form that England seeks to levy them, Johnson finds administrative chaos: "dominion without authority, and subjects without subordination." When colonial rhetoric joins natural law to English rights, Johnson forces the two apart again, using the standard eighteenth-century understanding of political theory. Either the Americans are "the naked sons of Nature," or "they are no longer in a state of nature." The choice is theirs, but by resorting to English rights at all, "these lords of themselves, these kings of *Me*, these demigods of independence, sink down to colonists, governed by a charter."

These arguments also prey deliberately upon American intellectual insecurities. Johnson exposes the slipperiness and unreliability in a language of protest. "The laws of Nature, the rights of humanity, the faith of charters, the danger of liberty, the encroachments of usurpation, have been thundered in our ears, sometimes by interested faction, and sometimes by honest stupidity." Most troubling of all is the "progress of sedition" in which "those who a few years ago disputed only our right of laying taxes, now question the validity of every act of legislation." Where, Johnson wants to know, will this progression end? Indeed, the breakdown in colonial government in the protests of the 1760s and 1770s appears to many Americans to be just such an alarming sequence. Johnson sees a "delirious dream of republican fanaticism" under a "congress of anarchy." For two centuries Americans had accepted the sacred importance of their colonial charters as their source of political identity and security; now, "without their charter, there would be no power among them, by which any law could be made, or duties enjoined, any debt recovered, or criminal punished." And for what? Johnson takes pains to show that the colonists enjoy "the same virtual representation as the greater part of Englishmen." Americans have lost nothing "except that of which their sedition has deprived them."

The interesting thing about this Johnsonian remonstrance is that it summarizes what Americans already have been saying to each other piecemeal for a decade. *Taxation No Tyranny* actually echoes the radical Boston lawyer James Otis's *A Vindication of the British Colonies* (1765), where Otis calls independence a state that "none but rebels, fools, and madmen will contend for." "God forbid these colonies should ever prove undutiful to their mother country!" writes Otis, in words that Samuel Johnson would have read with approval. "Whenever such a day shall come it will be the beginning of a terrible scene. Were these colonies left to themselves tomorrow, America would be a mere shambles of blood and confusion." Despite their many differences, the conservative English Tory in Johnson and the radical American Whig in Otis express many of the same fears. The skill in Anglo-

American writings of the period lies not in the parroting of "country" rhetoric or even in the refinement of it but in the way writers handle and exploit these fears in the exchange of ideas across party lines.

A vital generic consideration also fosters exchange. *A Defence of the New England Charters, A Vindication of the British Colonies,* and *Taxation No Tyranny* are all the same kind of expression. Jeremiah Dummer, James Otis, and Samuel Johnson write within the classic era of the pamphlet, a genre that dominates the formulation of political ideas in eighteenth-century culture and in the Revolution in particular. The highly polemical and topical nature of such writing, together with the natural responsiveness of pamphlets, one to another, make them the center of the contrapuntal development in revolutionary thought. Not least in this impact is the special license that pamphlets give to writers with extreme views. Eighteenth-century newspapers remain vulnerable to prosecution for libel and breach of privilege and to direct communal pressures in ways that the pseudonymous, one-shot pamphlet does not. The lower profile, smaller publication runs, and irregularity of the pamphlet are its own protections in a time when freedom of the press is still more of a question than a right.

The exact form of the eighteenth-century pamphlet is another advantage. A few printers' sheets folded into folio, quarto, or octavo pages, depending on length, the pamphlet lends itself to easy publication, to the briefest of collaborations between author and printer, to any style or range of argumentation, to minimal expense and quick profit, and to informal modes of distribution. Each of these strengths are expressly significant in early America, where limits in technology, capitalization, and cultural attainment all favor the crude levels of performance and production that pamphleteering so easily tolerates. Of course, all of these characteristics also abet the uncertainties and relative failures in articulation already noted.

Beyond technology are ideological considerations that bring the pamphlet and the Enlightenment together with special force in revolutionary America. Insofar as the Enlightenment conceives of conflict as the struggle of knowledge against ignorance, the rapid diffusion of right information becomes a vital key to victory. Publication represents the first line of attack, and the pamphlet quickly becomes the primary medium for the new citizen reader; it will remain the clearest path to an informed public until the supremacy of the newspaper early in the nineteenth century. No revolutionary culture has ever had a higher literacy rate than do some of the politically volatile areas of the thirteen colonies. (Although accurate figures for the period are not available, approximations suggest that 85 percent of all adult males in New England are able to read compared to roughly 60 percent in England.) Political leaders, aware of the opportunities for communication that exceptional literacy provides and worried about the undeveloped nature and distance between their communities, hope that cheap, readily available commentary on important issues will in itself shape American destiny. One of the breathtaking assumptions of revolutionary intellectuals about their period and place is their belief that widespread publication of correct ideas will make all of the difference in human history. Never in the long story of printing has the ephemeral pamphlet been drafted with greater expectations.

To these high notions must be added the low and continuous irritant of conflict. Recent historical understanding of the contentiousness in colonial life indicates that clashes of all kinds are endemic and perpetual – between American and British interests, between colonial governors and their assemblies, between eastern and western needs within colonies, between colonies over border and trade problems, between North and South, between an incredible variety of religious groupings, between colonial settlers and Native-American populations, and between everyone over land everywhere. Pamphlet production thrives on these controversies because the topicality, spontaneity, and loose form of the genre allow invective and banter to compete on the same terms with rational argument. Adrift in a culture still between oral and print modes of communication, the pamphlet often comes closer than even the printed sermon to the rhythms and personal pressure of speech.

The result in the revolutionary pamphlet is often a bizarre mixture in which rectification and excoriation vie for tonal control. The frustrations involved are palpable. Knowledge should end conflict in an enlightened culture, and yet the perceptive colonial observer finds strife begetting strife on every side. The first remedy in dealing with these difficulties is writing them out, the dissemination of relevant information within the correct idea. Alexander Hamilton, at twenty in *The Farmer Refuted* (1775), seems to have believed that real differences will disappear if his opponent, in this case Samuel Seabury, will read Grotius, von Pufendorf, Locke, Montesquieu, and Burlamaqui with the right care. "I might mention other excellent writers on this subject; but if you attend, diligently, to these," Hamilton condescends to add, "you will not require any others."

The notion that the right answer can be derived from correct readings dictates a painstaking narrative style in writing after writing. Over and over, the pamphlets of the period patiently rehearse the essential connections between legal philosophy, social contract theory, and the American situation in a step-by-step presentation of the truth and its sources from the beginning of history down to the present moment. Behind the earnest insistence upon presentation is an even more earnest assumption about reception: the true narrative, if complete, will convince the rational reader. It follows, however, that continuing conflict implies more than ignorance; ignorance alone, after all, will accept refutation.

The far more likely sources of enduring conflict are willful error and the near certainty of a self-interested plan to maintain it – unforgivable blemishes on the spread of the Enlightenment. Thus, the alternative strategy in American pamphleteering, often ranged alongside the sweet rationality of the first, relies on a spirit of invective and outraged condemnation. This second response ignores failures in understanding to concentrate instead on the presence and exposure of conspiracies. The development of the pamphlet in revolutionary America is about these competing tones and the eventual mastery of them in combinations of reason and anger, explanation and vituperation – a mastery that will convince Americans of the need for Revolution when orchestrated in *Common Sense*.

II

If one document can explain the several hundred American pamphlets on the crisis in politics between 1764 and 1776, it would be John Adams's *A Dissertation on the Canon and Feudal Law* (1765). Adams begins with the assertion, taken from Bishop John Tillotson, that ignorance is the greatest cause of human misery, and he closes with the injunction that "every sluice of knowledge be opened and set a-flowing." In between comes a controlling premise: only the spread of knowledge among the people can preserve liberty. *A Dissertation on the Canon and Feudal Law* uses this framework to draw out a contrast between Adams's presumptions about European ignorance and the American Enlightenment. In Europe, a confederacy between the clergy and feudal princes has kept the people in ignorance of their rights until the Reformation, which has renewed the struggle for knowledge. The first Americans, as part of that Reformation, establish their settlements "in direct opposition to the canon and feudal systems," substituting "the Bible and common sense" for "the ridiculous fancies of sanctified effluvia from episcopal fingers." Inevitably, the Stamp Act of 1765 figures as "the first step" in a European conspiracy to introduce the canon and feudal law to America.

Three elements in Adams's argument compel him to seek the broadest popular publication of American disagreements with England. First, Adams's view of European corruption and ignorance projects "a direct and formal design on foot, to enslave all America," and colonial writers must expose that design. But if this duty to spread the alarm seems obvious enough, the compulsion to publish American views remains *whether or not* a writer shares Adams's sense of conspiracy. Since "liberty cannot be preserved without a general knowledge among the people," the American way requires "the preservation of the means of knowledge among the lowest ranks." "Care has been taken," Adams observes, "that the art of printing should be encouraged, and that it should be easy and cheap and safe for any person to communicate his thoughts to the public." Adams, right or wrong, performs a patriotic function in publishing his pamphlet in the *Boston-Gazette*. He is participating in the communal expectation that informed citizens will communicate their thoughts in writing to the waiting public.

If Adams is even partially correct in his thinking, a third overriding consideration enters into his compulsion to write out every difference with Europe. Again, no conspiracy is necessary for Americans to celebrate their separation from European forms of corruption or for them to express a fear of contamination. The perception of difference is its own threat. Adams in 1765 shares with many other colonial intellectuals a growing mission to rescue history from its European failures. As he summarizes the thought, in a journal entry from December 30th:

[Americans] think that the Liberties of Mankind and the Glory of human Nature is in their Keeping. They know that Liberty . . . has been hunted and persecuted, in all Countries, by cruel Power. But they flatter them selves that America was designed by Providence for the Theatre, on which Man was to make his true figure, on which science, Virtue, Liberty, Happiness and Glory were to exist in Peace.

This is a mighty message to convey to a fallen world, and it transforms the provincial who delivers it into a figure of international importance. Not for the last time, American identification of an external threat presumes a contingent moral superiority.

A Dissertation on the Canon and Feudal Law may be pompous, but it is never complacent. Its terms demand a new commitment to knowledge in a literary call to arms. "We have been afraid to think," Adams concludes in reviewing the failure of Americans to assert their rights against British authority. His solution is clear: "Let us dare to read, think, speak and write. Let every order and degree among the people rouse their attention and animate their resolution." Adams's agenda, properly rendered in prose, describes every major pamphlet of the period:

Let them all become attentive to the grounds and principles of government, ecclesiastical and civil. Let us study the law of nature; search into the spirit of the British constitution; read the histories of ancient ages; contemplate the great examples of Greece and Rome; set before us the conduct of our own British ancestors, who have defended for us the inherent rights of mankind against foreign and domestic tyrants and usurpers, against arbitrary kings and cruel priests, in short, against the gates of earth and hell.

It is as if these words become every writer's guide. Pamphlet after pamphlet dutifully blends the principles of government, the law of nature, the meaning of the British Constitution, and the history of classical, English, and American politics in an interpretation of the crisis at hand. Most, as well, distinguish between ecclesiastical and civil frames of reference even as they conflate religious and political rhetoric in a secular writing. The conclusions of individual investigations differ, but the methodology remains the same. Meanwhile, the tedium of repetition serves yet another purpose; the rhythms in pamphleteering gradually smooth the irregularities in revolutionary thought.

Although conflict between English and American interests is a constant in colonial politics, the year 1764 marks a significant escalation. The change can be seen in a subtle transition. After 1764, colonists prefer the term "Americans" to "Englishmen" in their newspaper descriptions of themselves, and in that year two pamphlets display a new feeling or degree of apprehension. In Virginia, continuing controversy over the payment of Anglican clergy, the Parson's Cause from 1758, reaches a new and prescient level of constitutional interpretation in 1764 in Richard Bland's *The Colonel Dismounted: or the Rector Vindicated*. In New England, Parliament's first attempt to levy additional revenue from the colonies in the Sugar Act prompts James Otis's *The Rights of the British Colonies Asserted and Proved*. Each pamphlet has been called the first paper of the Revolution. Both involved an important colonial legislative leader of the moment, and both achieve notoriety for delineating a major facet of colonial protest. Both efforts also stimulate controversy and lead to more radical writings by their authors. Taken together, they cover North and South, politics and religion, light satire and solemn assertion. Yet, between them, they also dramatize the inconsistencies in protest. Not until 1776 do colonial writers get past the intellectual problems that Bland and Otis exhibit in their most celebrated writings.

Richard Bland has been forgotten because he dies in 1776, or just as the Revolution begins, and because most of his writings have been lost. The leading expert in colonial legal history in 1764, he is also the most important member of the Virginia House of Burgesses in the generation before Patrick Henry and Thomas Jefferson; he serves in the House for thirty-three years, from 1742 until 1775. Writing to William Wirt in August of 1815, Jefferson would claim for Bland that "he wrote the first pamphlet [*The Colonel Dismounted*] on the nature of the connection with Great Britain which had any pretension to accuracy of view on that subject." Bland's effort tries to separate internal and external government – a distinction that would percolate in Anglo–American debate for a decade to come. England, the argument runs, should control matters of external government, while internal government must be left to freeborn Americans in keeping with their liberties and privileges as English subjects.

The distinction between internal and external government places a limit on the authority of king and Parliament in British America and allows for a right of resistance when that limit is passed. Bland will "upon every occasion yield a due obedience" to his king, "but submission even to the supreme magistrate is not the whole duty of a citizen. . . . Something is likewise due to the rights of our country and to the liberties of mankind." Parliament remains supreme: "I do not deny but that the Parliament, as the stronger power, can force any laws it should think fit upon us." Still, "any tax respecting our INTERNAL polity which may hereafter be imposed on us by act of Parliament is arbitrary, as depriving us of our right, and may be opposed." Later, as opposition to British authority grows, colonial theorists come to see Bland's distinction as one without a difference, but it is an important rallying cry in the 1760s.

Bland struggles to remain a good British-American subject by leaving the "something due" American rights and the license to "oppose impositions" in suspension. *The Colonel Dismounted* relies on the certainty that George III and Parliament would never extract an inordinate submission; "we have nothing of this sort of fear from those guardians of the rights and liberties of mankind." Unfortunately, Americans have everything to fear in 1764. Passage of the Stamp Act in the next year fulfills Bland's worst hypothetical case of a "tax respecting our INTERNAL polity" and places him in an untenable philosophical position. The situation demonstrates how one pamphlet, *The Colonel Dismounted*, could compel and inscribe a sequel, *An Inquiry into the Rights of the British Colonies* (1766). In a typical pattern for the period, the first decision to write now requires a second farther along the continuum of resistance; writing itself becomes a radicalizing act. Bland is one of the moderates who temporize over the thrusts of Patrick Henry in the House of Burgesses, but the Stamp Act controversy forces him away from the comfort of automatic loyalty and toward the refinement of an American theory of opposition.

An Inquiry into the Rights of the British Colonies in 1766 is unavoidably a tortured document. Bland, the legal scholar, realizes that the letter of the law can make him a traitor. He drops the satirical mode of *The Colonel Dismounted* and now agonizes in the role of colonial champion. "I must speak freely," he observes, "I am considering a Question which affects the *Rights* of above two Millions of as loyal Subjects as belong to the British Crown." Simultaneously, he fears that the actual decision to become a champion means that he will "be charged with Insolence," and, in a courageous response to that anxiety, he prints his own name, "Richard Bland, of Virginia," on the title page of the document. The gesture, unique for the times, literalizes the issue of colonial spokesman by removing the thought of mediation. Stepping from behind the conventional veil of anonymity, Bland turns himself into a living type for the writer who delivers "the Sentiments of an honest Mind with Freedom."

The pamphlet itself is a checkerboard of contrasting assertions and assurances of loyalty, on the one hand, and discussions of the right of resistance, on the other. Once again, Parliament is supreme, though once again, the colonies are not to be subject to internal taxation by authority of Parliament. "The Colonies," claims Bland, "are subordinate to the Authority of Parliament; subordinate I mean in Degree, but not absolutely so." Where, then, is the line? Bland tries to draw a distinction between the law of England and the law of Nature with recourse to the latter when the first proves insufficient, but he is too good a lawyer to rest in this conclusion. For while the usual historical review reveals the British Constitution to be in decline or worse, the rights of English subjects remain civil guarantees founded in compact, and the duty of colonists is still "to lay their Complaints at the Foot of the Throne, and to suffer patiently rather than disturb the publick Peace." But this conclusion is intolerable even to its author. And so Bland persists: "if this Justice should be denied, if the most humble and dutiful Representations should be rejected, nay not even deigned to be received, what is to be done?" The open-endedness of the question, and the way it breaks into colonial rhetoric at each crucial juncture, is one test of creativity in pamphlet writings of the period.

What *is* to be done? Bland turns away from his own natural inclinations in law for an answer in politics. *An Inquiry into the Rights of the British Colonies* recalls the debates of the Corinthians and the Corcyreans over the rights of colonies in the first pages of *The Peloponnesian War*. The actual exchange in Thucydides supports the notion of fair dealing, but the antagonism of Corinth and Corcyra ripens into conflict despite every reasonable argument; conflict, in turn, triggers general war and leads the Greeks to their ruin. Bland lets the Corcyreans speak directly from his own pages. Every colony, they tell the Corinthians, becomes an alien when treated with injury and violence.

Stymied by history and law, unwilling to end with even an indirect prediction of war ("the Subject is delicate"), Bland reaches for the framework of science. *An Inquiry* shifts suddenly into a refutation of the use of Newtonian physics by anticolonial writers. These writers construe the technical language of first movers, of revolving orbs, and of equal force to make Great Britain "the Centre of Attraction to the Colonies." To the contrary, argues Bland, "the Laws of Attraction in natural as well as political Philosophy" prove that "Bodies in Contact, and cemented by mutual Interests, cohere more strongly than those which are at a Distance and have no common Interests to preserve." The odd sudden placement of the scientific theme here is a good example of thematic breakage in revolutionary discourse. Something of a non sequitur, the passage also strangely undercuts the largest hope in Bland's pamphlet: namely, that the colonies "ever remain under a constitutional Subordination to Great Britain!" For if Bland insists repeatedly upon "the deepest loyalty" and "an unshaken Attachment to the Interest of Great Britain," the law of gravity, as he presents it, suggests a greater attachment between or among the more proximate colonies.

The discrepancy between political hope and scientific argument goes to the essence of changing colonial apprehensions. Challenges to colonial rights from England have begun to create the need for images and arguments of an American solidarity. Bland, in describing the crisis of 1766, knows that for the colonies "the closest Union becomes necessary to maintain in a constitutional Way their dearest Interests." He also realizes that the supposed objectivity of science might serve the cause, and his resort, a frequent one in the period, is to the language of astronomy. The Enlightenment habit of relating scientific knowledge to human improvement is especially clear where order in the motion of the stars presumably figure a predictability in human occurrence. A decade later, the Declaration of Independence will begin with words about the course of human events cohering in separate and equal station through the laws of nature, and Americans in 1776 will first hear these words read in the Philadelphia Observatory on the platform built to observe the transit of Venus.

For all of their differences, Richard Bland in Virginia and James Otis in Massachusetts epitomize the same larger colonial dilemma in the middle 1760s. True, in writing the most notorious pamphlet of the decade, *The Rights of the British Colonies Asserted and Proved* (1764), Otis rejects Bland's distinction between external and internal government. True again, he conflates civil and natural law where Bland finds more of a contrast, and he restricts Parliament more than Bland is willing to do, but the overriding similarities in their major writings indicate a general colonial attitude beyond personal, regional, and philosophical differences. Definitions of loyalty are the real issue in these pamphlets, and at the center of that subject is a cultural paradox.

Americans in the middle 1760s have not yet drawn a meaningful line between obedience and protest even though British attempts to tax the colonies has made protest the basis of self-definition. Hence, *The Rights of the British Colonies Asserted and Proved* assumes that "it is the duty of every good citizen to point out what he thinks erroneous in the commonwealth," and it condemns the failure of Americans to do so. "There has been a most profound and I think shameful silence," observes Otis, "till it seems almost too late to assert our indisputable rights as men and citizens." At the same time, "the power of Parliament is uncontrollable but by themselves, and we must obey. . . . let the Parliament lay what burdens they please on us, we must, it is our duty to submit and patiently bear them till they will be pleased to relieve us." In the end, Otis depends on the unilateral response of English politicians sitting in London. "And 'tis to be presumed the wisdom and justice of that august assembly always will afford us relief."

Like Bland, Otis remains hopelessly entangled in his admission that Parliament holds sovereignty over the American colonies, and, in another similarity, he writes his own sequel distinguishing between power and right. In *A Vindication of the British Colonies* (1765), Otis will discover a "difference between power and right, between a blind slavish submission and a loyal, generous, and rational obedience to the supreme authority of a state." Even so, the stridency of adjectives like "slavish" and "generous" aside, Otis's questions are also Bland's. Where does obedience end and submission begin? What should be done when power ignores rights? Bland and Otis simply cannot articulate more consistent responses in the middle 1760s, and their failures involve a weakness in logic that keeps the English world from taking them as seriously as it should have done. Why should English leaders accept the logic of colonial lawyers like Adams, Bland, and Otis when the law itself appears so decidedly against the legality of colonial assertions?

A pamphlet by Martin Howard, Jr., a prominent lawyer in Rhode Island and one of very few American Tories not intimidated into silence by communal protest, helps to clarify the colonial dilemma. Howard's reply to Otis and others in *A Letter from a Gentleman at Halifax* (1765) prefigures Samuel Johnson's more adroit exposure of colonial argumentation a decade later in *Taxation No Tyranny.* Warning that loose comparisons between England in 1641 and America in 1764 "sound like sedition," Howard shows that existing theories of sovereignty allow for no equivocation in an admission of supremacy. "The jurisdiction of Parliament being established, it will follow that this jurisdiction cannot be apportioned; it is transcendent and entire, and may levy internal taxes as well as regulate trade." Attempts to distinguish between law and rights through colonial charters and the common law prove similarly defective; one must take all of the common law or none. Then, too, the so-called American right of representation in Parliament "is but a phantom" when examined in legal terms.

It is hard to argue with these claims in the cold light of historical precedent. Howard rather than Otis presents the conventional wisdom of the times. "One cannot but smile at the inconsistency of these inherent, indefeasible [rights] men," writes the gentleman from Halifax. All the same,

Howard fully realizes that his explanations break down under "the frequent abuse poured forth in pamphlets and newspapers against the mother country." Incredibly, "the pride of some and the ignorance of others" have been victorious, and "the cry against mother country has spread from colony to colony." The irony of Howard's defeat with winning arguments hints at the refraction of truth in the history of ideas. Not logic and reason but setting and tone give credence to the writings of Bland, Otis, and others; not the theory but new forms of theorizing capture the colonial imagination.

At one level, oppositional pamphleteering in America in the 1760s involves patterns of mutual recognition and reinforcement within a new colonial leadership. It is in this decade that lawyers replace ministers and Crown administrators as the intellectual elite in America. The rhetorical patterns of the oppositional pamphlet – the conflations of natural law, political philosophy, and common law – duplicate the colonial legal profession's approach to authority and self-mastery. John Adams, writing to Hezekiah Niles in 1818, recounts this perception in a description of his mentors from the 1760s, Jeremiah Gridley and James Otis: "It was a maxim which [Otis] inculcated on his pupils, as his patron in profession, Mr. Gridley, had done before him, '*that a lawyer ought never to be without a volume of natural or public law, or moral philosophy, on his table or in his pocket.*' " American pamphleteering applies just these combinations in the 1760s. One reason it is so effective politically is because it advertises the identity and merits of the colonial legal fraternity.

At another level, radical pamphleteering speaks directly to emerging communal affinities in American culture. Philosophical inconsistencies in works like *The Rights of the British Colonies Asserted and Proved* push these writers toward rhetorical extremes where their words serve a purpose beyond mere argument. In Otis's seminal pamphlet, it is not just that Americans can congratulate themselves collectively as "*the noble discoverers and settlers of a new world,*" nor that the rejection of "arbitrary" government allows them a government for "the good of *the whole,*" but that they can also hear Otis say "absolute power is *originally* and *ultimately* in the people." Patriotic identity attaches itself to the new idea that government begins – and ends – in the people.

There is a submerged, more radical discourse in such writings that begins to shape a different awareness of country. Typically, Otis's own use of astronomy – "gravitation and attraction have place in the revolution of the planets" – seeks an analogy between the physical world and the moral world, where "the first principle is *equality* and the power of the whole." Politically, the principle of equality requires "several powers properly combined," but, as the first principle, it extends to every other political consideration. Otis raises possibilities within the radical continuum that Americans will take centuries to recognize in full. "Are not women born as free as men?" he asks in his introductory remarks. For every colonist who heeds Otis's insistence that Parliament is supreme, several others seem to have been listening to a more abstract promise about human rights.

In fact, the emotional rhythms of *The Rights of the British Colonies Asserted and Proved* have little to do with the theme of parliamentary jurisdiction. Instead, they celebrate a fresh dispensation that the people have managed to create for themselves. For Otis, the year 1688 represents a sharp rupture with the past and a new constitution, not just another step in British liberties or an extension of the old one: "by the abdication [of James II], the original compact was broken to pieces . . . by the Revolution it was renewed and more firmly established, and the rights and liberties of the subject in all parts of the dominions more fully explained and confirmed." These thoughts carry well beyond the writer's intention to prove "that no parts of His Majesty's dominions can be taxed without their consent." The eighteenth-century reader who accepts the fullest implication of Otis's words begins to think that revolution might be the answer to insurmountable problems.

Plainly, much depends on whether that reader is American or English. The impulses that appeal to colonists utterly repel their English counterparts. In London, where literary production is still largely a matter of patronage and of leisure and where political position still depends on aristocratic station, the American lawyers who write out their vocationalism in political pamphleteering are vulgar upstarts at best. Virtually no one in England accepts the constitutional arguments in American pamphlets. Even *The Annual Register,* published there by oppositional Whigs, finds in 1766 that "advocates for the colonies carried the idea of liberty to the highest pitch of enthusiasm" and urges, in consequence, that an American "irregular spirit of enthusiasm should be timely checked, by making [the colonists] sensible of their dependence." The pervasiveness of this assumption in England can be appreciated in a single fact: Parliament passes the Stamp Act of 1765 by the resounding margin of 245 to 49, and it does so despite strong colonial protest against previous measures like the Sugar Act of 1764.

The emotional appeal of American pamphleteering does not translate easily into an English frame of reference, and that failure may be the clearest indication of the growing distance between the two cultures. The same language serves distinct purposes and has different effects on the two sides of the Atlantic Ocean. It may even have been that similarity of language increased acrimony by encouraging false understandings. Although English debate over the American situation is intense and serious in 1766, most members of Parliament summarily reject "arguments of *natural* lawyers, as Locke, Selden, and Puffendorf, and others." Such arguments, in the language of *The Annual Register,* "are little to the purpose in a question of constitutional law." British politicians dismiss colonial claims based on natural law through their own presumed familiarity with the theory. Missing in this familiarity, however, is the subtler understanding of a different context for ideas. Parliament misconceives the sincerity of American intentions by failing to comprehend the importance of natural-law philosophy in colonial discourse. Meanwhile, colonial leaders misconstrue parliamentary miscomprehension as a sign of corruption or worse.

These compounding failures in cultural awareness deserve elaboration. While they do not mean that the Revolution is inevitable in 1766 or after, they suggest that more is at issue in Anglo–American confrontations than conventional descriptions stress in a narrative of administrative blunders, inadequacies, instabilities, divisions, and corruption. The succession of short-lived British ministries in the 1760s compounds Anglo–American conflict without, however, being the source of it. Yes, the ministries of William Pitt, the Earl of Bute, George Grenville, the Marquis of Rockingham, Pitt again, the Duke of Grafton, and, finally, Lord North all hold power between 1761 and 1770, but every administration receives substantial support on colonial policy. Large parliamentary majorities pass the controversial colonial measures of the 1760s and 1770s, including the Intolerable Acts of 1774. Identification of the underlying sources of difference between England and America in these years would have required a truly inspired leadership; containment of them, even more. The pamphlet literature of the period is a sign of largely unrealized cultural differences and a neglected gauge, today, for measuring the range of those differences.

III

The American pamphleteer who reaches the largest audience in the world of the late 1760s is John Dickinson in *Letters from a Farmer in Pennsylvania.* Only Thomas Paine in the next decade would have a more instantaneous impact on colonial thought. Readers everywhere seem to have recognized a special contribution to the genre when Dickinson's twelve epistolary essays to "*My dear* Countrymen," first appeared in *The Pennsylvania Chronicle.* Other colonial newspapers reissue the essays as they are printed in *The Chronicle* between December 1767 and February 1768. Collected in a single pamphlet immediately after the last letter, they quickly go through seven editions in the colonies and several in England. Even today, American perceptions of the Revolution are shaped decisively by *Letters from a Farmer in Pennsylvania,* and it is important to understand why. The most detailed, sustained, learned, and ambitious pamphlet publication by an individual of the period, it also

offers tonal and philosophical controls that speak directly to cultural impera-
tives then and now.

Intellectually, Dickinson is the most thorough and effective of the colonial
lawyers who argue that Parliament cannot tax the colonies. His education at
the London Inns of Court shows in the Pennsylvania Farmer's frequent cita-
tion of British law and of writers like Locke, Coke, Hume, Montesquieu,
Tacitus, Harrington, and Machiavelli. These sources lead him to assume that
the social compact protects the inalienable right of property; thus, any
attempt to tax the property of an unrepresented citizen is contrary to English
law. Emotionally, and Dickinson is a master of the transition, this intellectual assumption translates into the celebrated cry of "Letter VII": "*We are
taxed* without our own consent, expressed by ourselves or our representatives.
We are therefore – *SLAVES.*" And yet Dickinson never sacrifices his British
readership to such polemics. The extraordinary balances in his prose keep
everyone in place.

Education and inclination together make Dickinson the most moderate of
colonial protesters, one who will actively oppose independence in 1776. The
Pennsylvania Farmer always imposes careful philosophical and stylistic limitations on political opposition. He considers the Townshend Acts of 1767
(externally imposed duties on American imports of glass, paper, paint, and
tea) to be as pernicious and unconstitutional as the Stamp Act before them,
and he challenges these laws across the gradations of resistance from legal
petition, to boycott, to force of arms. Invariably, though, the rhetoric of
Letters from a Farmer in Pennsylvania seals off the last alternative of actual
rebellion. "Letter I" detests "inflammatory measures" ("I should be sorry that
any thing should be done, which might justly displease our sovereign, or our
mother country"). "Letter III" terms liberty "a cause of too much dignity to
be sullied by turbulence and tumult"; the colonists must be "dutiful children, who have received unmerited blows from a beloved parent." "We
cannot," warns the Farmer, "act with too much caution in our disputes."
"Letter IX" inveighs against popular violence and rage; "Letter XI," against
popular reform; and "Letter XII," against the unseemliness of "*ill-formed
zeal.*"

The right kind of restraint requires a blend of controls. Dickinson begins
by asking for "a firm, modest exertion of a free spirit," but the equilibriums
involved are quite complex. "Letter I" balances protest over the Townshend
Acts ("a dreadful stroke aimed at the liberty of these colonies"), against a
modesty of temperament ("I have waited some time, in expectation of seeing
the subject treated by persons much better qualified for the task"), and the
freedom of the writer's essential theme ("so should not any honest man
suppress his sentiments concerning freedom") against a tougher summons of

spirit in the subscript of "November 5th" (the day William of Orange confirms the Glorious Revolution by accepting Parliament's Declaration of Right). If the Farmer seems to give with one hand while taking with the other, it is because he sees that the living whole, "a free spirit," cannot be simplified – especially in America.

Meeting the problem of definition head-on in "Letter III," Dickinson explains why Americans have remained so inarticulate on the subject: "it will be impossible to determine whether an *American's* character is most distinguishable, for his loyalty to his Sovereign, his duty to his mother country, his love of freedom, or his affection for his native soil." Each element – loyalty, duty, freedom, and affection – must be kept in mind and in practice. Dickinson struggles more than any other colonial intellectual to keep these conflicting affinities aloft when they confront each other. As a result, mixed metaphors and images figure prominently in *Letters from a Farmer in Pennsylvania*. Conceptions of peace and war, of objectivity and passion, of assurance and apprehension chase each other and then mesh on the page.

Dickinson wants to bring necessary ambiguities together in a theory of union. He is certain that a proper proportion will incorporate the differences of obedience and freedom, power and law. Characteristically, "Letter II" notes that "we are as much dependent on *Great Britain,* as a perfectly free people can be on another." "The *legal authority of Great-Britain,*" runs "Letter XII," is "like the spear of Telephus, it will cure as well as wound." Dickinson chooses the simile in order to eliminate the pessimism in improbable reconciliations. As the hero Telephus receives succor from the rust of the spear that has wounded him, so the colonies can extract "surprising remedies" from parliamentary "unkindness." Everything is possible, Dickinson seems to be saying, if colonial readers will only see the truth of their multiple interests.

Americans extract more than the reluctance of the revolutionary from this vision of themselves. In Enlightenment terms, the Pennsylvania Farmer personifies the ideal life. He evinces "a contented grateful mind, (undisturbed by worldly hopes or fears, relating to myself)." The sources of his tranquillity appear in his introductory remarks: a liberal education, property, and place ("My farm is small; my servants are few, and good; I have a little money at interest"); retreat from "the busy scenes of life" after having known them; the means to pursue "a greater knowledge" ("a library, which I think the most valuable part of my small estate"); and, finally, the companionship of others like himself ("two or three gentlemen of abilities and learning, who honour me with their friendship"). From the platform of these advantages, the Farmer hopes to "have an effect greater than he could reasonably expect." Actually, the effect is greater than anyone could have expected, one reason *Letters from a Farmer in Pennsylvania* deserves closer attention.

If the Enlightenment in the eighteenth century stands for one thing, it is that proper education and free exercise of the right of property will produce independence and tranquillity of mind. The Pennsylvania Farmer functions as the crystallization of this idea in the American pamphlet tradition. In biblical terms, the idea can be reduced to a single phrase repeated over and over in litany form by colonial pamphleteers: "they shall sit every man under his vine and under his fig tree." The passage, a symbolization of the union between communal peace and individual prosperity, appears in both the First Book of Kings, where it refers to the rule of Solomon, and the Book of the Prophet Micah, where it predicts the coming of the Messiah. Dickinson takes the fuller rendition in Micah 4:4, giving it his own special emphasis in "Letter V," where "the beautiful and emphatic language of the sacred scriptures" makes the right of property "the foundation of all the rest." In his version, " 'they should sit *every man* under his vine, and under his fig-tree, and *NONE SHOULD MAKE THEM AFRAID.*' " But what if these happy property owners *are* made to be afraid? *Letters from a Farmer in Pennsylvania* is about this reversal of implications.

Dickinson's Farmer should be tranquil; manifestly, he is not. British incursions on colonial rights have robbed him of a natural equanimity. Keeping within the image of vine and tree in "Letter IX," he exclaims that "the question is not, whether some branches shall be lopt off – The ax is laid to the root of the tree; and the whole body must infallibly perish, if we remain idle spectators of the work." The impact of such words depends first on the presumption of an available happiness. Americans who are *not* happy in the 1760s should be so. As they ask themselves, in Stephen Hopkins's typical version of the question from *The Rights of Colonies Examined* (1765), "Why should the gentle current of tranquility that has so long run with peace . . . be at last obstructed, be turned out of its true course into unusual and winding channels by which many of those states must be ruined, but none of them can possibly be made more rich or more happy"?

The phraseology of ruin and obstruction that interrupts the tranquillity in Hopkins's river metaphor implies a specific difficulty of the time as well as an attitude toward it. The colonies have experienced an artificial boom based on external credit and wartime spending during the French and Indian War, but a reaction automatically sets in as the war ends in 1760, bringing a recession that continues through the middle of the decade. Buying power drops for most colonists. Though population growth continues to soar, trade declines and then fluctuates wildly. Bankruptcies of overextended merchants and a growing trade deficit add to difficulties and a general foreboding. In this atmosphere, the British decision to tax colonial imports more than increases apprehensions; it encourages Americans to blame their troubles on politics rather than the marketplace. Political unrest, it should be noted, is greatest in Virginia and the New England coastal cities, where the tobacco trade and urban mercantile centers are hardest hit.

With prosperity the assigned norm and sometimes an assumed right, comparisons of past and present in the 1760s tend to meld liberty, tranquillity, virtue, and prosperity together in the name of their opposites – tyranny, anxiety, corruption, and economic misfortune. The parallel constructions recur so frequently in colonial discourse in part because they contain the one argument that Loyalists and British writers can never counter. To the extent that the absence of tranquillity and prosperity imply a comparable loss in freedom, it is enough for colonial writers to find that Americans are, in fact, anxious. Some agency must be responsible for the facts of unhappiness and misfortune as such, and the logical candidate in the 1760s is British policy.

John Dickinson molds these patterns of protest into a concise formula in *Letters from a Farmer in Pennsylvania*. How can Americans with the best chance in the pursuit of happiness still appear to be so far from their goal? For every educated property owner who struggles to make ends meet in the recession of the 1760s and who senses a discrepancy, the Pennsylvania Farmer offers an answer in "Letter XII":

Let these *truths* be indelibly impressed on our minds – *that we cannot be HAPPY, without being FREE* – that we cannot be free, *without being secure in our property* – that *we* cannot be secure in our property, *if, without our consent, others may, as by right, take it away* – that *taxes imposed on us by parliament,* do thus take it away.

Just as the enlightened sequence of truth, freedom, happiness, security of property, and tranquillity can be entered at any point and taken in either direction, so their opposites, insecurity and external taxation, stop every virtue and pollute the entire realm.

These leaps in logic are grounded in a rhetorical claim of absolute precision. Alive to the difficulty of correct expression in "Letter III," Dickinson in "Letter IV" asks for that clarity in principle and intention that "will give certainty to our expression and safety to our conduct." The greatest identified danger in *Letters from a Farmer in Pennsylvania* is always confusion. "To suffer our ideas to be confounded by *names* on such occasions," the Farmer admonishes in his last communication, "would certainly be an *inexcusable weakness*, and probably an *irremediable error*." Dickinson prides himself on a meticulous accuracy. "I have looked over *every statute* relating to these colonies from their first settlement to this time," he announces at the beginning of "Letter II." Dickinson's learning and erudition show on every page. Singular sources of satisfaction to colonial readers, they are the hardest traits to convey to a modern audience.

To grasp the true power of this pamphlet is to realize that the Farmer's expression of his knowledge is also the source and definition of his freedom. As his peroration runs, only those people "DESERVE liberty, who so *well understand* it . . . and so *wisely, bravely,* and *virtuously assert, maintain,* and *defend* it." The capacity to assert one's understanding means everything in this context. A definition of freedom offered in "Letter VI" stresses the faculty of judging for oneself when privileges have been invaded. The exercise of that judgment *is* the exercise of freedom, just as prior knowledge is the essential prerequisite to correct judgment. The writer renders a decision based upon an understanding of country and a separate understanding of previous communal expression on the subject; his words are freedom in action.

Dickinson is the master of both understandings. He announces his true purpose, "the meaning of these letters," in "Letter III": "to convince the people of these colonies, that they are at this moment exposed to the most imminent dangers; and to persuade them immediately, vigorously, and unanimously, to exert themselves, in the most firm, but most peaceable manner, for obtaining relief." In the cause of freedom there can be no higher mission, and the Farmer underlines the charge with his last words. Although not his own, this final passage proves all the more effective for kindling emphatic recognitions in his immediate audience, "My *Dear* COUNTRYMEN."

Poignantly, Dickinson closes *Letters from a Farmer in Pennsylvania* by reclaiming the stutter in revolutionary discourse. He transforms hesitation into the loftiest eloquence by taking Jeremiah Dummer's words from *A Defence of the New England Charters* in 1721 and giving them new life in 1768. " 'How little soever one is able to write,' " says Dickinson through Dummer, " 'yet when the liberties of one's country are threatened, it is still more difficult to be silent.' " The repetition forges a literary convention out of the original statement. The right to speak extremely (because in extremity) receives fresh credence. And what is actually said increases the pressure to say more. The hesitation in oppositional discourse has shifted from the voice of the writer to the characterological surface of the speaker – to the attractive image of the peace-loving farmer. The voice, by way of contrast, is now in full cry. Its fluency in the transforming repetition signifies a larger change in the nature of American pamphleteering.

The growing urgencies of protest – the monotony of mere repetition, the demand for eloquence, the insistence upon an ever more imminent danger, above all, the need for a heightened response – these urgencies are changing the meaning and the direction of words. While Dickinson seeks to reunite colony and mother country, he also contributes to a language of separation. Resisting the danger from abroad requires a firmer sense of colonial unity, and that act of identity inexorably pushes Americans away from previous associations with Europe. "Let us consider ourselves as . . . *separate from the rest of the world, and firmly bound together* by the *same rights, interests* and *dangers,*" pleads the Farmer in the end. The order to unite encourages an inadvertent corollary: increasingly, the language of protest will be phrased with other Americans in mind and not with the hope of a British response.

The pamphlets of the late 1760s and early 1770s illustrate the shift in orientation. When "Britannus Americanus," writing in the *Boston Gazette* in March of 1766, finds the same love of freedom and constitutionalism in Old and New England, he might be celebrating Anglo–American ties within the British Empire but for the point of the comparison, which is to prove that Americans are "utterly unaccountable to, and uncontroulable by the *people* of Great-Britain, or any body of them whatever." Many Americans still feel uncomfortable with the notion of "standing upon *equal* footing" with England in 1766, but, having been aroused by British taxing schemes, they laugh together over the reductio ad absurdum in the *Boston Gazette* that they, in turn, might "make a law to tax their *fellow subjects* in England." British readers, including sympathetic ones, do not share in this laughter. The price of humor for Britannus Americanus is the loss of his English audience.

The more profound the opposition grows, the more it raises practical questions that Americans can ask only of themselves. Daniel Leonard, another prominent Massachusetts lawyer, will become a formidable Loyalist pamphleteer in rousing exchanges with John Adams, "Massachusettensis" against "Novanglus" in late 1774 and 1775, but earlier, in November 1773, he still wavers enough to bring the predicament of protest into stark focus. Writing for the *Massachusetts Spy*, Leonard agrees with previous commentators that British measures have been "illegal" and "intolerable," and, like them, he wonders what should be done about these encroachments. The difference in 1773 has to do with the level of response. As Leonard writes, the thought of rebellion is less shocking to all parties. Though he will stay loyal to the Crown, Leonard dwells not on the philosophical duties of the English citizen but on the practical mechanics of American politics. By 1773, "the only question is, whether it be prudent to risque resistance."

The question of probable success or failure is replacing the more agonizing quandary of freedom versus loyalty. And that question, "the only question" left, belongs less to the English-speaking world at large than it does to specific colonial leaders. Americans, Leonard urges, must measure the risk in rebellion carefully. Accordingly, his essay discriminates within its nominal audience, "*all Nations of Men,*" in order to address "*more especially the Inhabitants of British North-America.*" It narrows the field of concern and, in that process, the term "British" begins to move from intrinsic category toward descriptive appendage. The real subject of debate turns more and more on the specific American circumstance that will trigger rebellion.

The occasional dimension of the pamphlet simultaneously follows and dictates the course of change. As physical conflict becomes more and more likely in 1774 and 1775, Americans must respond more directly to the divisions in their midst. Communal pressure is forcing Loyalists into silence or flight, and colonial solidarity, always an interest, now emerges as the controlling priority in Whig writings. Two pamphlets depict the new situation: Thomas Jefferson's *A Summary View of the Rights of British America* (1774) and David Rittenhouse's *An Oration Delivered February 24, 1775, Before the American Philosophical Society.* Very different from each other, both nonetheless presage a mode of address that will erase uncertainties in the name of recognized inevitabilities. In 1776, all local discomforts – loss, displacement, confusion, violence, injury, chaos, and death – will yield to ideological horizons in the spread of the Enlightenment. Jefferson and Rittenhouse foreshadow the speed of that transformation just before the moment. Not a rupture, not even a blemish, the Revolution will be read as natural event, a part of the history and science of the New World.

A Summary View of the Rights of British America takes the bold step of making the king of England a primary adversary. The step is bold because it is also well nigh irrevocable, and its importance at this moment in 1774 cannot be overestimated. As long as Parliament remains the main target of colonial protest, Americans can qualify their opposition in the larger claim of loyalty to king and country. Jefferson, in selecting George III as his real opponent in *A Summary View,* sacrifices that safer stance; loyalty is suddenly contingent. "But can his Majesty thus put down all law under his feet?" he asks. It is the old question, but Jefferson now answers it with a direct attack on the Crown: "let him remember that force cannot give right." When he adds that "it is neither our wish nor our interest to separate from [Great Britain]," he is also announcing the negative possibility. "This, Sire," Jefferson concludes on the necessity of liberty, "is our last, our determined resolution." His words add the insult of direct address to the deepening threat of separation.

Rhetorically the same shift in address is immensely liberating – so liberating that the eloquence of Jefferson's formulation will soon secure his place as drafter of the Declaration of Independence, where again the king will figure as essential foe. Before 1774, colonial writers encounter frustrating dramatic and intellectual difficulties in making Parliament the main source of their protest. For Parliament is not only faceless and multivoiced and, therefore, hard to particularize, it also symbolizes institutional liberty in an eighteenth-century understanding of Anglo–American culture. Nothing in the legacy of

1688 welcomes an American attempt to find tyranny in parliamentary encroachment. (England is said to have regained liberty *through* Parliament and
against the king.) Jefferson, for his part, does not absolve Parliament, but he
repossesses familiar language from the Whig theory of history. In a theme
that had long enthralled the English-speaking world, he concentrates instead
on "the most precarious of all tenures, his Majesty's will."

The innovative alignment of the colonies against their king also figures
powerfully in the dynamic of New World politics. *A Summary View of the
Rights of British America* converts mundane historical fact into a vital possibility. The truism that no European king has ever stood on western shores
becomes, in Jefferson's hands, a matter of conscious choice among emigrating
peoples. We are close to a wholly new conception: namely, that monarchy
itself might constitute an unnatural form of government on the fresh American strand. Jefferson's argument is fourfold: that all peoples have a natural
right of emigration; that the first Americans, as an emigrating people,
voluntarily choose to remain under the laws of England ("the emigrants
thought proper to adopt that system of laws, under which they had hitherto
lived in the mother country"); that the nature of this choice creates separate
legal systems linked only by a common executive, the king of England; and
that this king "is no more than the chief official of the people, appointed by
the laws, and circumscribed with definite powers, to assist in working the
great machine of government."

Jefferson is not the first to expound a theory of constitutionalism in which
the Anglo–American relationship is based upon the notion of a common
executive – Franklin, Adams, and James Wilson all hold similar views by
1774 – but he first converts the idea into a vivid story for Americans to
believe in. The story itself thrives on a dangerous negation; none of its four
main points are remotely acceptable to a British audience. The notion of a
natural right of emigration has no standing in English law. Neither does the
assumption of a voluntary colonial compact with England; nor of colonial
legislatures free of Parliamentary jurisdiction; nor of a king who functions
only as chief officer of the people. These thoughts border on treason in
eighteenth-century England. Even the Virginia convention must reject them
in the moment. They are, in the understatement of Jefferson's autobiography,
"too bold for the present state of things."

The complex form of Jefferson's story reveals his deeper purposes. *A Summary View of the Rights of British America* takes shape as a "Draft of Instructions
to the Virginia Delegates in the [First] Continental Congress." When the
Convention rejects this draft, Jefferson's colleagues in Williamsburg publish
and distribute it under its present title, and other publishers soon reprint it
in both Philadelphia and England. As such, *A Summary View* seems to have

fallen between three stools: sometimes an official legislative document, some-times a letter to the king, and sometimes a political pamphlet. Jefferson and his radical colleagues manipulate all three forms to drive their compatriots toward rebellion.

One power of the pamphlet genre is its flexibility in allowing for other forms. As a proposed "instruction to the said deputies," A *Summary View* partakes of official sanction even though it represents a minority view; inevita-bly, many who read it in 1774 assume that it represents established policy. The form of a legislative resolution also enables Jefferson to express personal ideas as the will of a collective presence. The first person plural pronominal address seems to come from all Americans, and this "we" is carefully disem-bodied so as to obscure the possibility of particularized differences. The title of the pamphlet, selected by Jefferson's colleagues, then reinforces this charac-teristic. A "summary view" implies an abridgment with overall authority; it pretends to cover the main points, leaving aside secondary differences.

Legislative resolutions rarely reach popular audiences in the way that this one does. It is Jefferson's letter to the king that absorbs readers then and now, and this transition – from formal resolution to emotional letter – occurs im-mediately in A *Summary View*. Jefferson's "instruction . . . that an humble and dutiful address be presented to his Majesty" merges with the idea of that address, though without much humbleness of tone. The king is the appropri-ate addressee because, as Jefferson tells him, he is "the only mediatory power between the several States of the British empire." There is no give in this letter. As official recipient, George III can hardly accept the role assigned him, that of a diminished "mediatory power." Neither can he have welcomed a communica-tion so explicitly "divested of those expressions of servility, which would persuade his Majesty that we are asking favors, and not rights." In the end, Jefferson's language deliberately seeks to offend. "Open your breast, Sire, to liberal and expanded thought," he orders, condescending to his king.

The artifice of a "humble and dutiful address" actually works as a political diatribe in pamphlet form, a rallying call to the real recipients of A *Summary View*, other Americans. And for these countrymen, apprehensive as they have to be in 1774, Jefferson adds a veiled admonition. "Let those flatter, who fear," he warns them; "it is not an American art." The brag and bounce in this assertion also contains a bullying tone that should not be overlooked. Unmistakably, those who continue to bow to their king are now somehow less than American. The threat is veiled in a rhetoric of solidarity, but both the reason and the high emotion of Jefferson's pamphlet are plain on the issue. At the heart of A *Summary View* in an interpretation of law in America that changes the king of England into an alien presence and loyalty toward him into an unnatural act.

The most curious aspect of *A Summary View* consists in the enormous political distance that it posits between England and America. Jefferson's description of the right of emigration under natural law leaves Americans closer in spirit to their Saxon ancestors than to their contemporaries in England. So distant are the latter that parliamentary encroachments appear as "acts of power, assumed by a body of men foreign to our constitutions, and unacknowledged by our laws." Jefferson's Americans speak a different conception of law than Englishmen – a conception based on "that freedom of language and sentiment which becomes a free people claiming their rights as derived from the laws of nature." The result is a bifurcation in behaviors and understandings. While natural law cuts across English law more decisively in America, the king and his colonial governors have been carrying specific power "beyond every limit known or provided by the laws."

England and America are on a collision course, and a collision on these terms is not one that the youthful Jefferson is inclined to avoid. Much of *A Summary View* is given over to the "arbitrary measures," "despotism," "series of oppressions," and "exercises of usurped power" that kings and their ministers have employed to disturb the natural harmony of British America. Amidst the litany of accusations and implied parallels to the Norman conquest of Saxon England, Jefferson finds himself at a loss for "terms reconcilable to Majesty, and at the same time to truth." Neither does the idea of a handful of American representatives in Parliament change matters. "Can any one reason be assigned," he wonders, "why one hundred and sixty thousand electors in the island of Great Britain, should give law to four millions in the States of America, every individual of whom is equal to every individual of them in virtue, in understanding, and in bodily strength?"

The man who asks this question no longer thinks in narrow terms about the repeal of specific measures. Everywhere, on every page of *A Summary View,* America will be better off without its king and royal governors. Jefferson's mood can be gauged by the timing of his pamphlet; he drafts it just after a colony-wide day of protest. "[T]he effect of the day, through the whole colony," his autobiography notes, "was like a shock of electricity, arousing every man, and placing him erect and solidly on his centre." Only an audacious statement will suffice in this setting. "An exasperated people, who feel that they possess power," he tells George III, "are not easily restrained within limits strictly regular." The writer of these words already has pledged his life, his fortune, and his sacred honor to the American cause. Excitement over *A Summary View of the Rights of British America* flows from its tacit recognition of the need for revolution. Jefferson burns his bridges in 1774, an act of courage that will lend a practiced equanimity to his eloquence in the summer of 1776.

David Rittenhouse, the astronomer and inventor of a world-famous orrery of the solar system, seeks the same distance from Europe that Jefferson finds through politics and law. If anything, Rittenhouse's effort is the more remarkable of the two because eighteenth-century astronomy emphasizes linkages, attractions, order, proportion, and the relation of forces – all elements that overcome distance. *An Oration Delivered Before the American Philosophical Society* (1775) is a scientific treatise that cannot resist political statement. Behind the compulsion is another American intellectual's fear of European influence. Like Jefferson, Rittenhouse hopes for a separate America before the Revolution. But why should separation work so well? Both writers envisage an America somehow safe in the natural harmonies of the New World. Rittenhouse, however, comes closer to the problems in that assumption because his subject, astronomy, forces firmer articulation of inchoate though controlling assumptions about the natural world.

Eighteenth-century scientists easily posit a moral universe, and, of all the sciences in Enlightenment thought, astronomy most nearly approaches a conception of deity. Rittenhouse utilizes these conventions in his presentation of the rise and progress of astronomy. "Every enlargement of our faculties," he observes, "every new happiness conferred upon us, every step we advance towards the perfection of the divinity, will very probably render us more and more sensible of his inexhaustible shores of communicable bliss, and of his inaccessible perfections." Yet increased perceptions do not explain why new shores in themselves should involve a greater bliss. Rittenhouse finesses the problem, using metaphors of light, motion, and divinity as mutually exchangeable quantifications of universal intelligence. In his own words, "[D]ivine energy supports that universal *substratum* on which all corporal substances subsist, that the laws of motion are derived from, and that wings *light* with angelic swiftness."

The light of discovery privileges the newly discovered object. To this implied premise, Rittenhouse adds the assumption that untouched objects – untouched by human hands – reflect pure purpose. The symbol of this perfection comes, readily enough, in the stars above: "yonder radiant orbs, traversing in silent Majesty the etherial regions, are the peaceful seats of innocence and bliss. Where neither natural nor moral evil has ever yet intruded; where to enjoy with gratitude and adoration the creator's bounty, is the business of existence." These thoughts lead directly to the nearer analogy of the New World, which, like the heavens, continues relatively untouched by such evils as "British thunder impelled by British thirst of gain." Rittenhouse's conclusion is an extraordinary one. "I am ready to wish – vain wish! that nature would raise her everlasting bars between the new and old world; and make a voyage to Europe as impracticable as one to the moon."

The astronomer apologizes for this digression, one that runs against the theme of perceptual enlargement. A more appropriate parallel, as he admits, would cite "that disposition of lands and seas, which affords a communication between distant regions, and a mutual exchange of benefits." But Rittenhouse, like so many eighteenth-century Americans, fears the "unnatural advances" of a European connection, and this fear of corruption feeds upon an inverse self-confidence in natural purity. The astronomer's contrasting emotions play themselves out along geographical lines. The liveliest moment of *An Oration* comes in its narrative of tyranny and luxury "advancing like a current irresistible, whose weight no human force can stem." These vices "have long since laid in the dust, never to rise again, the glories of Asia . . . and have nearly completed their conquest of Europe." Only the untouched and, therefore, still harmonious natural world of America remains.

Division with England cannot come fast enough for those who divide the Anglo–American world between European corruption and American purity. Symbol and act of renewed purification, the Revolution will grant Rittenhouse's most extravagant wish. War accomplishes what nature cannot in reconstituting barriers between the Old and New Worlds. And if these new barriers prove less than everlasting, difficulties in transportation still discourage generations of Americans from seeking a European experience. Indeed, many republican leaders welcome the inconvenience. No less an authority than Thomas Jefferson asks "why send an American youth to Europe for education?" As he tells John Bannister in 1787, "an American coming to Europe for education, loses in his knowledge, in his morals, in his health, in his habits, and in his happiness."

War with England obviously fulfills certain intrinsic American needs. The Revolution confirms an already obsessive and often tedious internal debate over the nature of American virtue. Less conspicuously, it shelves troubling philosophical questions concerning American identity in the natural world. With such questions in abeyance – quandaries about nature and country will preoccupy the greatest writers of the next century – revolutionary discourse is left to elaborate a narrative of American purity in the New World. One consequence is a series of easy identifications. For the several generations around the Revolution, "virtue," "nature," and "America" are mutually compatible and, at times, interchangeable terms of reference.

How the story actually works toward cultural objectifications can be seen in a common symbol. David Rittenhouse might have thought little of the alternating stripes of red and white in the new flag of the United States, but he surely must have nodded assent over the rest of the design when it is announced on June 14, 1777. Congress orders "that the Union be 13 stars white in a blue field, representing a new constellation." The hieroglyph epitomizes the astronomer's hope. Joining the conviction of the Enlightenment and religious faith, the Revolution transfigures the stars into a type for new world republicanism. Under this symbol of the new constellation, amidst presumed seats of innocence and bliss, citizens are to enjoy the creator's bounty. In a secularizing vision, the land of plenty will soon be, in Rittenhouse's phrase, "the business of existence."

IV

The first catalyst of change in 1776 is literary in form. Thomas Paine's *Common Sense* appears in Philadelphia on January 10th of the year. His pamphlet runs through a first printing of one thousand copies in a week and, according to its author, one hundred twenty thousand copies in three months, a phenomenal number for the times. No one questions its impact on immediate thought. Two of its most important first readers, Benjamin Franklin and George Washington, speak of, respectively, its "prodigious" influence and its "unanswerable reasoning." Other commentators quickly assign it a unique place in the changing political scene. "[*Common Sense*]," claims a writer in *The New York Constitutional Gazette* on February 24th, "introduces a new system of politics as widely different from the old, as the Copernican system is from the Ptolemaic." Overwhelming when it is issued, *Common Sense* lives as literature today, the one pamphlet from the period that still captures the imagination of the American reader.

This success – immediate, unique, and enduring – stands somewhat in the way of interpretation. Scholars have not stressed the innate qualities of the pamphlet so much as they have interpreted its impact. Paine is said to have collared the language of the people; *or* to have established psychological equivalencies between his own situation and that of the thirteen colonies; *or* to have caught the oppositional rhetoric of colonial politics at the crucial moment; *or* to have brought the peculiar perspective of a lower-class Englishman to American problems. True enough in themselves, these assumptions linger on the surface of analysis. They have missed the deeper levels of Paine's essay, where the ultimate dynamic of the Revolution is at work.

Three elements are worth isolating in explaining the power of Thomas Paine's literary achievement: one rhetorical, one philosophical, and one political. Rhetorically, Paine ends the impasse that loyal resistance imposes on colonial argumentation. Even Jefferson feels obliged to conclude his attack in *A Summary View* with pious hopes for "love and harmony through the whole empire," and James Wilson continues to speak for most Americans when, on February 13, 1776, he repeatedly disavows any desire for independence on the part of "humble, unaspiring Colonists" in *An Address to the Inhabitants of the Colonies.* Paine cuts through these contortions at a stroke; the king of England is the acknowledged enemy of *Common Sense.* To the familiar but still intimidating cries of "Treason! Treason!," he substitutes blunt assent for the clever evasions of previous writers. Figuratively speaking, *Common Sense* refashions Patrick Henry: this *is* treason; now make the most of it.

Philosophically, Paine excels all other writers of the moment in creating political thought out of religious and scientific imagery. Jefferson will come to match his skill, but in 1776 only Paine proves truly capable of wedding a living religious voice and scientific language to secular political pamphleteering, and this accomplishment is a large part of his appeal. In *Common Sense,* nature reveals, reason explains, and God ordains that "the birth-day of a new world is at hand." This event partakes of "the glorious union of all things"; it marks the beginning of "a continental form of government" that will make America "the glory of the earth." God reigns above this creation as "the king of America." On earth, "the Word of God" appears as the rule of law in the emerging Republic. Easily, then, "in America the law is king."

Meanwhile, in Europe, the hereditary succession of kings is "unanswerably" a parallel to original sin. Since "the palaces of kings are built on the ruins of the bowers of paradise," it follows that "reconciliation and ruin are nearly related." Scientifically, monarchy is an unwanted complexity against "the simple voice of nature and of reason," where "the more simple any thing is, the less liable it is to be disordered, and the easier repaired when disordered." Reconciliation, therefore, is *"a matter exceedingly perplexed and complicated"* – "INDEPENDENCE *being a* SINGLE SIMPLE LINE." The history of religion and the geometry of science concur. In showing that "there is something very absurd, in supposing a continent to be perpetually governed by an island," Paine resorts to the conventional Newtonian metaphor of the times: "In no instance hath nature made the satellite larger than its primary planet." The entwining imagery of religion, science, and politics works to remove every hesitation, every fear of the unknown, every anxiety over the lost conveniences in British rule.

The prescience of Paine's positive vision for America also depends upon the careful conflation of religious and political imagery. *Common Sense* outlines the vital aspects of the unfolding American experiment before they happen: the continental scope of republicanism, its representative form, even its denouement in a national convention and written constitution. Significantly, Paine can suggest so much only because he possesses a set of religious ideas about what should happen. The spontaneous creation of a continental union simply cannot be conceived in strictly secular terms in 1776. The language of political reference then in use will not justify the extrapolation.

Instead, Paine describes an impending millennium of republican culture, and the contrivance of God's new Israel proves exceedingly useful in this regard. "The Reformation was preceded by the discovery of America," explains *Common Sense*, "as if the Almighty graciously meant to open a sanctuary to the persecuted in future years." Those future years have now come to pass, and they are safe only in "the distance at which the Almighty hath placed England and America." Paine, who has lived in both worlds, can insist that "the authority of the one, over the other, was never the design of Heaven." To the contrary, separation and a hatred of things English is part of God's plan. "As well can the lover forgive the ravisher of his mistress, as the continent forgive the murders of Britain," observes Paine. "The Almighty hath implanted in us these unextinguishable feelings for good and wise purposes." It is God's design, not human events, that gives this vast and largely unpopulated continent a single voice.

The third isolatable element in Paine's achievement, a peculiar politics, enables him to convert guilt over lost loyalties into anger and a new definition of country. It is here that the workings of *Common Sense* have been least understood because also least pleasant to contemplate. Critics have noted Paine's creative objectification of colonial unrest as patriotism and his corresponding articulation of the emotions of the mob. But how does he put the unrest of the moment to such explosive use, and what does it mean to articulate the emotions of the mob? Answers to such questions are difficult; they involve fault lines between the elitism of the published word and the lost emotive context of that word in the speech and will of the people. *Common Sense*, more than any other writing of the period, tries to bridge the divide.

The distinction between the anger of colonial Americans and their ability to express that anger fully in formal prose is one effect of the decorum of loyalty already noted in the pamphlet tradition. Figures like Richard Bland, James Otis, John Dickinson, and even Thomas Jefferson all mean more than they can actually say in print. Within the oral culture, however, anger is a more unbridled source of definition. Popular uprisings occur frequently enough in eighteenth-century America for the mob to operate as an intrinsic part of colonial life and as a vital extralegal arm in important communal decisions. If these upheavals are originally episodic events geared to local issues of the moment (the punishment of outlaws and other deviants, land title disputes, impressment controversies, customs enforcement, problems in local defense, and intraneighborhood conflicts of all kinds), they become a more widespread and cohesive phenomenon in the late 1760s and early 1770s. Beginning with the Stamp Act controversy, mob action is a regular and dominant force in the colonial challenge to imperial policies. It is also the clearest indication that people in every colony anticipate their leaders' opposition to British rule.

Why do we hear so little about rioting and the nature of the mob in the major literature of the Revolution? Loyalists, often the recipients of the mob's attentions, do describe their distress in private writings, but revolutionary leaders generally withhold comment in their fear that further publicity will push the people's right of resistance toward a justification of public disorder. The more chaotic events become, the less these leaders wish to discuss or write about the situation. Even radical Whigs worry about inflaming the populace. A ploy of accountability in imperial politics, their restraint in pamphleteering is also a strategy for keeping the lower orders in line.

The great exception to the rhetoric of restrained feelings is, of course, *Common Sense,* and Paine's anger finds an immediate outlet in America. When he introduces his pamphlet, Paine calls upon "every Man to whom Nature hath given the Power of feeling." He magnifies emotion in explicit contrast to those who seek to restrain it. The greatest danger in an essay obsessed with "proving enmity (or enemyship)" is not the British but rather "men of passive tempers." More than modest exertion, the American situation requires a total commitment to "those feelings and affections which nature justifies." These feelings, when most deeply probed by Paine, are almost always ones of rage. The true guardian of appropriate emotion in *Common Sense* is none other than Satan, who speaks, though unnamed, from Milton's *Paradise Lost:* "never can true reconcilement grow where wounds of deadly hate have pierced so deep." Forgiveness is an unnatural feeling in this world. "There are injuries which nature cannot forgive; she would cease to be nature if she did," Paine observes.

Paine repeatedly justifies and encourages the fact of hatred, bringing that emotion to bear first against the king of England, next against traitors in America, and only then on the positive goal of building a continental republic. "Men read by way of revenge," he explains, and his own reading in *Common Sense* is fueled by images of blood, ashes, suffering, cruelty, villainy, corruption, monstrosity, and hellishness. In April of the year, when critics call him "furious," Paine welcomes the accusation and turns it back upon them. "There are men, too," he responds as *The Forester,* "who have not virtue enough to be angry."

The point to remember is that Paine's natural and intended audience is the American mob. It is not just that Paine appropriates the language of the people. He uses anger, the natural emotion of the mob, to let the most active groups find themselves in the general will of a republican citizenry. Recognizing that "the mind of the multitude is left at random, and feeling no fixed object before them," Paine writes to give the mob specific direction in the act of independence. *Common Sense* identifies three ways of achieving independency: "by the legal voice of the people in Congress; by a military power; or by a mob." The beauty of action in the moment of 1776 is that it combines all three. Congress, soldiery, and mob can be all one if Americans will only recognize "the present time is the true time." In the moment, writes Paine, "our soldiers are citizens, and the multitude a body of reasonable men."

The explosive response to *Common Sense* comes in the mob's recognition of its own purpose and dignity. After a decade of pamphleteering on the rationality of moderate opposition – a rationality that necessarily regards the mob as a shameful by-product – Paine argues that anger and public outrage are the central vehicles of colonial identity and, hence, of cultural salvation. Recent theories about mass behavior and its modes of expression in nationalism help to illustrate the colossal effectiveness of this strategy. The cultural critic Elias Canetti has identified four central traits and a controlling activity of the mob, or crowd as he calls it, in his *Crowds and Power* (1962): the crowd wants to grow, it seeks equality within itself, it loves density, and it needs direction. Its most conspicuous activity comes in its destructiveness. Wherefore, in its early growth, the crowd or mob builds an identity by destroying representational boundary images; the doors and windows of houses are useful targets. In fact, symbolic violations of hierarchy of just this kind characterize the American mob before and during the Revolution.

Common Sense moves along these axes. Its rhetoric begins in an intellectual attack upon monarchy that culminates in a specific call to arms; the goal is to destroy all linkage with Britain. Three positive elements of cohesion then support this impulse to destroy: first, discovered mutuality in a language of equality; next, a realization of density in the projected solidarity of union; and last, a recognition of direction in group identification with an expanding continental republic. Colonial readers who accept these incentives strike a simple bargain. They sacrifice local, provincial identity, the symbol of which is their connection to England, for an enlarged American view.

There are dangers in Paine's strategy. The call for a citizen who will "generously enlarge his views beyond the present day" runs certain risks. Critics then and now have noted the cold comfort and potential isolation in Paine's abstractions of enlargement. Where are the compensating notions of attachment, the affecting and familiar links, in Paine's "the universal order of things" and "the RIGHTS OF MANKIND"? How, exactly, is the new American supposed to "hold out to his neighbour the hearty hand of friendship"? Paine's answer relies on the projected cohesion of his mob in action. For not only is the crowd the natural symbol of the isolated figure, but the crowd as nation begins to take on a special power of identity in this last part of the eighteenth century. The first to cut himself free of colonial links, Paine is also the first to recognize the absolute priority of a national argument in revolutionary America. As Elias Canetti will later elaborate on Paine's realization, "We can take it for granted that no member of a nation ever sees himself alone."

The national argument in *Common Sense* is more an expression than a formal idea, but this, too, can be a strength if taken with the realization that nationalisms are not distinguished by originality of conception or thought but by the style in which they are imagined. The style and tones in which Paine first imagines a republic of states united on the American continent are emotional rather than intellectual, and they revolve around an angry, suffering, embattled self-assertion. That self takes a ubiquitous pronominal form. The ever-present "we" of the pamphlet comprises neither colonies, nor voting citizens, nor leaderships of any kind. It concentrates, rather, on every discriminate American self in collective union. Disturbingly, this narrating self then shrinks in scope during successive stages of argumentation. Excluded by the third section of *Common Sense* are "all those who espouse the doctrine of reconciliation." The designation encompasses not just Loyalists and Tories but also "weak men who *cannot* see, prejudiced men who *will not* see," and, in a much larger category, "moderate men, who think better of the European world than it deserves."

A consummate but generally unrecognized irony emerges from the growing list of restrictions. The test of the worthy citizen narrows even as Paine insists upon the largest view of country. True Americans must declare themselves angry enough to act against England. Only colonials who have suffered "the present sorrow" of America are allowed to judge "the offences of Great Britain," and having suffered, those who seek reconciliation are unworthy of the name of citizen; they "have the heart of a coward, and the spirit of a sycophant." Paine reserves a special wrath for the inhabitant who does nothing at all in this crisis: "there is no punishment which that man doth not deserve." In the end, a defeated British soldier deserves more respect than a citizen caught on the wrong side. "The one forfeits his liberty the other his head."

Behind the threat is the unmediated commonality of *Common Sense*. Citizens gain security and transcend the limits set upon individual identity when they mass together, but the act of joining also establishes psychological patterns of exclusion; you are for the mob or it is against you. Paine is not the last to understand the power of this appeal in a democracy. Exclusionary tactics in civic membership, hidden enemies (within and abroad), melodramas of suffering and victimization, challenges against patriotic standing, the assignation of faintheartedness to identified opponents, and, above all, the anticipated communal cohesion that comes in the successful explosion of righteous anger – these are devices that Americans use in 1776 and still use to imagine their national community.

Paine realizes intuitively, as no writer before him quite does, that imagining a democratic American community requires a different series of strategies in a writer. Consider the contrast of John Adams and other radical pamphleteers meeting with three hundred and fifty supporters under the Liberty Tree at Dorchester in August 1769. Adams, jotting in his diary, wishes to "Tinge the minds of the People" and to "impregnate them with the sentiments of Liberty," but he needs simultaneously to "render the People fond of their Leaders in the Cause" and to secure the place of authority, his own included, "hearty in the Cause." Accordingly, the act of writing seeks both to inspire the people and to demonstrate a visible leadership in control of the course of events. Paine, on the other hand, offers words that address every citizen directly and without mediation of any kind, and his words have a very different purpose in mind.

Common Sense strives to empower the people, "a truly legal authority," over every group distinct therefrom. Paine takes his title from the very term in eighteenth-century politics that distinguishes between the complexity of special knowledge and the natural simplicity of the common good. Rhetorically, "common sense" operates as a check upon those men of place and learning who use their advantages to protect themselves and their class in a language of controlled differentiations. When Paine uses the idea – "nothing more than simple facts, plain arguments, and common sense" – he means three things: that anyone can understand his pamphlet, that everyone should, and that no other narrative or explanation or ceremony is necessary for action to follow comprehension. The language of common sense touches the readiest understanding; it has no literary or political tolerance for a leadership that would control thought.

In the conjunction of concept and literary work, *Common Sense* struggles against every gradation that might stand in the way of common action. "Where there are no distinctions there can be no superiority," writes Paine in his vision of the independent states, "perfect equality affords no temptation." The well-to-do are a special problem in this scheme for revolution ("The rich are in general slaves to fear, and submit to courtly power with the trembling duplicity of a spaniel"). Everything that distances the power or the importance of the people is suspect – everything. For Paine, in the first significant use of a favorite trope in American politics, even the vaunted checks and balances of the British Constitution signify "an house divided against itself."

Much more is at stake in the moment of 1776 than conflict with England. The question of home rule raises an immediate and troubling sequel: Who will rule at home? There is no more vexed query in America in the 1770s and early 1780s, and of all the leaders of the Revolution, only Tom Paine offers a completely spontaneous, ingenuous reply. In the ultimate challenge of the Revolution, he welds the relation of ruler and ruled together in the simplest of terms. The people can oppose "the unmeaning name of king" in *Common Sense* because the power of government already has been rightly and actively theirs in every moment of decision that they might want to name.

V

Other revolutionary leaders strain against the leveling spirit of Paine's pronouncement. They want the magic of *Common Sense* without its simplifying sweep and without its overriding anger. Yet, in straining, these leaders also see that their exertions cut across symbiotic strengths. The stark emotive power of Paine springs from his acceptance of the power of the people, and the effect of that realization on a new American elite is a mixture of fascination, frustration, and dread. We glimpse all of these impulses in John Adams's famous summary. To Benjamin Waterhouse in 1805 he confides:

I know not whether any Man in the World has had more influence on its inhabitants or affairs for the last thirty years than Tom Paine. There can be no severer Satyr on the Age. For such a mongrel between Pigg and Puppy, begotten by a wild Boar on a Bitch Wolf, never before in any Age of the World was suffered by the Poltroonery of mankind, to run through such a Career of Mischief. Call it then the Age of Paine.

This invective conveys more powerfully than any argument the nature of the divide in revolutionary and postrevolutionary rhetoric. The vitality of the mongrel comes from below. How promiscuous should the role of the people be in a people's government? That is the question for every writer in 1776. Adams can be so acerbic because he instantly recognizes and articulates the threat posed. Writing James Sullivan in May of 1776, just four months after *Common Sense* appears, Adams admits that "the only moral foundation of government, is the consent of the people," but he also asks "to what extent shall we carry the principle?" The rest of his letter condemns the bottomless inclusions that the principle encourages. "Depend upon it, Sir," Adams advises, "it is dangerous to open so fruitful a source of controversy. . . . It tends to confound and destroy all distinctions, and prostrate all ranks to one common level." His personal mission in 1776 is clear, and it goes beyond the accomplishment of independence.

Adams writes a pamphlet of his own in 1776, *Thoughts on Government*. Second only to *Common Sense* in influence, it is also a direct response. At the time, Adams's autobiography reports a conversation with Paine on the subject: "I told him . . . I was as much afraid of his Work [as] he was of mine. His plan was so democratical, without any restraint or even an Attempt at any Equilibrium as Counterpoise, that it must produce confusion and every Evil Work." *Thoughts on Government*, originating in a letter to Richard Henry Lee, agrees with *Common Sense* on the need for republican government and engages in its own brand of revolutionary rhetoric, extolling the empire of laws, elective accountability, and regular rotation in office. There, however, the similarities end.

If the contrasting initiatives of *Thoughts on Government* sound familiar, it is because they supply the effective blueprint that Americans act upon after they, to use the author's delicate phrase, "are put out of the royal protection." Adams rejects Paine's notion of a single democratic assembly for a more complex bicameralism. He favors an independent judiciary, balances between branches of government, and, most important of all, the delegation of power. "The first necessary step, then," he writes, "is to depute power from the many to a few of the most wise and good." Where Paine counts on the power of the people, Adams draws upon an enlightened restriction through law. "You and I, my dear friend," he tells Richard Henry Lee, "have been sent into life at a time when the greatest lawgivers of antiquity would have wished to live."

Adams's self-confidence rides as high as Paine's, which is in itself impressive when one considers the state of government and law in America in 1776. As the Revolution begins, there are no functioning courts in North America. The separate colonies lack effective local executive authority, and depend upon an untried and fundamentally weak central government. All foundational legitimacy has been lost in the sudden irrelevance of colonial charters. It is with perfect credence that Samuel West can use his election sermon in 1776 to prove that the people, "having not the civil law to regulate themselves by, became a law unto themselves; and by their conduct they have shown that they were regulated by the law of God written in their hearts."

These weaknesses in government actually work in Adams's favor and against Paine in the long run. Stressing "the present exigency of American affairs," Adams and his allies shift the literary adventure in revolutionary thought from loose pamphleteering toward the construction of governmental institutions, an enterprise necessarily left to leadership or, in Adams's understanding, "to a few of the most wise and good." Paradoxically, the idea of a constitution as higher law – above government and derived from the people – aids this shift. The presumed special nature of constitutional writing encourages the circumvention of standard legislative institutions, where "the new men," Paine's natural allies, will gain increasing authority over the course of the Revolution. A separated enterprise, the average constitution of the period is written by a small number of men in special committee, sometimes by a single hand. John Adams will draft the Massachusetts Constitution of 1780 more-or-less on his own.

The struggle that Adams and Paine symbolize also has generic repercussions that have been forgotten. The volatility of revolutionary pamphleteering encourages radical over conservative impulses. *Thoughts on Government* may carefully gesture toward the people, but Adams also knows that his learned insistence upon "forms of government" might lead to popular censure. Quoting Milton, he begs Richard Henry Lee to protect authorial anonymity lest " 'a barbarous noise environs me / Of owls and cuckoos, asses, apes, and dogs.' " There is a subtle subversion of form in this recognition. One of the elusive shifts in early republican literature is the way Adams and other moderates use the pamphlet form to undercut its original importance. When they are finished, the age of the pamphlet is no more.

As radical forces turn against authority in western Massachusetts in 1778, the reaction of conservative pamphleteers is to regret the need for any response at all and to disclaim any claim to originality ("I pretend not to offer you any new, and cunningly devised arguments to convince you"). As "Impartial Reason" in *An Address to the Inhabitants of Berkshire County, Mass.*, William Whiting protests against anarchy and licentiousness: "I can't but take notice, how shamefully that ancient maxim, *vox populi est vox Dei* (the voice of the people is the voice of God) has been prostituted in this country." The persona of "Impartial Reason" easily distinguishes between the proper voice of elected representation and the "blasphemy and treason" of the mob, but Whiting, himself a member of the Massachusetts legislature, seems to expect more answers from the "arm of power" than from his own power of language. Curiously, he also worries that the attempt alone will replace impartial reason with anger ("ere I am aware, I should catch the epidemic disease myself, and a flame of passion, begin to rage in my own breast"). One of the growing realizations in pamphleteering is the recognition of never-ending acrimony in the act. Certainly, this writer shares a number of worries about the efficacy of his effort.

In a far more influential pamphlet from 1778, *The Essex Result,* Theophilus Parsons turns the same constitutional crisis into a noble adventure of controlled intellectual activity. Parsons, too, qualifies the meaning of *vox populi est vox Dei*. "No man will be so hardy and presumptuous," he writes, "as to affirm the truth of that proposition in its fullest extent." His candor signals changing times. Specifically, in the "arduous task" of forming a constitution, Parsons asks republicans "to look further than to the bulk of the people." Where they should look is also clear; the virtues required – wisdom, firmness, consistency, and perseverance – "will most probably be found amongst men of education and fortune." Only through these priorities will "the supreme power be so deposed and balanced, that the laws may have in view the interest of the whole." Only in this way can Americans expect a lasting constitution, "one that will smile amidst the declensions of European and Asiatic empires."

The overall impact of *The Essex Result* could not have been greater. Drafted in response to the proposed, and soon rejected, Massachusetts Constitution of 1778, this single work supplies many of the basic assumptions, gestures, and terms of American constitutionalism, including the special prominence of a bill of rights, some specifics of checks and balances, and the names and certain functions of "the house of representatives" and the "senate." But Parsons's major contribution in the moment is to lift the idea of constitution making out of the turmoil of the democratic process and away from the venue of occasional writing. Fearing that "the idea of liberty has been held up in so dazzling colours, that some of us may not be willing to submit to that subordination necessary in the freest States," Parsons finds his solutions in the idea of a correct constitution. He reduces the problems of uncertainty, chaos, and passion to the idea and unity of official and published form.

Reduction, in this case, furnishes the vision that the framers of the Federal Constitution will use to appeal to the American people. The rewards that Parsons reserves for the wise leader able to construct "the best form of government" are "a statue of gold to his memory" and "unrivalled lustre" in the annals of posterity. Well before such fame, though, this figure is already metaphorically distinct from the people:

The man who alone undertakes to form a constitution, ought to be an unimpassioned being; one enlightened mind . . . perfectly acquainted with all the alienable and unalienable rights of mankind; possessed of this grand truth, that all men are born equally free, and that no man ought to surrender any part of his natural rights, without receiving the greatest possible equivalent; and influenced by the impartial principles of rectitude and justice. . . . He ought also to be master of the histories of all the empires and states which are now existing, and all those which have figured in antiquity, and thereby able to collect and blend their respective excellencies, and avoid those defects which experience hath pointed out.

The parallels and the contrasts to John Adams's earlier description of the American writer in *A Dissertation on the Canon and Feudal Law* are instructive. Knowledge remains the same, but Adams's pamphleteer from thirteen years before "animates" and "rouses" the people, whereas this "unimpassioned" writer of constitutions uses his knowledge to overcome feeling and to resolve turmoil through skills that "possess," "master," "collect," "blend," and "avoid."

The mix of tones in works that try to both arouse and collect the people is perhaps the most palpable characteristic of early republican writing in the 1780s. Naturally geared to timeliness and excitement, the political pamphlet always exhibits these tendencies, but now more confusion enters into the choices involved. A more uncertain manic-depressive quality overtakes writers in the genre. An anonymous contributor from New Hampshire describes the phenomenon perfectly in *Address to the Public, Containing Some Remarks on the Present Political State of the American Republicks, etc.* (1786). "Amicus Republicae," as he styles himself, predicts that either virtue will make the Republic "wealthy, honorable, powerful, and happy" or vice will plunge it "into a state of the greatest calamities." He and other friends of the Republic see no middle path, no alternative to absolute success or total failure. The upshot is an obvious and active ambivalence in the observing writer: "every judicious and honest mind must, when it considers the present licentious disposition of many persons, be depressed and elated alternately by hope and fear."

Vacillation between the hope of success and the fear of failure helps constitution-makers in the 1780s and begins to erode the literary base of the more spontaneous pamphleteers. The duty of the citizen to write out a conception of country remains a literary constant still recognized by all, but, by the early 1780s, the personal attempt in pamphlet form produces mostly dismay and frustration. In performing this acknowledged "duty of a citizen," Thomas Tudor Tucker in Charleston, South Carolina, easily visualizes the ideal republic and its constitutional basis. As "Philodemus" in *Conciliatory Hints, Attempting by a Fair State of Affairs, to Remove Party Prejudice* (1784), he defines the true commonwealth as one in which "all authority is derived from the people at large, held only during their pleasure, and exercised only for their benefit" and a constitution as "a social covenant entered into by the express consent of the people, upon a footing of the most perfect equality with respect to every civil liberty." The balances in these familiar revolutionary generalizations are conventionally sound, but they no longer seem sufficient to clarify Tucker's actual situation or political agenda.

The pamphlet of the 1780s is a litany of ills. Although a talented figure like Tucker will soon enter the Continental Congress and will eventually become treasurer of the United States, a host of complexities stand in the way of his understanding and service in 1784. The "fatal influence of slavery" destroys everything, including "the boasted Characteristic of Rationality." Philodemus also wonders what to do about returning Tories, and he worries about the dangers in accepting a British conception of constitutionalism. From the other side, he fears "a government approaching to Democracy." The times are filled with "factious men assuming the mask of patriotism," with "novices in politics," with "secret combinations," with "irregularities and civil dissension," and with "a wilderness of confusion." Worst of all, Tucker knows that "our present Constitution was framed in a time of distress and confusion" and sees that it "is not founded on proper authority."

Pamphlet writing in the 1780s is about Tucker's "wilderness of confusion." It presides over a litany of ills beyond its own solution, and it looks increasingly toward another kind of writing enterprise. Salvation in Tucker's *Conciliatory Hints* means one thing: a new constitution "paramount to all acts of the Legislature, and irrepealable and unalterable by any authority but the express consent of a majority of the citizens collected by such regular mode as may be therein provided." The new challenge, shared by so many early republican intellectuals in the 1780s, lies in the framing of constitutions. Pamphleteering has begun to wait upon that eventuality.

Political writing in America has arrived at a divide – a divide that the political pamphlet will not survive intact. The volatility and immediacy of the pamphlet extend back to an oral culture, to speech and the need for protest. The desire for order, regularity, and permanence in the hope for a new constitution carry forward or toward print. The difficulties of the 1780s and time itself will place the most important revolutionary leaders of the 1770s on the side of print and constitution writing. The Philadelphia Convention of 1787, where many of these leaders will serve, brings the last flurry of pamphlets to absorb the entire nation, but the die is cast. In that flurry, the anger, frustration, localism, and rhetorical excess of the anti-Federalists give way to a new kind of pamphlet that completes even as it breaks the genre.

Alexander Hamilton will swallow his own volatile temper in *The Federalist* (1787–8) to take aim at "passions and prejudices little favorable to truth." *Federalist No. 1* gives "a lesson of moderation to those who are ever so much persuaded of their being in the right in any controversy." Dismissing the "torrent of angry and malignant passions," "the bitterness," and "the specious mask of zeal for the rights of the people" of his enemies, Publius assumes for himself "the evidence of truth" and the high ground of "a judicious estimate of our true interests, unperplexed and unbiased by considerations not connected with the public good." Hundreds of pages later, *Federalist No. 85* will conclude on the same "lesson of moderation."

The Federalist succeeds because it approaches Americans with a new act of imagination. Longer and more ponderously organized than any other pamphlet, calculated to reach from scattered and ephemeral pieces to comprehensive collection and permanent book, *The Federalist* is virtually unreadable as a pamphlet. Against the ordinary pamphleteer's embattled apologies for urgency, insufficiency, abruptness, and brevity, Publius archly promises comprehensiveness, enlargement, agreement, amiability, and candor. He does not so much raise points as, in Hamilton's opening phrase, "give a satisfactory answer to all objections." And both the nature and the source of these shifts are clear. *The Federalist* is a commentary on another sort of writing. It takes its subject, its purpose, its values, its organization, even its tone and voice from the new Federal Constitution. Publius is a successful pamphleteer, but his victory salutes a final triumph over his own genre. His gaze, also that of the country, is on the literature of public documents.

5

❦

THE LITERATURE OF PUBLIC
DOCUMENTS

I

The disruptive modes in sermonizing and pamphleteering in eighteenth-century America compete with the predisposition toward consensus evident in so much writing of the period. As the first chooses perception through crisis, so the second emphasizes the possibilities in reason and progress. Separate narratives, they both contribute to revolutionary discourse – sometimes in the same breath. The skill in revolutionary writing demands the promiscuous manipulation of these tendencies in prose that often tries to be provocative and encompassing at once, but an accident of history tips the balance between them. Acrimony grows on all sides in the 1780s and, with it, an intellectual preoccupation; early republicans yearn for a better definition of their experiment in government. Constitutionalism will control that quest, and its impulses are consensual in form.

From the first, American constitutionalism differs from its English equivalent in its commitment to the written word. The biblical conjunction of sovereignty and the book of law, the need for an artificially imposed order in the wilderness, and the politics of Anglo–American relations – these factors all encourage a literal documentation of governmental forms as the reference point of communal identity. Since every act of founding a new community is also a challenge to the status quo ante, the challenge itself, however implicit, must be laid to rest in new claims of authority, placement, and acceptance. Invariably, then, community in America begins in some act of writing. If such writings tend to confirm traditional beliefs, they also reconstitute those beliefs in a moment of registered agreement, and these moments in themselves soon become a prerequisite to group identity.

This means that colonial leaders respond to the uncertainty and flimsiness of their new social forms by inscribing fundamental law more generally, more frequently, more compulsively in official documents. By way of contrast, their English counterparts put fundamental law to paper mostly in the form of individual rights and only when faced with an explicit political challenge; Magna Carta and the Bill of Rights of 1689 provide the standard examples.

In America, the need to address beginnings — instead of assuming them from time immemorial — puts a special pressure of comprehensiveness on official language, and that pressure is immediate; there is no time in the formality of colonial origins to let institutions evolve as they did in England. Instead, words and the formal presentation of them must substitute for custom and the absent past. Social compacts must also be constitutions of government. The whole artifice of colonial charters, covenants, compacts, ordinances, fundamentals, and constitutions represent a perpetual crisis in definition, a steady search for the words that will complete identity in a new moment of agreement. And the very steadiness of that search is also an underlying source as well as a symptom of developing facility.

Documents like the Mayflower Compact of 1620 and the Ordinance and Constitution for Virginia of 1621 create social and political structures as much as they assert individual rights. The desire to "covenant and combine ourselves together into a civil Body Politick," in the first instance, and "to settle such a forme of government," in the second, requires a psychology of framing. As the Mayflower Compact claims to "enact, constitute, and frame . . . just and equal Laws, Ordinances, Acts, Constitutions, and Officers," so the Ordinance and Constitution for Virginia strives "to make our Entrance, by ordaining & establishing . . . supreame Counsells." These documents and others like them also take the form of a writing upon another writing. As responses in kind to the charters of colonial incorporation (in these two cases from James I, king of England), they engender intertextual tensions, operating at once as glosses upon the king's grant and as extensions of it.

These preoccupations — faith in the written word, the psychology of framing, the specific language of ordination and establishment, and the textual mediation of power received and power assumed — are touchstones in measuring the growth of a literature of public documents. They also point to the very crux of the Revolution as literary achievement in the records of ultimate foundation, The Declaration of Independence in 1776 and the Federal Constitution of 1787. For in such methodologies of composition, collections of peoples engage in similar acts of origination from colony to colony, and the congruences allow them to unite after more than a century of limited contact and cultural divergence. Union, as such, need not have taken place; there is no single people to claim the collective identity of "American" in 1760. More to the point, union could not have taken place if "the spirit of 1776" had not received from previous generations the will and the art of reconstitution. "Many" become "one" only because colonial peoples have imbibed a confidence and a skill in political reformulation *before* the Revolution.

II

The concise uses of language in the Declaration of Independence have encouraged a search for particular sources even though the broadest influences pertain. We have seen how the nature of a consensual literature and the ideology of the Enlightenment dictate strategies of assimilation in prose. Nowhere is this characteristic more important than here, in the highest expression of the American Enlightenment. "All its authority," runs Jefferson's summary of the Declaration of Independence in 1825, "rests then on the harmonizing sentiments of the day."

Precision lies in the form of the Declaration and not in the intellectual influences upon it. If the language of self-evidence and of equality seems to come from John Locke's *Second Treatise of Civil Government* (1690), it can be found just as easily in Algernon Sidney's *Discourses Concerning Government* (1698) and, by the 1770s, everywhere in colonial America. Reference to "the pursuit of happiness" may suggest specific writers in the Scottish Enlightenment (Francis Hutcheson, David Hume, Adam Smith, Lord Kames) or, alternatively, Jean-Jacques Burlamaqui, but the idea is a general preoccupation in moral philosophy by 1776 and a regular formula in the political writings of John Adams, George Mason, James Wilson, James Otis, and others. The Declaration actually weaves three essential strands together – the constitutional writings of colonial America, Whig political theory, and English common law. Skill enters in the writer's proficient construction of a unified text from them.

Most of the Declaration, in both word and thought, follows directly from earlier documents written by Americans – more specifically, from earlier compacts, resolves, and state constitutions. All but four of the document's twenty-eight charges against the king of England appear in preceding state constitutions (specifically, the constitutions of New Hampshire, South Carolina, and Virginia). Similar lists of grievances fill colonial newspapers, and these are the elements that absorb eighteenth-century readers. The phraseology of the opening paragraphs resembles the preamble to the Virginia Constitution, adopted in June of 1776, and George Mason's Declaration of Rights for Virginia, adopted and widely circulated in the same month. Even the famous conclusion – "we mutually pledge to each other our Lives, our Fortunes, and our sacred Honor" – is a paraphrase of the Mecklenburg Resolves of North Carolina, published in May 1775.

Yet, in virtually every instance, the language of the Declaration is sharper and more succinct than its background sources. In part, these improvements reflect what John Adams, writing to Timothy Pickering in 1822, calls Jefferson's "happy talent of composition" and "peculiar felicity of expression."

In part, however, they bespeak the compressed energy and economy of under-standing that occurs when form and thought truly cohere in a mastery of genre. This point needs to be properly understood. Eighteenth-century American writings are not generally known for such mastery, but they achieve an unparalleled maturity in the literature of public documents.

The blend of combinations is what counts in the Declaration. Tonally, the languages of science and politics join to convey an aura of inevitable conse-quence within self-evidence (the causes and constraining necessities that impel and dissolve bands in the course of human events). Thematically, the same sense of inevitability turns the Whig theory of history into a passionate source of story ("The history of the present King of Great Britain is a history of repeated injuries and usurpations, all having in direct object the establish-ment of an absolute Tyranny over these States"). Colonists, already familiar with extended narratives of royal despotism from *Common Sense* and other popular writings, easily blame a king for the miseries of history. The Declara-tion uses "a long train of abuses and usurpations" to elide troubling complexi-ties; its self-confidence in form is never clearer than in what it decides *not* to talk about. The plan to recover lost rights from a tyrant makes use of neither the vocabulary of rebellion nor the existing debates over parliamentary jurisdiction – vexed subjects in colonial life.

Inevitability also flows from the nature of repetition in the Declaration, a characteristic that illustrates yet another level of creativity. Heavily syllogis-tic, the language of the document moves from major premise (the people have the right to overthrow a leader who engages in a deliberate design of tyranny) to minor premise (the king of England is such a tyrant) to conclu-sion (the people of the American colonies have no choice but to overthrow). There is genius in stressing the minor premise, the king as tyrant. For within the laborious proofs of the Declaration – "let facts be submitted to a candid world" – one fact remains utterly implicit: the presumption of a single peo-ple desirous of overthrow. As late as June of 1776, Jefferson, in his autobiog-raphy, sees "that the colonies of New York, New Jersey, Pennsylvania, Dela-ware, Maryland, and South Carolina were not yet matured for falling from the parent stem." He also reports fierce debate in America over the crucial units of meaning: colonies or citizens, representatives or constituents, "the murmurs of some" or "the opposing voice of the freer part of the people."

Does the Declaration create thirteen separate peoples who agree or one national people? The opening sentence, where "one people" dissolves bands with "another," implies a single identity, as do three other capitalized uses of the word "People" and the promiscuous mix of bare signatures at the end of the document; citizens sign the Declaration, not state representatives. But the careful title, "The Unanimous Declaration of the Thirteen United States of America," can be construed either way. Other uses of the word "people" maintain a deliberate tension; and from the other side, plural references to the states dominate syntax ("these United Colonies are, and of Right ought to be free," "as Free and Independent States, they have full power," and so on). Plainly, the psychology of opposition welcomes ambiguity: the dual principles of government – the colonies as states *and* a confederation thereof – remain deliberately uncertain. Readers of the Declaration are left with a choice within unities. Reiteration of the word "people," ten uses in all, creates identity, but the overriding definition of people *against* the king takes many forms, and all of them reinforce the common cause.

There is craft in the subtlety of such balances, but real vision lies beyond them. The document's creative integrations fuse in a powerful generic consideration. Thomas Jefferson and most of his colleagues in the second Continental Congress are eighteenth-century lawyers steeped in the English common-law tradition. They know that a *declaration* is the foremost form of pleading in a legal action and that it is the only form to be brought before a king for redress or vindication. "Pleadings," explains Blackstone in his widely read *Commentaries on the Laws of England* (1765–9), "are the mutual altercations between the plaintiff and defendent. . . . The first of these is the *declaration, narratio,* or *count,* anciently called the *tale;* in which the plaintiff sets forth his cause of complaint at length . . . with the additional circumstances of time and place, when and where the injury was committed."

Colonial Americans also know how to use a legal declaration for political ends. Both the English Petition of Right in 1628 (a demand of the House of Commons declaring essential rights and sent directly to Charles I) and the Bill of Rights of 1689 (a similar act, declaring the rights and liberties of English subjects after a listing of evils under James II) are declarations of this kind. Jefferson and his colleagues are part of an Anglo-Saxon revolutionary tradition – part of what the historian G. M. Trevelyan, describing the Revolution of 1688, calls "the triumph of the Common Law and lawyers over the king." The point is not just that English colonists in America know what to write and how to write it in 1776, but that they look upon the writing thereof as the highest patriotism, as nothing less than the whole meaning of history in their time.

The nexus of literary ingenuity and historical implication allows the drafters of the Declaration to manipulate genre without breaking the form. The long list of grievances against the king imitates common-law practice, where a declaration sets forth every conceivable cause of action "at length" to guard against a nonsuit or failure of proof in any one count. Formulaic overkill also feeds the Whig conspiratorial view of royal power as one continuous and excessive abuse of ancient rights and natural liberties. Elsewhere, appeal to "the Supreme judge of the world" evokes the modes of the courtroom and so does the final oath ("we mutually pledge to each other our Lives, our Fortunes and our sacred Honor"). In fact, the form of this conclusion is a direct parallel to the pledge of surety that every plaintiff offers against the charge of a frivolous suit in a common-law action.

The language and forms of legality carry the Declaration another step from the unseemliness of rebellion by associating legal action with "the Laws of Nature." The same maneuver solidifies "the people" in the unifying symbol of "plaintiff" and lends formality, ceremony, and credibility to conflict. Time and again, form and content work together. As the balance of plaintiff against defendant in "mutual altercation" confirms the Declaration's sweeping claim of "separate and equal station," so the whole conceit of English courtroom pleading supports "the voice of justice and consanguinity" of American protest.

The symbolism of the king as defendant is peculiarly momentous. Its crude effectiveness daunts even *The Annual Register,* which, in publishing the Declaration in England in 1776, removes the words "King of Great Britain" from the list of grievances against him. Two years later, *The Register* still speaks of how "the American declaration of independence astonished [members of Parliament] with a new, awful, and unexpected situation of public affairs." As the defendant in the Declaration, the king must "put in a *plea,*" in Blackstone's explanation of the procedures, "or else the plaintiff will at once recover judgment by *default.*" The transformation in colonial self-presentation is from humble supplicant to righteous accuser. All thought of political negotiation disappears in the legal charge of guilt or innocence, a determination already fixed against the king in Whig mythology.

There is genuine, explosive power in these devices, and the ensuing punch sets the English world on its heels. That power is all the greater because the originality of the conception grows out of familiar form. The document casts the basis of colonial action in a language and context that every educated member of the British Empire instantly grasps. Read aloud and then posted in every American village, the Declaration succeeds in its plea for recognition because it is so instantly recognizable. Different appreciations have come to dominate modern understanding, but this, too, is part of the lasting power of the document. Ancient accusations against a king have become timely admonitions within twentieth-century culture, reminders to every citizen that self-evident truths remain unfulfilled. Perhaps, in the resonance of language and form, there always have been two Declarations: the immediate assertion of eighteenth-century revolutionaries and the larger claim of revolution itself. The hallowed artifact is always fresh as the signifier of aspirations still unreached.

But if time-bound and timeless connotations compete, as they do in any substantial work of literature, they also meet in a more literal fascination. Americans rarely separate the universal ideas of the Declaration from specific attachment to the document itself. The conjunction seems natural because the Declaration has functioned simultaneously as the first articulation and the ultimate expression of cultural life. This language, and no other, has been accepted without question. Americans celebrate neither June 7th, the day Richard Henry Lee proposes independence to Congress, nor July 2d, when Congress actually declares independence, but July 4th, the date when Congress accepts Jefferson's modified draft of language as its own. There is relevance in this concentration on the text. The ability to write out American independence with such consummate skill is the best evidence of a cultural capacity in the moment; celebration thereof, the clearest indication of achievement in a republic of laws.

III

While one-half of the first national compact has been revered, the other half is forgotten. No one now remembers the Articles of Confederation, the first document of national government, and there is irony in the contrast because the Articles fulfill the spirit and even the intention of the Declaration. That irony deepens in the revolutionary elite's own hesitations. John Dickinson, for an assigned committee of the second Continental Congress, pens the first draft of the Articles of Confederation in June 1776, but this draft is revised and then totally transformed in long and sometimes bitter debates on the floor of Congress and in state ratifying assemblies. Not until November 1777 does Congress approve the Articles of Confederation; not until March 1781, almost five years after the Declaration, do the Articles finally go into effect.

The Articles of Confederation bend and then break because they must settle the very ambiguities that the Declaration of Independence is allowed to evade. Where does sovereignty truly lie amidst the Declaration's "Free and Independent States"? Early republicans are not prepared to answer that question as a group in 1776, or, for that matter, in 1777 or 1781. They vacillate between the relatively strong central government of Dickinson's first draft of the Articles ("The said Colonies unite themselves so as never to be divided by any Act whatever") and the final version ("Each State retains its sovereignty, freedom, and independence"). Ultimate divisions of this kind create serious problems within the understandings of a consensual literature. The Articles raise the issue of sovereignty but do not settle it in credible or agreed-upon form, a difficulty that will cause some of the same participants to try much harder in 1787 when the costs of disagreement have become clearer.

The change in expression between 1777 and 1787 is complex but quite specific. At one level, the Revolution stands for the challenge of local rights to central authority, while at another, it seeks to make the people the fundamental authority of all government. These themes enjoy a symbiotic relationship in opposition to British rule and, initially, in resistance to a strong American confederation. No one really questions or separates the issues. But the rise of "new men" in the state legislatures of the 1780s, coupled with attacks on state power from local (usually western) communities, complicates a people-based rhetoric and frightens leaders at both the national and the state levels. The response of these leaders in 1787 is to divide revolutionary impulses by subsuming one challenge into the other. They neutralize distrust of centralization by recasting, rather than displacing, a familiar rhetoric. In a word, they turn the authority of the people into a justification for national sovereignty.

The respective preambles of the Articles of Confederation and the Federal Constitution convey the shift perfectly. Compare, on the one hand, "To all to whom these Presents shall come, we the undersigned Delegates of the States affixed to our Names send greeting," with, on the other, "We the People of the United States in Order to form a more perfect Union . . . do ordain and establish this Constitution for the United States of America." The first words of the Articles of Confederation are immediately lost in distinctions and vested particularities; the first of the Federal Constitution dissolve those distinctions and particularities in the empowering presence of the people. Fully aware of previous difficulties, the framers of the Constitution turn the people themselves into the authors of the Constitution, cleverly conflating the act of writing with the process of ratification.

Note, as well, the insistence on continuity. Rhetorically, the Convention of 1787 supplies "a more perfect" consequence of union, not a new form of government, and the new document can be superior to the Articles mostly because it rests upon them. Fully one-half of what is written in the Articles appears somewhere in the Constitution. The Articles first articulate the phrase "The United States of America" in official language. They first give assurance of "perpetual union." They initiate the crucial policy (popularized by the Northwest Ordinance) of admitting new states on the same footing. They suggest the language of enumeration as a doctrine of limited powers. They outline at least the prospect of dual citizenship. They assert the equality of all citizens in privileges and immunities, and they eliminate travel limitations and trade restrictions between the states. These are not mean achievements either in initial conception or in their abiding significance.

The Articles of Confederation prove vulnerable not in their innovations but in their assent to political circumstance. The limitations that hurt most – a weak executive in a committee structure, restrictions on the taxing power, and the requirement of overwhelming majorities for confederated action – come from dominant patterns in the colonial compacts and previous plans of confederation like the Albany Plan of Union (1754). In the 1770s, Whig arguments against the king make such curbs on power politically irresistible. Soon, though, when Americans argue more among themselves than with their king, the virtues of the 1770s become the frustrations of the 1780s. Congress loses much of its ability to govern in the interim, and institutionalization of the oppositional modes in revolutionary thought is one reason.

At the same time and amidst every difficulty, the Confederation grows into more than a temporary convenience for waging war. Certainly, the Articles deserve credit for helping to expand the realm of political possibilities in the early 1780s, and the explicit nature of that achievement also demonstrates how the public document differs from other literary acts of imagination. The first rule in such writing is that the new must somehow always appear familiar; since mere plausibility in thought and language is never enough, creativity must also satisfy a stricter standard of acceptability. Minimally, the Articles of 1777 conduct the idea of union from theory into regular political discourse and practice. No longer just a hope or an idea, "union" begins to function as an answer within republican life; it can be discussed in a different way in 1787 if just because more Americans are eager to see the existing institution work.

All of these hopes and fears bring subtle changes to the writing of public documents. Between 1776 and 1787, revolutionary leaders become less convinced about the self-evidence of truth in political forums. The weakness of the Confederation, growing factionalism, Shays's Rebellion, severe land disputes, economic depression, these facts – the very facts that bring the delegates of the Constitution Convention to Philadelphia – also make Convention delegates less certain of agreement and more worried about the textual basis on which agreement might rest. While the writers of the Constitution still believe in the text as the basis or foundation of all agreement, their uncertainties within this faith create a new aesthetics of control in what is written. They work harder for agreement. These differences appear symbolically in Benjamin Franklin's famous closures as he signs first the Declaration of Independence and then, eleven years later, the Constitution.

Signing the Declaration, Franklin supposedly observes, "we must, indeed, all hang together, or most assuredly we shall all hang separately." The Declaration functions as both the artifice behind Franklin's witticism and the artifact of the solemnly sworn policy that he enunciates. The members of the Continental Congress not only "hang" together in grouped signatures, they swear to do so in the Declaration, and their oath guarantees the "facts" they submit to "a candid world." The world is "candid" because it will accept facts as given and because it will further accept a right of revolution based upon them. Facts are submitted, again in the words of the Declaration, "to prove this." Meanwhile, more than humor rides on Franklin's psychology of opposition. Colonial solidarity in 1776 depends upon the unacceptable alternative: punishment for treason in an English courtroom.

By 1787, clear enemies and incontestable facts, let alone proofs, are much harder to come by. Placed in the exact same ceremonial situation at the Constitutional Convention, Franklin achieves a similar certainty but by a far more circuitous route. James Madison describes the event in his reports of the Convention:

Whilst the last members were signing [the Constitution] Doctr. Franklin looking towards the Presidents Chair, at the back of which a rising sun happened to be painted, observed to a few members near him, that Painters had found it difficult to distinguish in their art a rising from a setting sun. I have, said he, often and often in the course of the Session, and the vicissitudes of my hopes and fears as to its issue, looked at that behind the President without being able to tell whether it was rising or setting: But now at length I have the happiness to know that it is a rising and not a setting sun.

Franklin's assumed text in this anecdote, the artist's painting, is hopelessly ambiguous without a larger context; people can and will differ over whether it depicts a rising or a setting sun, just as the delegates themselves have differed in a final argument over whether the new Constitution will mean prosperity and peace for America or anarchy and civil convulsion.

Franklin has taken a central role in these last-minute bickerings, and the substance of his contribution has been to raise an unavoidable epistemological uncertainty. "For having lived long," he tells the Convention on September 17th, "I have experienced many instances of being obliged . . . to change opinions even on important subjects, which I once thought right, but found to be otherwise. It is therefore that the older I grow, the more apt I am to doubt my own judgment." The point of this comment is to encourage his divided colleagues to settle for an "apparent unanimity" where "real" accord is impossible and to urge them to incorporate that subterfuge into the Constitution itself. Knowing that the delegates are divided, that they *cannot* hang together, Franklin successfully moves that the Constitution be approved "by the unanimous consent of *the States* present," the majority of each delegation being for ratification.

In accepting Franklin's "convenient" motion, the framers of the Constitution, as reported in Madison's *Notes of Debates in the Federal Convention,* see and welcome, "the ambiguity of the proposed form of signing." Unanimity, of course, is less than the truth. Three leading members of the Convention – Edmund Randolph, Elbridge Gerry, and George Mason – refuse to sign the Constitution on the final day of the Convention, and three others – Luther Martin, Robert Yates, and John Lansing, Jr. – withdraw earlier because of their unhappiness with the emerging document. The unanimity injected into the language of the Constitution is instead a useful fiction, a myth of glorious harmony that the framers wield in the ideological struggle to elicit and then to enforce allegiance in the fight over ratification. But unanimity can be mobilized without hypocrisy in this fashion because the text itself has been accepted as an inevitable repository of epistemological ambiguities. Philosophical uncertainty, in Franklin's sense, has become a vital source of political flexibility and literary creativity.

Franklin's strangely useful pessimism about human understanding might appear idiosyncratic but for the fact that it is shared, even amplified, by a more important leader of the Convention – by James Madison, Father of the Constitution. At issue is how a writer turns a necessarily ambiguous text into a tool of ideological conformity. The whole problem of consensus is a vexing one in Madison's writings. The most famous Federalist Paper, *No. 10*, may argue that disagreement and faction will yield to "the extent and proper structure of the Union," but *Federalist No. 37*, also from Madison's pen, reveals paralyzing philosophical uncertainties that call the entire realm of human agreement into question. Here, in one of the darkest thrusts of the American Enlightenment, Madison describes three intruding levels of chaos in human existence: "the obscurity arising from the complexity of objects," "the imperfection of the human faculties," and the failure of language itself ("the medium through which the conceptions of men are conveyed to each other adds a fresh embarrassment").

When these elements are compounded in the actual process of human perception – "indistinctness of the object, imperfection of the organ of conception, inadequateness of the vehicle of ideas" – we are left with a world of impenetrable "gloom," one filled with "dark and degraded pictures which display the infirmities and depravities of the human character." This world is so impoverished with its "discordant opinions," "mutual jealousies . . . factions, contentions, and disappointments" that Madison's "man of candor" regards mere agreement with surprise and the presumed unanimity of the Constitutional Convention with "wonder" and "astonishment." Only "a finger of that Almighty hand" can have supplied such a level of understanding in mere men. As he tells Jefferson just a month after the Convention, "it is impossible to consider the degree of concord which ultimately prevailed as less than a miracle."

The point of *Federalist No. 37* is that real agreement becomes impossible without imposed manipulation and design – a manipulation and design that can be traced to the pen of Madison as easily as he has traced them to the finger of God. His talk of miracles and Providence may trade on the colonial tradition of unanimity in the community of saints as the human expression of God's will, and it surely echoes a covenant tradition in American constitutionalism that begins in 1629 with the transfer of the charter of the Massachusetts Bay Company to the New World ("every of us doth hereby freely and sincerely promise and bind himselfe in the word of a christian and in the presence of God who is the searcher of all hearts"). But Madison, "the man of pious reflection" in *Federalist No. 37*, is more a child of the secular Enlightenment. The substructure of his statement, and particularly the metaphor about a guiding finger, suggests how the writing of the Constitution involves an aesthetics of conscious human control, how the document itself depends upon questions of craft. The Constitution operates as a place where "theoretical propriety" and "extraneous considerations" can meet and where a molding hand resolves the difference.

How are we to know that the Constitution represents a rising and not a setting sun? What is it about the text itself that leads fallible observers to the same conclusion? The rhetoric of the framers urges us to answer these questions by thinking of the Constitution as the expression of a shared truth devised by the elected representatives of an enlightened people. We are urged, in other words, to mystify the text in question. Quite another set of answers comes to mind if we think of the text as created text, as a manipulated and manipulative work, as the imposed truth of a conscious and philosophically sophisticated elite, as the concrete product of James Madison, Edmund Randolph, James Wilson, and Gouverneur Morris – the four men who in 1787 actually write succeeding drafts from the Virginia Plan of late May, through the Report of the Committee of the Whole in mid-June, to the copy reported by the Committee of Detail in early August, to the Constitution as submitted by the Committee of Style in mid-September. The craft of the document is one of its most ignored features.

IV

National deliberations have rarely developed into intellectually impressive events. The Federal Convention stands out not just because of the oft-noted genius of its participants but because of their practiced talents as men of letters. The Constitution is a marvel of concision, emerging as it does from four months of florid effusion and often bitter debate. It contains just five thousand words of the plainest prose, cast within a one-sentence preamble and seven brief articles. Neither verbiage, nor allusion, nor admonition interrupts its prescriptive clarity; there is very little linguistic novelty, almost no philosophical innovation, and minimal elaboration. But these evasions are counterbalanced by a series of more subtle commitments. Brief rather than cryptic, the Constitution confirms a familiar past. Every word belongs to the realm of common understanding in eighteenth-century American experience, and many of them are taken directly from the constitutions of the states and from the Articles of Confederation in a reaffirmation of republican principle.

Chief among the drafters' skills is their ability to grasp and then wield a common understanding. Like John Adams, who watches anxiously from England, the framers use the state constitutions as the repositories of an American identity in the 1780s. Use, however, signifies more than a knowledge of documents; it also means making constitutional language one's own. Adams, as drafter in his own right of the Massachusetts Constitution of 1780, offers A Defence of the Constitutions of Government of the United States of America (1787–8) as "a specimen of that kind of reading and reasoning which produced the American constitutions." His themes are "the well-ordered constitution" as the holder of "futurity in America" and the state constitutions as the true history of an emerging republicanism.

Consensus over Adams's assumptions is a matter of practice. Between 1776 and 1784, every state except Rhode Island and Connecticut writes and adopts a new constitution. Seventeen new constitutions in all are written in America during the course of the Revolution, and the number is one key to interpretation. Even the best writer struggles through lesser works before a masterpiece becomes possible. Just so, the framers in Philadelphia prepare themselves in the workshops of congressional and state assemblies. Forty of the fifty-five delegates already have served in both. Half of that number have participated directly in the writing of state constitutions and territorial ordinances. The quantum jump in quality of language and conception between the Articles of Confederation and the Constitution actually occurs step-by-step in state convention after state convention.

The framers take the measure of their own growing ability in the very first speech of the Convention. Edmund Randolph begins his criticism of the Articles of Confederation by exonerating the authors of that document for errors made "in the then infancy of the science, of constitutions, & of confederacies." Infancy, in Randolph's terms, refers to an understanding that is just ten years old, and it includes many of the men sitting around him in Independence Hall; obviously, much has been learned in the intervening decade by American revolutionaries, many of whom are still only middle-aged. A new sophistication in the science of constitutions has reduced a series of primal uncertainties. What does it mean to write out a constitution when the ideal model of the British Constitution assumes an unwritten status? To whom does one address such a document amidst raging debates about the locus and feasibility of sovereignty? How and where, precisely, does fundamental law lie upon a page also dedicated to the artificial machinery of modern government?

The state constitutions that intervene between 1776 and 1787 curb the unfamiliar by placing it within familiar form. They, in effect, bring the framers to a greater awareness of genre. Only in repetition do possibilities become apparent. Generic skill is clearest in the framers' many shorthand references to state constitutions on the Convention floor; their mastery, in their self-confidence amidst every difficulty. Even though they are politically divided, they remain collectively committed to the sequent toil of successive drafts of the Constitution. They share a series of assumptions about the way narrative, form, and style control unruly content, and they have learned what to avoid in each other. Their borrowings from the state constitutions are, in consequence, all the more impressive because so discriminating. Witness the careful circumvention of controversial terms like "national," "republic," and "federal."

The framers' knowledge of genre is especially evident in their willingness to seek form as a primary source of meaning. Compared with the looser prolixity of the state constitutions, the generalities of the Constitution lie within a precise arrangement of tone and structure. The seven articles are clearly deployed in descending order of length, concern, and difficulty. The first three articles – on the legislative, executive, and judicial branches – give the crux of the Constitution. Each moves from description of a branch of government into issues of qualification and selection for office and then to an enumeration of powers and limits.

Each article also demonstrates that the engaged delegates have come to understand the deepest workings of constitutional language. The hardest lesson, one that the Committee of Detail articulates on July 26th, involves simplicity. Edmund Randolph and John Rutledge, for the committee, see the necessity of a scope, style, and tone that will trust to form over detail. As they draft a constitution that will be properly "fundamental," they agree "to use simple and precise language, and general propositions" and "to insert essential principles only, lest the operations of government should be clogged." This spirit of restraint, captured in Madison's *Notes of Debates in the Federal Convention,* can dominate the writing process precisely because it claims clarity of form as its goal. Randolph and Rutledge distinguish sharply between "the construction of a constitution" and the more open-ended enumeration of mere law; only the former requires "the shortest scheme that can be adopted." The accessibility of the framers' document absolutely depends upon this distinction. The Federal Constitution can be twice as clear as forerunners like the Massachusetts Constitution of 1780 in part because it is less than half as long.

The Constitution itself literalizes appropriate form. The empowering presence of the people, as the prerequisite to all government, comes first in "we, the people." This preamble is then joined by the specific articles of government to a conclusion that portrays union on the very face of the document. The signers of the Constitution appear neither in alphabetical order, nor by presumed importance or seniority, nor in haphazard fashion. They are grouped, instead, by state with the states themselves appearing in *geographical* order from north to south, starting with New Hampshire in the north and working in sequence through Georgia in the extreme south. The United States thus appear on the page in familiar map form – the perfect icon in answer to Madison's fears about indistinct objects, imperfect perception, and faulty language.

This iconicity reflects the Constitution makers' sense of their work and of themselves as "framing" and "framers." Most famously, Madison in *Federalist No. 51* uses "framing a government" to evoke the necessary controls (internal and external) that distinguish a government of men from one of angels. The metaphor of framing, a general one in the discourse of the delegates at the Convention, conjoins act and object, creation and control, regularity and contrivance with the overarching notion of order as the ultimate source of many different meanings.

In Johnson's *Dictionary of the English Language* (1755), "frame" includes "to form or fabricate by orderly construction and union of various parts," "to make," "to regulate," "to invent," and, from the noun, "a fabrick, any thing constructed of various parts or members," "any thing made so as to inclose or admit something else," "order; regularity; adjusted series or disposition," "scheme," "contrivance," "projection." The Constitution, self-consciously the fabric of union, is all of these things, but most particularly it encloses and, thereby, creates form in the midst of chaos. *Without* the weaver's fabric, the frame signifies only a void. Alexander Hamilton, no friend of the original plan, turns this opposition of order and chaos into the rallying call for ratification when he asks on September 17th, "Is it possible to deliberate between anarchy and Convulsion on one side, and the chance of good to be expected from the plan on the other?"

The frame, together with the framers' effort, insists upon what might have been thought to be missing: recognizable form. It is both a claim of accomplishment and a rejection of prevalent fears. Just how prevalent these fears have become in 1787 can be seen in George Washington's own pessimism over the "little ground on which the hope of a good establishment can be formed." "I *almost* despair of seeing a favourable issue on the proceedings of our Convention," he writes to Hamilton on July 10th, "and do therefore repent having had any agency in the business." Framing is that act of agency depersonalized, the very method of establishing common ground or good form. As noun, "frame," it is also the act accomplished, the proof of common ground.

The belief in boundaries intrinsic to the metaphor also eases the three central innovations of the Constitution, all of which involve a chilling open-endedness in conventional eighteenth-century political thought: first, the *amorphous* and *changeable* people as the foundation of all authority; second, the constitutional *separation* of powers in government; and, third, the *sharing* of sovereignty between the nation and states. None of these ideas lends unifying form to the early American mind, and all three generate uneasiness and debate. Framing is the visual aid for an assumed congruity. The eighty-five *Federalist Papers* build around these premises. They argue that the new national fabric is a uniformity woven of apposite parts and not a weak tissue, not a mere contrivance.

To be sure, the arguments themselves are easy to accept only in retrospect, but if they also require an act of faith in the troubled 1780s, the visual possibilities in framing encourage a useful personification. In the ratification process, *who the framers are* counts for as much as *what has been framed*. As Madison warns Edmund Randolph in January 1788, "[H]ad the Constitution been framed & recommended by an obscure individual, instead of a body possessing public respect & confidence . . . it would have commanded little attention from those who now admire its wisdom." The personages who enter the Convention also emerge immeasurably greater in Madison's description of what they accomplish. Their act of framing, in all of its unifying implications of craftsmanship and communal success, constructs a public body worthy of respect and confidence out of conspicuous individuals who often disagree.

Two other considerations reinforce the literary ability that the delegates bring to Philadelphia. By 1787 a majority of Americans embrace the Convention as the appropriate institutional arrangement for contemplating national union. Political legitimacy insures the high quality of its participants as well as their self-confidence and mutual awareness. In the first month of the Convention, Madison, Franklin, and George Mason all write that they can hope for much from a Convention made up of, in Madison's words to William Short, "the best contribution of talents the States could make for the occasion." Franklin, writing to Richard Price, sees "the principal people in the several states" around him. "America," adds George Mason to his son, "has certainly, upon this occasion, drawn forth her first characters."

Not uncontested, the legitimacy of the forum nonetheless brings the recognition of a golden opportunity to bear on the proceedings, and when troubles mount in late June and early July that knowledge is saving. On June 26th, Madison and Hamilton warn that, because they are "digesting a plan which in its operation wd. decide forever the fate of Republican Govt.," failure will mean "it would be disgraced & lost among ourselves, disgraced & lost to mankind forever." Three days later, Hamilton summarizes the importance of the moment. "It is a miracle that we are now here exercising our tranquil & free deliberations on the subject," he observes. "It would be madness to trust to future miracles." Then, on July 5th, Gouverneur Morris uses the theme to make his colleagues "extend their views." Each delegate, "a Representative of America," must also think as "a Representative of the whole human race; for the whole human race will be affected by the proceedings of this Convention." In these and other exhortations, the framers define a special purpose. They engage in what Herman Melville will later term "the shock of recognition," the moment in which creativity takes its own measure to move beyond itself.

The second consideration suggests a more subtle and generally forgotten influence, one that also enables Madison's "best contribution of talents" to understand and thrive upon itself. The delegates who attend the Convention conceive of themselves as eighteenth-century gentlemen of letters. Much has been made of their adept use of committee structures, their secrecy and restraint before publication, their willingness to suggest solutions without insisting upon personal investment, and their ability to compromise over language. By and large, these characteristics are exactly what one can hope for in the exemplary writers of the time. The true gentleman of letters privileges reason over emotion, writes for a small group of social peers, circulates drafts among those peers for correction, avoids publication until agreement is reached, and leaves his work unsigned. In short, the very qualities that critics have cited as weaknesses in early American fiction, poetry, and drama become strengths in the literature of public documents. The retreat to committee arrangements for compromise reveals only the most obvious of these strengths.

Surely the most remarkable trait of the Convention has to do with the delegation of sensitive writing tasks *within* committees to embattled figures like Edmund Randolph, James Wilson, and Gouverneur Morris. These men take strong stands in debate on the floor of the Convention, and yet their colleagues can trust them to express the general will when writing by assignment. The official selflessness of the man of letters is crucial in this frequent behavior pattern. Not until the 1830s do Americans learn for certain that the aristocratic, thoroughly conservative Gouverneur Morris penned the final draft of the Constitution. News of his authorship in 1787 would surely have hurt chances for ratification, but Madison, a sometime opponent of Morris, knows that the gentlemanly tradition minimizes the danger of publicity. As he tells Jared Sparks in 1831, "[A] better choice could not have been made, as the performance of the task proved."

The role of the man of letters channels authorial identity into a social or corporate orientation. Half a century later, writing to William Cogswell in 1834, Madison is still insisting on the essence of that collective spirit. "You give me a credit to which I have no claim, in calling me '*The* writer of the Constitution of the U.S.,'" he explains. "This was not like the fabled Goddess of Wisdom, the offspring of a single brain. It ought to be regarded as the work of many heads and many hands." More than modesty dictates Madison's response. His notion of "many heads and many hands" is the source of all agreement in the writing of the Constitution. The aesthetic of the man of letters blends perfectly into a politics of ratification.

Unjustly ignored today, Washington's letter delivering the Constitution to Congress is a model of this convergence. Sent "By *unanimous Order of the Convention*" on September 17th, the letter uses the undifferentiated, first-person plural pronoun to incorporate every level of decorum: "In all our deliberations on this subject [differences among the several states] we kept steadily in our view, that which appears to us the greatest interest of every true American, the consolidation of our Union." A gentlemen's agreement over language is also a national consensus in spite of difference. The litany of pronominal possessives conflates framer and ordinary citizen, "our deliberations" and "our view" referring to the framers' decisions but merging with "our Union," the perspective of every true American.

Washington then alludes to differences that might have been expected but that never materialize. Again, the guiding decorum of the framers as gentlemen is also the larger decorum of the true American perspective. In Washington's words, "the Constitution, which we now present, is the result of a spirit of amity." Those who disagree must remember that the document grows out of "mutual deference and concession" and that it, therefore, "is liable to as few exceptions as could reasonably have been expected." The acceptable exceptions already have been made. By extension, a challenge to any part of the final document violates the decorum of amity, forgets "the greatest interest of every American," and endangers "our prosperity, felicity, safety, perhaps our national existence." These words follow the tactic already traced in the preamble of the Constitution, and they prefigure the framers' larger strategy in the ratification debates. The people share in the act of writing through the related act of ratification. Agreement *with* the document looms as the acceptable interpretation *of* it.

The evolution of these strategies can be seen in the framers' final debates. At sometime in the rearrangement of twenty-three loose articles into the tightened, final version of seven, a majority decides that their text should not be opened to reinterpretation. The Committee of Style presents the Constitution's ultimate amendment clause on September 12th with its stipulations on how subsequent changes are to become "part thereof," a phrase subsequently changed to "Part of this Constitution." The word "part" in this context means "extension." One need only compare such language with the relevant clause in the Articles of Confederation, which allows for the possibility of "alteration" within the articles themselves.

Amendments to the Constitution are *added on* to a document that remains intact despite every revision. The whole discussion of constitutional change takes place between September 15th and 17th, amidst the framers' rejection of calls for a second convention and their decision to resist the right of state ratifying conventions to alter language in the document. As Edmund Randolph notes, their stance leaves the people with just two alternatives regarding the Constitution, "accepting or rejecting it in toto." "Conventions," observes Charles Pinckney for the majority, "are serious things, and ought not to be repeated."

The major literary consequence of ratification is the addition of a Bill of Rights. But even these restrictive adjustments – the bargain struck after two years of debate in the first Congress and the state assemblies – have the effect of magnifying the overall document. The original framers reject the need for a Bill of Rights because, as Roger Sherman argues on September 12th, "the State Declarations of Rights are not repealed by this Constitution; and being in force are sufficient." Sherman's argument, accepted by the Convention, assumes that the Constitution must always be read in conjunction with the state constitutions. When anti-Federalists demand instead that the Constitution supply an independent guarantee of individual rights, their insistence has the ironic effect of letting the document stand on its own. The traditional Anglo–Saxon freedoms of speech, religion, press, the right to bear arms, and trial by jury lend another level of identification and allow the Constitution to emerge as an autonomous and complete expression of republican government and American politics. The first ten amendments also seal off the original document. When they are passed and then *added to* the text in 1791, they insure that all further changes will be supplementary rather than integral to the language of the framers.

Lengthy debate over the amendments in the summer of 1789 confirms the realization of form in the Constitution. Notably, Congress spends almost as much time arguing over the placement of amendments as it does discussing their substance. The strongest proponents of a Bill of Rights and perhaps an

initial majority in Congress want to re-draft the preamble of the constitution, but attempts to do so please no one. Those who prefer to incorporate
the amendments into the body of the document fail for similar reasons;
friends deplore the loss of a separate statement on basic rights, and opponents
resist alterations that would spoil an existing lucidity. James Jackson of
Georgia seems to have spoken for many on the floor of Congress when he
argues that the Constitution as ratified must be left untouched. To amend
internally would leave the document "patched up, from time to time, with
various stuffs resembling Joseph's coat of many colors." In the end, Roger
Sherman, opponent of a Bill of Rights on the Convention floor in 1787,
moves the successful proposal in Congress to add amendments "by way of
supplement." Debate and the drafting of its own language in the amendment
process drive Congress back on the original structure in framing.

Madison, for one, is quick to see that the Bill of Rights strengthens the
new government. The amendments, he writes to Jefferson in December
1788, will "give to the Government its due popularity and stability." Of his
own considerable role, first, in crafting those amendments so that they do
not interfere with enumerated constitutional powers and, second, in shep-
herding them through the federal government, he is typically discreet. "I
should have acted from prudence," he tells Edmund Randolph in 1789, "the
very part to which I have been led by choice." There may be no more succinct
gauge of creativity in the literature of public documents.

Choice is instinctively prudential in such writing; the claim of inevitability,
its best defense. In keeping with these tones, the amendments themselves take
the plainest, most laconic expression. They are like the Constitution itself – in
direct contrast to the elaborate prose of the state constitutions and state declarations of rights. Each of the first ten amendments is a single sentence with the
longest employing one hundred and six words and the shortest just sixteen;
five amendments are thirty words or less. In the consensual apparatus of
writing out agreement, debate means less rather than more. "Nothing of a
controvertible nature," Madison explains to Edmund Pendleton during the
process, "ought to be hazarded by those who are sincere in wishing for the
approbation of $\frac{2}{3}$ of each House, and $\frac{3}{4}$ of the State Legislatures."

Making prudence the whole of choice must be understood against a struggle for ratification that could have gone either way. For if Delaware, New
Jersey, Connecticut, Maryland, and South Carolina accept the Constitution
with relative ease, the vital large states – Pennsylvania, Massachusetts, Virginia, and New York – engage in prolonged contests and pass the Constitution by narrow and bitter margins. Massachusetts ratifies by just ten votes
out of a total of three hundred and fifty-five cast; Virginia, by ten out of one
hundred and sixty-eight; New York, by three out of fifty-seven. North

Carolina first rejects the Constitution altogether, reconsidering a year later in 1789. When recalcitrant Rhode Island finally joins the new government in 1790, it is by two votes from a total of sixty-six. Americans are a divided people in 1788. The surprise is not in their differences but in the speed with which they resolved conflict in their first decade under the new Constitution.

v

Communal acceptance of the Constitution remains one of the mysteries of early republican life. In literary terms, the shift involves nothing less than the crystallization of a genre, the moment when decisive accomplishment transforms an art form and everyone's understanding of it. The reasons for this change of perspective in the writing and reading of constitutions are various. When John Adams, using hindsight in 1815, summarizes the period as "the age of revolutions and constitutions," the phrase contains a vital expectation. Constitutions resolve revolutions.

The assumption, one widely shared by early republicans, is that constitutional forms define revolutionary accomplishment and, thereby, American culture itself. Not for the last time, the written word is the comprehended act. But even this predilection only begins to explain the strength and scope of a new faith. In the 1790s, Americans turn their disputed document into the universal symbol of an era. The Constitution now fixes all previous aspects of revolutionary activity, especially the disruptive or chaotic parts, into a text for all to read. Aaron Hall of New Hampshire offers an early version of the controlling truism. "Till this period," he declares in an oration from 1788, "the revolution in America has never appeared to me to be completed; but this is laying on the cap-stone of the great American Empire."

The expectations in closure change how the Constitution must be regarded. If ordaining and establishing a republican form of government in America at the end of the eighteenth century possesses a universal significance in human history, as the framers in Philadelphia themselves claim so frequently, then the artifact of ordination and establishment, their document, easily becomes more than mere language. In its simplest form, these pressures turn the text of the Constitution into an independent repository of moral value. Republican virtue resides not in the act of clarification, a frequent call in the early 1780s, but in the clarifying result, the battle cry of ratification in 1788. The Constitution becomes not a symptom of virtue but the extent of virtue then possible.

Adams, writing his *Defence of the Constitutions* in the same year as the Federal Convention, shows the way by insisting that constitutionalism enables virtue and not vice versa. "The best republics will be virtuous, and have been so," he argues, "but we may hazard a conjecture that the virtues have been the effect of the well-ordered constitution, rather than the cause." Adams and other early republican intellectuals use their readings in British empirical thought to claim that institutions, not the manners and morals of a people, guarantee good government. What they add on their own in 1787 and after is the notion that a written text, the Constitution, can function as such an institution – the *central* institution.

Madison's writings play heavily on the theme. The Revolution, he explains in the *National Gazette* for January 19, 1792, distinguishes between European "charters of liberty . . . granted by power" and American "charters of power granted by liberty." As with Adams, constitutionalism defines the meaning of revolutionary action. Madison's "revolution in the practice of the world" becomes a matter of wielding and understanding official language properly. "In proportion to the value of this revolution; in proportion to the importance of instruments, every word of which decides a question between power and liberty . . . ought to be the vigilance with which they are guarded by every citizen."

Madison claims that American constitutions, as expressions of liberty rather than of power, are infinitely more precious but also inevitably more complicated than their European counterparts. This complexity "requires a more than common reverence for the authority which is to preserve order thro' the whole." The charters of government in America are the worthiest objects of reverence because "[a]s truths, none can be more sacred" and "[a]s metes and bounds of governments, they transcend all other land-marks." These public documents are the ultimate sources of definition in the culture. In consequence, texts like the Constitution require more than understanding. The citizen's highest duty is to protect and preserve "charters of government . . . superior in obligation to all others, because they give effect to all others." "How devoutly it is to be wished, then," concludes Madison, "that the public opinion of the United States should be enlightened; that it should attach itself to their governments as delineated in *great charters* . . . that it should guarantee with a holy zeal, these political scriptures from every attempt to add to or diminish from them."

The many valences of Madison's appeal – the careful balances and proportions of liberty and power, value and vigilance, effect and obligation, together with the conflated symbolism of transcendent landmarks, sacred truths, political scriptures, enlightened opinion, and holy zeal – keep the idea of constitutionalism at the center of every frame of early republican reference, whether scientific, political, economic, geographical, or religious. Individuals, society, and government are to cohere in the attachment to constitutionalism. Americans, so attached, will act out their commitment to the Revolution and define themselves accordingly through their appreciation of the documents of origination. As the ultimate spirit of consolidation in American culture, as the highest expression of the republican experiment, as a symptom of the advanced stage in the Enlightenment, and as one of the most discussed documents on the face of the earth in 1790, the Constitution must evoke the reverence that Madison stipulates.

Spontaneous and enduring, that reverence also has obscured an overall achievement in the literature of public documents. Other official writings from the period, some of consummate power, have been lost in the shadow of the Constitution. In several ways, "The Virginia Statute of Religious Liberty" (1786) provides a more moving and coherent statement of Enlightenment principles. Drafted by Thomas Jefferson, it places an awareness of mental powers ("Almighty God hath created the mind free") against darker realizations ("the impious presumptions of legislators and rulers . . . being themselves but fallible and uninspired men"). An ensuing list of injuries, incapacities, corruptions, briberies, temptations, fallacies, and intrusions represent the excesses of religious establishment. Truth alone – also gendered separately as female virtue against masculine error – stands against these dangers. Even so, "truth is great and will prevail if left to herself"; only "human interposition," literally violation, can "disarm her." Truth's natural weapons are free argument and debate. They are, however, sufficient; "errors ceasing to be dangerous when it is permitted freely to contradict them." In Jefferson's formulation, the Virginia legislature enacts its own implied marriage to truth by wrapping itself in the same protections of freedom and nature: "we are free to declare, and do declare, that the rights hereby asserted are of the natural rights of mankind."

The Northwest Ordinance from 1787, also an ignored expression of the American mind, is the cardinal achievement of Congress in the first ten years of the Republic. The clearest and most compelling picture of union in the period, the Ordinance guarantees the spread of republican government across the continent. It is drafted by Nathan Dane of Massachusetts, and its provisions mandate and orchestrate the appropriate stages of development from wilderness to territory to something like colonized status to full equality in statehood. Here, as well, are most of the central ideals of the culture rendered as practices: the assurances of due process in law, of equal inheritance, of the general availability of property, and of freedom of travel; the call for a systematic plan of public education; the protection of minorities in the promise of "utmost good faith" toward Native-American peoples; the extension of "the fundamental principles of civil and religious liberty" to all persons regardless of citizenship; and, most courageously for the times, the prohibition of slavery throughout the territory. In analyzing "the celebrated

'*Ordinance*' " as "the model of all subsequent territorial governments," Timothy Walker's seminal *Introduction to American Law* (1837) finds that "for brevity, comprehension, and forecast, it has no superior in the annals of legislation."

Brevity, comprehension, and forecast: these virtues mark the extraordinary general achievement in public documents by the writers of the early Republic. As works of literature, documents like the Constitution, the Statute of Religious Toleration, and the Northwest Ordinance set a standard for new generations of writers to reach for. They also assure that the tenuous bond between aspiration and realization will never be lost completely. More, as in any living literary tradition, they lend themselves to further interpretation in each additional expression, or, in this case, in the further exposition of democratic and republican principles; they sustain and guide the skills of continuing interpretation.

As with any other literary masterpiece, the Constitution encourages even as it dominates thought. All but forgotten are the first important arguments concerning strict and loose construction of constitutional language: the debate originated by George Washington, as president, but written out by his secretaries of state and of the treasury in early 1791. Jefferson, offering his opinion on February 15th of that year, and Hamilton, just a week later, take the constitutionality of the projected United States Bank as their assigned subject, and their dispute has remained the most cogent single exchange on federal power (limited or implied) across two centuries of constitutional debate. Subsequently, Hamilton's *Report on Manufactures* (1791) and Jefferson's "Kentucky Resolutions" (1798) extend their respective views. The issue they raise, central authority versus state rights, eludes resolution by the very nature of the federated Republic, but its ramifications are already clear in these four documents taken together – all from the first decade of the new government.

The loftiest of constitutional interpretations, those of John Marshall as Chief Justice of the Supreme Court, help to explain the power and excitement in all other interpretations. "[W]e must never forget," Marshall explains in *M'Culloch* v. *Maryland* (1819), "that it is a constitution we are expounding." He never does, and neither do other early republican intellectuals who wish to be heard. As the singular experiment in thought of the period, the Constitution always guarantees an audience when it is the subject. Marshall's choice of language is also instructive. "To expound" means to set forth or declare in detail; as well, "to explain" or "to interpret," especially where scripture or religious formularies are concerned, and also to offer a particular interpretation, to construe in a specified manner, chiefly in law.

Marshall's opinions resonate with all of these possibilities. Chief among all of them, however, is his assumption of a vital and absorbing enterprise, one that Americans will accept as their primary intellectual concern. When, for example, he first establishes the right of judicial review in *Marbury* v. *Madison* (1803), Marshall begins by assuming "a question deeply interesting to the United States." But why is it so interesting? After all, the question itself is a simple one and easily answered ("not of an intricacy proportioned to its interest"). No, the reader's interest in this case, and in all of Marshall's major opinions, come from the assertion that the Constitution is somehow in jeopardy. As Marshall puts the matter in converting legal principle into dramatic story, there is a danger of "doctrine [that] would subvert the very foundation of all written constitutions" and that "reduces to nothing" the Federal Constitution. Americans *must* listen because Marshall's answer to that doctrine will touch "the basis on which the whole American fabric has been erected."

Opinions like *Marbury* v. *Madison, M'Culloch* v. *Maryland, Dartmouth College* v. *Woodward* (1819), and *Gibbons* v. *Ogden* (1824) are essentially celebrations of the achievement of the framers. "Expounding" the Constitution is every citizen's link to that achievement. In the America of *Marbury* v. *Madison,* "where written constitutions have been viewed with so much reverence," the "very great exertion" of the framers signifies the "original and supreme will" of government as well as "the greatest improvement on political institutions" of the age. Any law repugnant to the Constitution is therefore necessarily void. The supreme importance of what the framers have done translates easily into the supremacy (and continuing excitement) of the document that they have rendered.

The framers, always invoked in these opinions, protect the vitality, the importance, and the simplicity of originating language. They are, in this sense, literary guardians as well as lawgivers and political leaders. In *Dartmouth College* v. *Woodward,* a "general spirit" in the Constitution excludes "unnecessary" or "mischievous" interpretations that "the framers of the constitution could never have intended to insert in that instrument." Because this spirit resides only in the strength of a common understanding, *M'Culloch* v. *Maryland* warns against turning the Constitution into "the prolixity of a legal code." Danger looms in too much complexity of interpretation. If expanded into a code, the Constitution "could scarcely be embraced by the human mind" and "would probably never be understood by the public." *Gibbons* v. *Ogden* follows with its own criticism of "powerful and ingenious minds" that "entangle and perplex understanding, so as to obscure principles which were before thought quite plain." Marshall's recurring standard, announced here, is that "the enlightened patriots who framed our constitution, and the people who adopted it, must be understood to have employed words in their natural sense, and to have intended what they have said."

These passages capture a final capacity in the literature of public documents. Marshall believes that ordinary language must encompass the most intricate of philosophical and political problems. And without exception, the leading documents of the period support his conclusion. Time and again, these formative writings subsume complexity in a narrative and form that speak directly and easily to the largest common audience. This is not to say that writers like Jefferson, Madison, Hamilton, and Marshall ignore underlying complexity; they overcome it.

Actual articulations of difficulty illustrate the point perfectly. Madison, writing to Jefferson on October 24, 1787, calls the Constitution "a task more difficult than can be well conceived by those who were not concerned in the execution of it." Franklin tells Pierre-Samuel DuPont de Nemours that the Convention should be compared to an infinitely complex game of chess in which every move is contested. From hindsight in 1818, John Adams thinks of thirteen clocks striking simultaneously, "a perfection of mechanism which no artist had ever before effected." In every case, the fact of difficulty gives way to a metaphoric projection of ease in competence and accomplishment. Madison's executor of a task, Franklin's chess player, and Adams's artist all know what to do and how to do it. Jefferson best describes the self-confidence involved. "It is a part of the American character," he writes his daughter in the anxious year of 1787, "to consider nothing as desperate; to surmount every difficulty by resolution and contrivance." The combination is illuminating: resolution (an act of will) permits contrivance (the ability to invent order in a crisis).

The literature of public documents flows out of this peculiar dynamic. Optimism, resolution, and contrivance, themselves minor literary virtues, nonetheless combine as the driving force in a creativity of almost unlimited effectiveness. They form, as Jefferson says, "part of the American character." Within the combination, we have found perhaps a dozen works of the first rank, starting with the Declaration of Independence in 1776 and extending through John Marshall's opinions in the 1820s. In fact, twelve works are a reasonable total for gauging the merit of a literary configuration, but the number becomes astonishing when the comparison drops to consider any similar time span in a civic literature. In its immediate impact, its cumulative character, its continuing importance, and its general influence, the early republican literature of public documents stands alone. There has been nothing quite like it before or since, this practiced skill in an official language that is also common to all; not in American culture nor in any other.

6

THE LIMITS OF ENLIGHTENMENT

I

A dominating frame of reference assimilates the crises in meaning and the contradictions in practice that it generates. The Enlightenment shapes early republican culture in just this way. It is both the source of ideas and the boundary placed upon them in revolutionary America, both the expression of broad aspirations and the enforcement of narrow instrumental controls. The literature of public documents offers a proximate case in point. The Federal Constitution of 1787 embodies the central aspirations of the Enlightenment. In daring to know and then in imposing their knowledge, the framers assume the capacity of reason to define and control human society. Their text, the Constitution, celebrates the association between correct human mechanism and universal improvement. Knowledge, through mechanism, forms a more perfect union that will establish justice, insure tranquillity, promote the general welfare, and secure the blessings of liberty for the people of the United States. Yet, at another level, the body and mechanics of the Constitution take back the scope and sweep of its preamble.

Not everyone in America is so insured, so promoted, so secured, so blessed. Quietly but emphatically, the Constitution eliminates whole categories from the rubric of "we, the people." In a shocking adaptation of the mathematical penchants of the Enlightenment, the Constitution, in Articles 1 and 4, perpetuates the institution of slavery and reduces all individuals who are not "free" to three-fifths of a person. Again in Article 1, it excludes Native Americans from the apportionment of representation and gives Congress an exclusive power in commerce over them. More subtly, it avoids all mention of one-half of the population under its jurisdiction, the women of the United States; all pronouns referring to gender are in the masculine form.

The calculation in such language is apparent from a simple elision. When the American woman actually finds a place in early drafts of the Constitution, it is as a fugitive slave. "If any Person bound to service or labor in any of the United States shall escape into another State," ran the original and unanimous language of August 29th, "He or *She* shall not be discharged . . .

but shall be delivered up to the person justly claiming their service or labor." Obviously pertinent in this setting, the feminine referent is altogether too singular, too solitary in its implications for the Committee of Style when it tests the appropriateness of constitutional language. Just as all explicit reference to slavery is removed from the final document, so the substitution of a simple and direct negative subject in the fugitive slave provision ("No person legally held to service") removes the subordinate conditional clause and, with it, all need for a subject pronoun that carries unsettling gender connotations.

The manipulation of language is deliberate, but how does one explain the recognition of discrepancy between theory and practice that such language implies? The simplest answer always has stressed the political needs and orientations of pragmatic statesmen. John Rutledge, representing South Carolina in the Federal Convention of 1787, reveals how bluntly a politics of interest could dominate thought. When Luther Martin of Maryland, as reported in Madison's *Notes of Debate in the Federal Convention*, argues on August 21st that "it was inconsistent with the principles of the revolution and dishonorable to the American character to have such a feature [slavery] in the Constitution," Rutledge responds that "Religion and humanity had nothing to do with this question — Interest alone is the governing principle with Nations — the true question at present is whether the Southn. States shall or shall not be parties to the Union."

Heeding Rutledge's warning, early national leaders follow a politics of interest over principle. Not one of the primary founders risks a public stance on abolition while in a position of responsibility even though most privately oppose the institution of slavery. Five of the first seven presidents (Washington, Jefferson, Madison, Monroe, and Jackson) own slaves, and all of the first seven, including John and John Quincy Adams, fully accept public silence on this issue as a price of highest office. The federal government will actually institutionalize silence, when Congress, in 1836, passes a "gag rule" to table without discussion all petitions and papers relating to slavery. These years of silence, 1789 to 1836, also mark the period of greatest expansion in American slavery; the shift from an imported African work force of four hundred thousand in the American colonies to an indigenous slave population of more than four million receives its greatest impetus in 1793 with the invention of the cotton gin.

Slavery is not the only discrepancy here. All of the major patterns of exclusion from citizenship grow stronger within the presumed benefits of an increasingly democratic culture — so much so that it is worth reexamining the conventional premise that these patterns represent "paradoxes" in the republican experiment. Black Americans, Native Americans, and women all lose ground in the first decades of the Republic even as the rights of citizenship are spreading to a broader population base: the workings of political interest and economic advantage only begin to explain these discrepancies. The discrepancies in themselves – particularly the violation of the natural rights of slaves and the subversion of Native-American property rights – receive thorough airings in public forums in the last third of the eighteenth century. Recent scholarship has documented a previously overlooked degree of protest in early republican pulpits, journals, newspapers, court records, petitions to federal and state legislatures, speeches, travel literature, pamphlets of all kinds, and the private correspondence of leading intellectuals. How then, the question remains, do early republicans justify inconsistencies that they themselves articulate?

Recognition of the contradictions in revolutionary aspiration begins in the moment of inception. "I long to hear that you have declared an independancy," Abigail Adams writes her husband, John, on March 31, 1776, " – and by the way in the new Code of Laws which I suppose it will be necessary for you to make [in the Second Continental Congress] I desire you would remember the Ladies, and be more generous and favourable to them than your ancestors." In parallels replete with mockery and irony, she appropriates the syllogisms of revolutionary rhetoric for her own purposes. Her major premise, "all Men would be Tyrants if they could," one often used by John Adams himself, supports a minor premise and direct accusation, "your Sex are Naturally Tyrannical," which, in turn, allows the standard eighteenth-century justification for Revolution as its conclusion. "If particular care and attention is not paid to the Laidies," Abigail tells John, "we are determined to foment a Rebellion, and will not hold ourselves bound by any Laws in which we have no voice, or Representation." Here, three months before the fact, are the theme, the logic, and much of the phraseology of the Declaration of Independence.

John Adams's response on April 14th deserves attention not just for its sexism ("We know better than to repeal our Masculine systems") but for its comprehensive catalogue of groupings excluded from power in the Republic. This negative catalogue, from the individual most responsible for guiding Congress toward independence, illustrates the priorities and the anxieties of revolutionary leaders caught in flux. Their question is not so much "What is an American?" as Crèvecoeur would have it in *Letters from an American Farmer* (1782) but, rather, "Who will be allowed to act as one?" In denying his wife's request, John Adams and his peers in Congress try to keep all of the margins in place:

As to your extraordinary Code of Laws, I cannot but laugh. We have been told that our Struggle has loosened the bands of Government every where. That Children and Apprentices were disobedient – that schools and Colledges were grown turbulent – that Indians slighted their Guardians and Negroes grew insolent to their Masters. But your Letter was the first Intimation that another Tribe more numerous and powerfull than all the rest were grown discontented.

Many issues are joined in this statement. The "discontented tribes" of America – workers, the poor, the young, Native Americans, blacks, and women – all enter into the universal appeal of the Revolution, while John Adams's ridicule ("I cannot but laugh"), his fear ("our Struggle has loosened the bands of Government every where"), and his pretended ignorance ("your Letter was the first Intimation") control the practical limits of achievement. It is not too much to suggest that the Republic continuously defines and redefines itself between these mixed and changing lines of hope against fear and that, in the process, the Revolution has partially fulfilled and partially reneged upon its promise each day for centuries on end.

The basic patterns in these tensions already appear in the exchange of Abigail and John Adams in 1776. Abigail argues from the premise of universal rights for a specific excluded grouping; John answers by universalizing her appeal to all excluded groupings in an exposure of special pleading. Abigail presents the basic recourse of the disenfranchised, their inclusion and participation in a "new Code of Laws," whereas John labels that expanded code "extraordinary," literally beyond the ordinary of what is to be expected. The development of the Republic in time will dictate that the extraordinary become ordinary, but in 1776 Abigail receives the answer that the disempowered regularly encounter; "be patient," John tells her. In context, this call for patience refers to the prospect of independence, but John and Abigail Adams are acutely aware that independence creates an immediate continuum of challenges, and Abigail knowingly sends another answer from out of that continuum. "I can not say that I think you very generous to the Ladies," she writes again on May 7th, "you must remember that Arbitrary power is like most other things which are very hard, very liable to be broken."

The Enlightenment supplies the lens through which both sides observe themselves in conflict, though it appeals to the powerful and to the powerless in different ways. Inasmuch as the Enlightenment emphasizes environmental conditioning over innate unchangeable character, it is radical in its thrust. And the symbol of its radicalism is an abiding faith in the efficacy of education and reason, the belief that learning transforms the present and, hence, the future forever. This is what Tom Paine means when he says in *Common Sense* that "a new method of thinking hath arisen" or that "we have it in our power to begin the world over again." It is also why Benjamin Rush, a signer of the Declaration of Independence, can expect a complete transformation simply by placing newspapers in every farmhouse. In his *Plan for the Establishment of Public Schools and the Diffusion of Knowledge in Pennsylvania* (1786), he also announces that "the golden age, so much celebrated by the poets" is already within reach; legislatures need only to establish "proper modes and places of education in every part of the state."

At the same time, the Enlightenment is a conservative force. It assumes that knowledge is harmonious in inclination, that it tends toward unity in form. The difference from Christian theology, from which it borrows much, is that it does not welcome the notion of apocalyptic conflict. Progressive in history, enlightened knowledge instinctively abhors the disobedience, turbulence, and insolence that Adams finds in discontented groups. Disruptions are the reversible signs of ignorance, symptoms of darkness that will disappear in the spread of light. Locality also gives way to universality in Enlightenment thought processes. Over and over in the period, writers and political figures strive for the largest view, and they expect to take solace in what they find there.

Conditions in the early Republic favor the conservative over the radical to the extent that the Enlightenment offers an attractive vision of unity. The virtues of progress, harmony, universality, and achieved perspective quickly attach themselves to the more concrete aspiration of political union and to its perceived concomitant, cultural homogeneity. *E Pluribus Unum,* taken from the first volume of the English *Gentlemen's Magazine* of 1731, furnishes a catch phrase for the wartime need of the whole when it is first selected by the Continental Congress for an official seal in 1776, but, six years later, when formally accepted as the national motto, it already signifies how "the many" dissolve in the solution of "the one." The radical impulses of the American Enlightenment never succumb to these homogenizing tendencies, but they are easily contained within them.

The examples of Tom Paine and Benjamin Rush convey the process of containment. For although both writers are unusually eloquent champions of minority groups, they allow the continuing urgency of the Revolution to overshadow invidious differences. As the war ends in 1783, Paine distinguishes sharply between "national character" and "local distinction" in his thirteenth *American Crisis* paper. Only the former is sacred. "Our great title is AMERICANS – our inferior one varies with the place." In the language of sacrifice, Paine argues that "something must be yielded up to make the whole secure. . . . we gain by what we give, and draw an annual interest greater than the capital." Local injustices must yield to a newly forming national identity. The goal, now that "the times that try men's souls" are over, must be to "conciliate the affections, unite the interests, and draw and keep the mind of the country together." Benjamin Rush's hopes for education in 1786 take a similar universalizing turn. His *Plan for the Establishment of Public Schools* will "convert men into republican machines." "Let our pupil be taught that he does not belong to himself," writes Rush, "but that he is public property."

The economic metaphors in these projections are indicative. Terms like "interest," "capital," "machinery," and "property" all betoken the instrumental side of the Enlightenment. As education symbolizes the radical thrust, so property and economic value sanction the conservative side of mastery, control, and order. John Adams is the first early republican to articulate how these premises converge. Stung into expression, perhaps by his wife's charges, Adams writes to James Sullivan on May 26, 1776, of the dangers in giving too much attention and sway to "the consent of the people." Consent is the moral foundation of government, but it cannot be its agent, and Adams proposes a property qualification for the participating citizen that will keep everyone in place. Otherwise, he tells Sullivan, there will be no end of controversy and altercation. "New claims will arise"; he warns, "[W]omen will demand a vote, lads from twelve to twenty-one will think their rights not enough attended to, and every man who has not a farthing, will demand an equal voice with any other, in all acts of state."

Property can qualify and contain the spirit of equality because property itself, in the conventional triad of entitlements, is a more circumscribed natural right than life and liberty. To be sure, John Locke's *An Essay Concerning the True Original, Extent, and End of Civil Government* (1690) reserves the property of the body and its labor to each individual (slavery is against both natural and positive law), but this absolute does not apply in the same way to real or landed property. In Locke's own words, "[I]t is plain, that Men have agreed to disproportionate and unequal Possession of the Earth." The basis of that inequality is also plain:

God gave the World to Men in Common; but since He gave it them for their benefit, and the greatest Conveniences of Life they were capable to draw from it, it cannot be supposed he meant it should always remain common and uncultivated. He gave it to the use of the Industrious and Rational (and *Labour* was to be *his Title* to it;) not to the Fancy or Covetousness of the Quarrelsome and Contentious.

Much remains implicit in Locke's statement of relative capacities and disproportionate rewards. What is proper industriousness, and when does it degenerate into covetousness? Who are the rational, and why do they deserve a greater benefit? How are the wrongfully contentious to be identified, and by what means are they deprived of property? For those in the act of drawing "the greatest Conveniences of Life" from the land, the task of reason is more obvious. As the statements of both Adams and Locke suggest, reason reconciles universal human rights with "a disproportionate and unequal possession of the earth." This is part of "the right Rule of Reason." No wonder, then, that eighteenth-century conceptions of property mediate between the theory and practice of the Enlightenment.

II

The most perceptive contemporary essay on discrepancies in the Enlightenment uses property to depict the recognition and acceptance of inconsistencies. Immanuel Kant, writing in 1793 "On the Common Saying: 'This May be True in Theory, but it does not Apply in Practice' " ("Uber den Gemeinspruch: 'Das mag in der Theorie richtig sein, taugt aber nicht für die Praxis' "), begins his discussion of political right by guaranteeing certain principles as a matter of natural law. These principles are "the *freedom* of every member of society as a *human being*," "the equality of each with all others as a *subject*," and "the *independence* of each member of a commonwealth as a *citizen*." Kant's principles would seem to guarantee the basic rights of all persons in the enlightened state, but his essay immediately qualifies the meaning of freedom, equality, and independence in practice.

Each of Kant's qualifications speaks to realities in American politics. Kant argues that *freedom* thrives only within a patriotic government, where patriotism requires that "everyone in the state, not excepting its head, regards the commonwealth as a maternal womb, or the land as the paternal ground from which he himself sprang." *Equality* does not obviate "the utmost inequality of the mass in the degree of its possessions, whether these take the form of physical or mental superiority over others, or of fortuitous external property." Finally, the *independence* of the citizen must be understood within accepted limitations: "The only qualification required by a citizen (apart, of course, from being an adult male) is that he must be his *own master* (*sui iuris*), and must have some *property* . . . to support himself."

The allure of the qualifying terms themselves in early republican ideology – patriotism, available property, and the independence of the citizen – helps to explain their power when turned toward exclusionary ends. In reality, subjected Africans, dragged from their homes into slavery on another continent, could hardly have regarded themselves (or been regarded) as springing from one maternal womb or from common paternal ground with other inhabitants of the New World. Native Americans, who can make such a claim, fall instead to the charge that relative superiority rightly determines degree of possession. Meanwhile, those without land and all women disappear from Kant's a priori definition of citizenship. Kant never advocates the exclusions, but his language encourages an acceptance that his principle would deny, and his discourse of mastery palliates discrepancy by fusing theory and practice.

Kant's adult male citizen, "his own master," presides as the symbol of the Enlightenment, and his ownership of property operates as both the tangible sign and logical extension of his capacity. Moreover, this conjunction of imposed reason and ownership flourishes with special vitality in the American Enlightenment, where combinations in politics and property are readily available to all free men. In America, even more than in Europe, improving the land epitomizes a rational, virtuous, masculine, and politically necessary control of the world. To return one more time to Locke's chapter on property, "subduing or cultivating the Earth, and having Dominion, we see are joyned together"; this is "the Voice of Reason confirmed by Inspiration." But only in America does the cultivation of property become the penumbra of transcendent truths. For if the ideal of education promotes the idea of reason everywhere, the cultivation of property marks the rational working out of God's plan, a phenomenon that Americans will soon term manifest destiny. In the unfolding of that destiny, reason and order turn into the same thing; so, at times, does the ownership of property and the control of other people on the land.

Put another way, the homology between reason in thought and order in land works off of a vital presumption in Enlightenment thought. The idea of cultivation can be such a literal symbol of advancing civilization in the New World because it so directly parallels the light of reason imposing harmony and order on darkness and chaos. The appeal of the vision is matched only by the facility with which Americans manipulate its terms. Within the homology, nature instructs, but it is also there to be used and even overcome — distinctions often lost sight of in the Enlightenment. The accompanying slide between reason as universal guide (in the discovery of principle) and reason as mere tool (in the mastery of fact and circumstance) is often as imperceptible, though Benjamin Franklin, as usual, sees farther and more carefully than others. "So convenient a thing it is to be a *reasonable creature*," he observes in his memoirs, "since it enables one to find or make a reason for everything one has a mind to do." The irony in these words touches an unarticulated battleground in Enlightenment thought: conflict is determined by who first defines and then exercises reason.

Within the rule of reason, the mechanics of exclusion find their logical place in the rational constructs of Anglo–American law. Specific restrictions on tenure in property law leave marginal groups in suspended animation. Early republican leaders, many of whom are legally trained, understand that ownership and use represent vastly different things in the possession of land. They exploit the difference, creating entrance requirements for other capacities (voting, for example) and easing the egalitarian entanglements in "life, liberty, and property." Only full title, ownership in fee simple, the capacity to devise and sell property without restriction of any kind, confers full citizenship in the early Republic, and the distinction rapidly becomes a means of filtering rights through assigned capacities.

Reconsider, for a moment, John Adams's enumeration of discontented tribes in the light of these legal restrictions on ownership. As "insolent Negroes" have "masters," so "Indians" have "guardians" in Adams's catalogue. Native Americans are wards of the state; the Indian trade and intercourse acts of 1790, 1793, 1796, 1799, and 1802 prohibit them from devising property to any other source than the government. In effect, they possess land but without title. Ultimate title resides in the United States of America, where it is a contingent remainder waiting to be fulfilled. The ensuing legal hold of early republicans over Native Americans is best expressed in Secretary of State Thomas Jefferson's record of a conversation with British Minister George Hammond on June 3, 1792: "What did I understand to be our right in the Indian soil? – 1. a right of preemption of their lands, that is to say the sole and exclusive right of purchasing from them whenever they should be willing to sell. 2. a right of regulating the commerce between them and the Whites." For President Washington a year later, Jefferson justifies the legality of preemption as "in the nature of a remainder after the extinguishment of a present right."

The impelling force of the doctrine is that possession *will* pass; a moment *will* come when the "present right" of Native Americans will be forever "extinguished," either having been relinquished by sale or lost through some failure in active possession. Politically, the doctrine accommodates the incessant demands and encroachments on Native-American lands throughout the nineteenth century. In treaty after treaty, Native Americans appear to have ceded their lands, but the technical release is much closer to a tenancy at will or a lease upon land, where a preempting and often peremptory owner expects possession sooner rather than later. Chief Justice John Marshall catches the direction of these pressures as he confirms the doctrine of preemption for the Supreme Court in *Johnson and Graham's Lessee* v. *McIntosh* (1823). The qualifiers in Marshall's assertions tell the story. "In the establishment of these regulations," he admits, "the rights of the original inhabitants were, in no instance, entirely disregarded; but were necessarily, to a considerable extent, impaired." Just how impaired is clear from another admission. "It has never been contended," Marshall finds himself saying, "that the Indian title amounted to nothing."

Adams's "insolent Negroes" come more rapidly and directly under the restriction of property. As property themselves – the property of another – slaves lose every capacity in the republic of laws. Three renowned early republicans (Patrick Henry, Benjamin Rush, and St. George Tucker) demonstrate how easily the amenities of ownership and the legal discourse of property evade the injustice of chattel slavery. When the Quaker Robert Pleasants charges Patrick Henry with owning slaves, the firebrand of American liberty responds that he cannot face "the general inconvenience of living without them." "I will so far pay my duty," writes Henry on January 18, 1773, "as to own the excellency and rectitude of [Christian] precepts, and to lament my want of conformity to them." Henry consoles himself in the hope that "a time will come, when an opportunity will be afforded, to abolish this lamentable evil," but for the moment, and for one steeped in the convenience of slavery, a lenient master is "the furthest advance towards Justice."

This convenience of ownership is not an exclusively Southern rationale. Although Benjamin Rush is a Pennsylvanian and the author of a famous essay against slavery in "An Address to the Inhabitants of the British Settlements in America upon Slave-Keeping" (1773), he still manages to own a slave throughout the revolutionary period. This slave, named William, finally wins his freedom in 1794 after eighteen years in bondage. As Rush's affidavit in May 1788 reveals, the moment of release for William comes "at such a time as will be just compensation for my having paid for him the full price of a slave for life." All paradox in the incident pales in the power of property to define behavior in American culture. At no point does the inherent injustice of slavery override the economic value of "just compensation," even though the same affidavit concludes that slavery is "contrary to reason and religion."

Inevitably, the possession of slaves as a right of property grows in power as slavery itself prospers in the early Republic. Success magnifies the conveniences and the value in ownership, and it undercuts the temporizing tones of leaders like Washington, Jefferson, and Henry, who hope that slavery somehow will disappear in the natural course of the Enlightenment. In exposing these hopes, the prosperity of the system projects a permanent institution, one that requires and receives a stiffer justification of apparent contradictions. St. George Tucker, the Virginia Blackstone, provides this harder line in deciding *Hudgins v. Wrights* in 1805 for the Virginia Supreme Court of Appeals. The Bill of Rights, observes Judge Tucker,

was meant to embrace the case of free citizens, or aliens only; and not by a side wind to overturn the rights of property, and give freedom to those very people whom we have been compelled from imperious circumstances to retain, generally, in the same state of bondage that they were in at the revolution, in which they have no *concern, agency,* or *interest.*

Yet if the right of property controls, it can never eliminate the troubling reality of people "retained" on the land. Stripped of all place in the Revolution, American slaves surface in the language of rebellion. They are the disembodied presence in their masters' litanies against enslavement, the nightmare figure behind the quest for independence. When, for example, the Virginians of 1776 devise a state seal, with "VIRTUS, the genius of the

commonwealth . . . treading on TYRANNY, represented by a man prostrate, a crown fallen from his head, a broken chain in his left hand, and a
scourge in his right," they borrow from traditional iconography, but the
image also reflects an aspect of daily life in revolutionary Virginia. The dusty
pictures of slavery that British Whigs conjure up from Roman tyranny, the
Spanish Inquisition, and Turkish despotism only begin to explain the compulsive allusions to chains in American rhetoric. "In the Southern Colonies,"
writes the South Carolinian David Ramsay in the opening chapter of *The
History of the American Revolution* (1789), "slavery nurtured a spirit of liberty,
among the free inhabitants." Revolutionary slaveowners bring special intensity to the ideological irony. "In them," adds Ramsay, "the haughtiness of
domination, combines with the spirit of liberty." Here and elsewhere, the
incongruity of tyranny next to liberty is resolved in a claim of property.

Women, as Adams's largest discontented tribe, face a restriction of similar
scope in their roles as wives and mothers. The first volume of Sir William
Blackstone's *Commentaries on the Laws of England* (1765–9) summarizes the
legal plight of the married woman in Anglo-American culture – a plight
that continues well into the nineteenth century:

By marriage, the husband and wife are one person in law: that is, the very being or
legal existence of the woman is suspended during the marriage, or at least is incorpo-
rated and consolidated into that of the husband: under whose wing, protection, and
cover, she performs every thing; and is therefore called in our law-french a *feme-covert.*

Disabilities turn into benefits in Blackstone's presentation of women. "So
great a favourite," he decides, "is the female sex of the laws of England."
Jefferson, no admirer of Blackstone's *Commentaries,* nonetheless illustrates how
the benevolent suspension of legal existence in the *feme-covert* (the "covered" or
"protected" or "hidden woman") carries into political practice. "The tender
breasts of ladies were not formed for political convulsion," he writes Angelica
Schuyler Church when she, in 1788, asks questions about the new Federal
Constitution. Women, he tells her, "miscalculate much their own happiness
when they wander from the true field of their influence into that of politicks."

The realized image of exclusion requires a description of presence without
place, a report in which restriction signals an assigned passivity. The hidden
woman, the preempted Native American (sometimes figured as the dying
Indian), and the submitting slave (without concern, agency, or interest) are
shadows in the social portrait of "every man under his vine and under his fig
tree," the republican refrain of communal happiness. As property lends a
picture of independence, so its absence renders the person without it invisible
and politically unimportant. So, too, invisibility is a verification in any
calculated evasion of Enlightenment principle.

This end point, the strange act of verifying unimportance, takes on special significance in democratic society and has unique consequence in a revolutionary one. *The Federalist* (1787–8) provides a dramatic model in the early Republic. It shows how patterns of dismissal in a hegemonic text can channel the flow of principle and, hence, the availability of rights, in a culture of consensus. Woman, as subject, appears just twice in the eighty-five papers of *The Federalist*, and the theme of each passage is a negative capacity: the dangers of female intrigue in politics in *Federalist No. 6* and the inability of married women to convey property in *Federalist No. 83*. The union may indeed represent "an empire in many respects the most interesting in the world," but the gender implications of Hamilton's summary in *Federalist No. 1* must be taken quite literally. As he tells us, "the important question [is] whether societies of men are really capable or not of establishing good government from reflection and choice."

Of the fourteen references to Native Americans in *The Federalist*, all but one concern hostility, conflict, and the need for greater federal control of the problem. The exception, curiously enough, involves an admission of failure in overall understanding. "What description of Indians are to be deemed members of a State, is not yet settled, and has been a question of perplexity and contention in the federal councils," writes Madison in *Federalist No. 42*. What is an Indian? Publius might as well ask. Earlier, *Federalist No. 24* already has imposed a working definition for policy purposes. "The savage tribes on our Western frontier," writes Hamilton, "ought to be regarded as our natural enemies." Barely visible, though portrayed as an encircling danger in *Federalist No. 25*, these tribes appear only as people of darkness in the (as yet) untamed wilderness.

Publius has more trouble with the subject of slavery, but even here his treatments remain cursory. In eighty-four of the eighty-five papers of *The Federalist*, there are but four references to American slavery; all are short, and just one, on the subject of importation in *Federalist No. 42*, takes a normative stand. Only in *Federalist No. 54* does Publius allow himself to be caught in an extensive analysis of "the mixed character of persons and of property." Elaboration here is simply inescapable. The constitutional proposal that counts slaves in the census for congressional representation has been a source of bitter national debate in 1788.

The political embarrassments that James Madison encounters in *Federalist No. 54* explain why early republican leaders resist detailed discussions of slavery whenever they can. If slaves are property, then they might enter into estimates of taxation, which are founded on property, but they should not enter into tabulations for representation, which are regulated by a census of persons. If instead slaves are "moral persons" – "if the laws were to restore the rights which have been taken away," Publius posits in a telling phrase – then "negroes could no longer be refused an equal share of representations with the other inhabitants"; or, one might add, an equal share in any other civil right.

Of the three constitutional provisions that allow for slavery without ever mentioning the term – representation (Art. 1, Sect. 2), the importation of slaves (Art. 1, Sect. 9) and the first fugitive law (Art. 4, Sect. 2) – only this first reference presents an insurmountable problem for Publius. Madison hardly mentions the fugitive law and easily handles slave importation, both in *Federalist No. 42*. In conventional Enlightenment terms, a "barbarism of modern policy" like the importation of slaves can be expected to disappear in time, possibly even in 1808, when the constitutional provision protecting it lapses. Representation, on the other hand, raises the cardinal principle of free government and forces Publius to deal more directly with slavery in a demo-cratic republic. In *Federalist No. 54* the mixed character of slaves as property and as persons turns out to be "their true character" under law. It is with "propriety" that the Constitution adopts the "compromising expedient" of counting slaves as three-fifths of a free person.

The argument from property law is an expected one within the patterns of marginalization just noted, and yet even Madison appears to have been uncertain about the result. Uncertainties, in fact, are never far from the surface in any of these arguments of exclusion. John Marshall's hesitations over the impairment of Indian rights, St. George Tucker's vehemence in the "imperious circumstances" of slavery, and Blackstone's complete removal of "the very being" of the married woman all contain within them the whisper of an opposing argument. There is the felt pressure of a righteous response, the tacit knowledge that some republicans will find the argument a shame-ful one.

This realization becomes acute in *Federalist No. 54*. Madison struggles with the ramifications of his claims, and the nature of his struggle brushes the very edge of the Enlightenment. It is as if the two virtues of the age, the rule of reason and universal aspiration, enter the lists against each other. Indeed, Publius's central argument comes from another persona altogether; it appears entirely in quotation marks that signify "the reasoning which an advocate for the Southern interests might employ on this subject." We listen to a voice within a voice within a voice – from Madison, to Publius, to southern advocate:

"Let the case of the slaves be considered, as it is in truth, a peculiar one. Let the compromising expedient of the Constitution be mutually adopted, which regards them as inhabitants, but as debased by servitude below the equal level of free inhabitants; which regards the slave as divested of two fifths of the *man*."

Missing in the voice of this distanced speaker is justice, where justice, in eighteenth-century terms, completes the recognitions of commonality and of right between lawgiver and subject. The language of peculiarity in *Federalist No. 54* is one of the first references to "the peculiar institution," and, as such, it violates the universal application on which the harmonies of the Enlightenment depend. Clearly, the speaker's direct association of the particular with separate verities ("as it is in truth, a peculiar one") would have jarred against the sensibilities of Madison's first readers. But why would Madison have wished to undercut his own argument? The southern advocate, after all, is his creation.

Publius is of two minds. Reaching through the mask after pages of silence, he divulges that the southern advocate "fully reconciles" him to the "propriety" of the constitutional solution, but part of him remains unconvinced, and that part wishes to be on record. If "such is the reasoning" of the southern advocate, he warns in his own voice, then "it may appear to be a little strained in some points." While failing to deter Madison's formal conclusions, this "strain" puts everyone on notice. Perhaps, as well, Publius cannot quite bring himself to mouth this shabbiest of all arguments in *The Federalist*. The greatest of early Roman consuls, Publius Valerius Poplicola is official lawgiver and first friend of the people. For this most exalted of all classical republican identifications to announce that servitude logically debases inhabitants to the degree of divesting them of two-fifths of their humanity is debasing in itself. Far better to cast the whole issue at one remove.

The interesting thing in Madison's calculated distance is his consciousness that slavery must at least acknowledge higher terms. The peculiar institution cannot stand for order and convenience in a part of republican life without some loss of principle and coherence in the whole. The philosophical distance between Madison, Publius, and the southern advocate may have been slight. All three are southern politicians on the issue of slavery, and the strain between them is "little" in *Federalist No. 54*. Even so, the deliberate invention of distance creates a tension beyond the gloss of discrepancies. We enter, however minimally, the radical hope of the Enlightenment, the insistence that humankind must use its discovered capacities to improve the lot of all people.

III

Moments of breakage in the dominant discourse indicate other ways of thinking, but they do not articulate the thought itself, and the problems in reconstructing opinions now lost are immense. Appearances and realities are substantially more difficult to decipher in the voices that speak without property behind them. The Lockean right rule of reason is a wholly different thing for those who are ruled, and the aspirations of the Enlightenment take on separate meanings among those who are barred from its dispensations. To be heard at all in eighteenth-century public forums, the defeated warrior, the debased slave, and the invisible woman must speak in fractions of them-selves. They must exploit the discourse that denies them. To catch the sound of these voices (frequently no more than a murmur in translation, a decontextualized outburst, an ambiguous image, or a gesture), the joint venture of historian and critic must probe the lost circumstances, the limited vehicles, and the hidden costs of performance. Creativity in these speakers often resides in strategies of survival now taken for granted.

Some constraints on marginal voices in the early Republic are specific; others general. Eighteenth-century Native-American efforts, now in fragmen-tary form, contend with the near certainty of their own disappearance. Slave accounts must fight to create the sound of their own worth. The narratives of women strive against gender restrictions that dignify accommodation over assertion. Simultaneously, all of these voices suffer within the controlling aesthetic of a consensual literature. They lack the communities of auditors in the public sphere that legitimize the word in eighteenth-century literature, and the handicap is a severe one. Because literary production is profoundly social throughout the period, the circles of white male citizens that nurture and sustain the gentleman of letters can successfully reject the voices beyond their ranks or, alternatively, appropriate them for their own purposes.

Predictably, the most famous Native-American utterance is one that early republicans love to hear. Chief Logan's speech about the gratuitous murder of his family in 1774 epitomizes the vanishing Indian, first, in Thomas Jeffer-son's *Notes on the State of Virginia* (1784–5) and, after, in endless editions of *McGuffey's Reader.* Memorized for generations and thematized in James Feni-more Cooper's *The Last of the Mohicans* (1826), it confirms the hopes and minimizes the fears of the dominant culture. Logan, a Cayuga chieftain among the Mingos in New York, espouses a familiar Christian charity ("I appeal to any white man to say, if ever he entered Logan's cabin hungry, and he gave him not meat; if he ever came cold and naked, and he clothed him not"). He fights only when treacherously attacked by an identifiable villain ("I had even thought to have lived with you, but for the injuries of one man"), and he suffers defeat with a stoicism that limits the agony for all concerned ("Logan never felt fear"). Most memorable of all, he disappears without a trace ("There runs not a drop of my blood in the veins of any living creature. . . . Who is there to mourn for Logan? – Not one"). The truly noble savage does not complicate his story – or the stories of others – by remaining behind.

Take, however, a more practical and characteristic Native-American address: the Seneca Chief Cornplanter's speech before President Washington in Philadelphia in 1790. Cornplanter, or Kiontwogky, refers back to the military campaign of 1779, when revolutionary troops under orders from General Washington ravage and destroy Iroquois civilization in the western parts of New York and Pennsylvania, but his real preoccupation is the continuing threat to Iroquois property six years after the second Treaty of Fort Stanwix (1784) supposedly has secured all remaining Native-American lands:

When your army entered the country of the Six Nations, we called you *Caunotaucarius,* the Town Destroyer; and to this day when that name is heard, our women look behind them and turn pale, and our children cling to the knees of their mothers. Our councilors and warriors . . . are grieved with the fears of their women and children, and desire that it may be buried so deep as to be heard no more. When you gave us peace, we called you father, because you promised to secure us in possession of our lands. Do this, and so long as the lands shall remain, the beloved name will remain in the heart of every Seneca.

Cornplanter's play upon alternative nomenclature confirms the contrast in civilizations. He speaks as the political leader of a distinct people and not, like Logan, as the tragic warrior whose worthiness transcends culture boundaries in a claim of universal sympathy. The distress of living women and children, the need to overcome cultural trauma, above all, the need to secure threatened lands — these concerns dominate Cornplanter's social agenda. The fullest implication of dissimilarity appears in the juxtaposition of Washington's names: "Father of His Country" against "Town Destroyer." To understand that Washington can be both "father" and "destroyer" is to see the absolute chasm between the new American states and Native-American tribes; the development of the one means catastrophe for the other. Cornplanter brings few illusions to this unequal conflict. As he says, it is "as if our want of strength had destroyed our rights."

The creativity of Cornplanter's speech comes in the conceit that Washington must still earn the title of father. Note, in addition, that all naming depends upon the tangibility and endorsement of property for its existence. Washington first merits the designation through his promise to secure Native-American possession of Iroquois lands, but "the beloved name" lasts only "so long as the lands shall remain." Cornplanter knows that he must speak through Anglo-American norms of property to be heard at all, but he cleverly uses the device to question the fondest epithet in all of early republican lore, that of Washington as the Father of His Country. Its very effectiveness suggests why this speech cannot be memorable in the dominant culture. Cornplanter mobilizes an ignominous legacy, one in which broken republican promises devastate a helpless people. How many, in regarding that legacy, wish to contemplate George Washington as the destroyer of towns?

Native-American perceptions flicker in the clash of ideological perspectives, in the slippages of translation, in the preoccupations of transcription, and in the misunderstandings that accumulate between a literate and an oral culture. In these fragmentary records, the sign of thought is sometimes clearest in processes of reversal. Thus, although Native Americans initially fail to comprehend how the rigid binding power of a written statement might differ from the more pliant meanings that memory and oral consensus generate in tribal exchange, they soon grasp their practical disadvantage in cross-cultural debate. Deliberations over the Treaty of Fort Stanwix between the Six Nations of the Iroquois Confederacy and the Commissioners of the United States in October of 1784 take a bizarre twist when the Iroquois negotiators are the ones who want a written record of proceedings while their white counterparts refuse that record, insisting instead on the traditional Native-American exchange of wampum belts to recall provisions of speech. The Iroquois have come to realize that the legalistic and adversarial strategies of their opponents manipulate the flexibility in oral performance and prey upon the freedom of interpretation that aurality allows. They have begun to see that written evidence alone protects them in an agreement with the United States.

The thoughts of eighteenth-century Native Americans attain print mostly in translated expressions of anger, sorrow, and loss – reasonable tones for participants who are witnessing the total destruction of their way of life. Still, the overall effect in the literature is a stylistics of plaint. We are left with patterns of lamentation that convey little of the underlying vitality in tribal culture. The Shawnee Prophet, Tenskwatawa, the most eloquent exponent of Native-American nationalism in the period, typifies the strengths and weaknesses of the genre. His speech before the Tuscarora branch of the Iroquois Confederacy in 1806 supposedly rallies all tribes to action, but the published record, especially the Prophet's peroration, is more a chronicle of paralyzing declension:

They [all tribes] will vanish like a vapor from the face of the earth; their very history will be lost in forgetfulness, and the places that now know them will know them no more. We are driven back until we can retreat no farther; our hatchets are broken; our bows are snapped; our fires are extinguished; a little longer and the white man will cease to persecute us, for we shall cease to exist.

The words themselves may be a true transcription. They accurately convey the plight of Native Americans, and their predictions are fulfilled when the battles of Tippecanoe and the Thames decimate the tribes of the Northwest

Territory in 1811 and 1813, but the overall tone also evokes classical thren-
ody and the popular eighteenth-century graveyard school of poets. That
melancholy tone, which will soon achieve its American apogee in William
Cullen Bryant's "Thanatopsis" (1817), stands for Anglo-American literary
sensibility in the early Republic. All in all, the Prophet's mood is suspi-
ciously conventional in its appeal, and the general effect of quiescence makes
his rhetoric seem even more dubious.

Early republicans hear and report what they want to hear and report.
Where, in this speech, are the radical conceptions of property and the galvanizing pride in Native-American ways that enable the Prophet and his twin
brother, Tecumseh, to consolidate the tribes of the Indiana Territory against
Governor William Henry Harrison? The Prophet's fatalistic description of a
dying culture, with its obverse of western lands now safe from savage attack
("our hatchets are broken; our bows are snapped"), supplies an attractive image
for white Americans to absorb. Shawnee hopes, in contrast, directly threaten
the dominant culture. Tenskwatawa and Tecumseh seek a separate, unified
Native-American nation that whites would be compelled to respect, and they
begin by challenging early republican ideas of property. All tribal territory,
argue the Shawnee leaders, must be held in common beyond the capacity of
individual tribes to cede or otherwise alienate. Here, in principle, is a direct
counter to the federal doctrine of preemption.

To the extent that the shock of devastation does dominate published
Native-American oratory, it presents other problems in interpretation. The
pathos of loss robs both speaker and listener of context. When, in the
Philadelphia meetings of 1790, the aged Seneca chieftain Gayashuta (Kaiagh-
shota) "wonders at his own shadow, it has become so little," the synecdoche
of personal outline for larger culture transmits nothing of the social complexity and agrarian prosperity that Gayashuta has witnessed all along the frontier in Iroquois towns of up to seven hundred people. Only a shadow is
disappearing in his speech. The theme of loss feeds the expectations of the
dominant culture. "We are afraid if we part with any more lands the white
people will not suffer us to keep as much as will be sufficient to bury our
dead," complains the Creek leader Doublehead (Chuquacuttague) at the
Treaty of Colerain in June of 1796. Unfair treatment is the obvious thrust of
this passage, but the language also imparts a message of breakdown, and, in
Enlightenment terms, this breakdown forms part of an irresistible antithesis.
Whatever the cost, Native-American disintegration computes as an acceptable price of early republican growth.

How does one sort the elements of integrity in these appropriated narratives? The task, in a sense, is to catch the separate awareness, the canniness of
address, and the assertion of value that sometimes punctuate these speeches.

For instance, even though the Seneca Chief Sagoyewatha, known as Red Jacket, responds to the missionary work of Joseph Cram in 1805 with yet another sketch of Native-American decline, he manages to turn the worn theme into a powerful assertion of cultural relativity and Native-American worth. "You have got our country, but you are not satisfied," Red Jacket accuses Cram. "You want to force your religion upon us." Unanswerable questions illustrate the point. "If [the Bible] was intended for us as well as for you, why has not the Great Spirit given it to us?" "How shall we know when to believe, being so often deceived by the white people?" "If there is but one religion, why do you white people differ so much about it?" Slowly, the sarcasm in these interrogatives builds into something much greater. Red Jacket exposes the insatiable nature of white expansion in the name of a more philosophical Native-American containment and contentment:

[God] has made a great difference between his white and red children. . . . Since he has made so great a difference between us in other things, why may not we conclude that he has given us a different religion, according to our understanding? . . . We are satisfied. Brother! We do not wish to destroy your religion, or to take it from you. We only want to enjoy our own.

Victories in debate of this kind afford glimpses of a character and perception beyond pathos. In a similar flash of recognition from late 1781, the Delaware leader Captain Pipe (Hopocan) wields a single question to destroy the logic for a British alliance in the Revolution. "Who of us can believe," Pipe asks British commanders in council at Detroit, "that you can love a people of a different colour from your own, better than those who have a white skin, like yourselves?" The power of the realization should not be forgotten in its failure to change the situation. Native Americans must choose sides between white opponents in the Revolution, and they lose everything no matter how they choose. "We were struck with astonishment at hearing we were forgot [in the Treaty of Paris of 1783]," the Mohawk Thayandangea, called Joseph Brant, reminds the British secretary for colonial affairs in 1785, "we could not believe it possible such firm friends and allies could be so neglected by a nation remarkable for its honor and glory."

Occasionally, adroit minds make the most of both difference and similarity in a claim of justice. On August 13, 1793, a letter from the Seven Nations to the United States of America protests white encroachment north of the Ohio River by resisting the whole notion of money for land ("money to us is of no value, and to most of us unknown"). A better alternative, the letter continues, would be to give the money set aside for Native-American lands directly to the poor white settlers who do want it and who now steal land in search of it. The near Swiftian play upon difference does not, however, prevent another satire based on the similarity of independent cultures. The same letter infers a confusion of "common justice" in federal proposals and concessions: "[you] seem to expect that because you have at last acknowledged our independence, we should for such a favor surrender to you our country."

Communications of this sort demonstrate that the collapse of Native-American peoples does not issue from a failure in understanding; neither is the larger failure culture specific. Little Beaver, a Wyandotte speaker at the 1790 conference in Philadelphia, bluntly assigns blame where it belongs. "Do then what you said," he tells federal representatives, "restrain your people if they do wrong." Manifestly, the weak United States governments of the Confederacy and federal union cannot restrain their citizens. Early republican authorities fail to enforce even minimal policies and regulations on an exploding and acquisitive frontier population.

One ideological contribution of the Enlightenment is to imply rational controls that do not exist in white expansion and government policy. In his "Observations Concerning the Increase of Mankind" (1751), Benjamin Franklin shows how the paradigm of light can seem to stand in Nature for the rational exclusion of "all Blacks and Tawneys," where Native Americans fall under the latter category. "And while we are, as I may call it, *Scouring* our Planet, by clearing America of Woods, and so making this Side of our Globe reflect a brighter Light to the Eyes of Inhabitants in Mars or Venus," writes Franklin, "why should we in the Sight of Superior Beings, darken its People?" Less agile than the ironic Franklin, George Washington poses a rudimentary conflict between refinement and savagery. In a letter to Congressman James Duane on September 7, 1783, he explains that "the gradual extension of our Settlements will as certainly cause the Savage as the Wolf to retire; both being beasts of prey tho' they differ in shape."

Commentary of this sort keeps its speakers remote from all feeling of human obligation and away from the emotional depths in Native-American responses. "Are you determined to crush us?" Cornplanter asks Washington in 1790. "If you are, tell us so; that those of our nation who have become your children, and have determined to die so, may know what to do." The primal eloquence of this comment comes in loss realized and properly measured, but Cornplanter's words rise to another level in their recognition that republican light and refinement reflect only power and not reason. That recognition, by extension, leaves early republicans wholly *without* eloquence.

Washington simply cannot be memorable in response. His formal answer to Cornplanter, on December 29, 1790, regrets the past, promises protection, gives "suitable presents," condemns "bad Indians," and proclaims justice. But justice in the realm of cross-cultural relations already has been stripped of its philosophical foundations in eighteenth-century thought. As

Jefferson, the theorist, already has foreseen in vindicating Virginia land claims in 1773–4: "whoever shall attempt to trace the claims . . . or reconcile the invasions made on the native Indians to the natural rights of mankind, will find that he is pursuing a Chimera, which exists only in his own imagination, against the evidence of indisputable facts." The fragments that remain in the lost record of Native-American expression catch the early Republic in its least favorable light.

IV

The poignancy of the Native-American situation lies in the ephemeral moment; that of slavery, in its growing permanence. If the first is more psychologically dramatic in eighteenth-century life, the second is far more ideologically ominous. Early republicans "discover" indigenous peoples and then immediately forget them by displacing them in the destructive push of their own prosperity, but they "create" slavery in the name of that prosperity, and it flourishes as part of republican growth. Slavery also interrupts Enlightenment norms and the rhetoric of American liberty in more decisive ways. As Patrick Henry expresses these troubling divergences to Robert Pleasants in 1773, "[W]hat adds to the wonder is, that this abominable practice, has been introduced in the most enlightened Ages, Times that seem to have pretensions to boast of high improvement." "Would any one believe that I am master of Slaves," Henry muses. Belief in the presumed contradiction questions many other eventualities. "I know not where to stop," Henry tells Pleasants, "I could say many things on this subject, a serious review of which give a gloomy perspective to future times."

Just how ominously slavery hangs over the republican experiment is evident when the same awareness comes from the mouth of a slave. "I have nothing more to offer than what General Washington would have had to offer, had he been taken by the British and put to trial by them," responds a black defendant after the Gabriel Prosser slave revolt of 1800. "I have adventured my life in endeavouring to obtain the liberty of my countrymen, and am a willing sacrifice in their cause." Awareness, in fact, is doubled and inverted in transmission. These words survive through a white Virginian who witnesses the trial of the insurrectionists in a Richmond courtroom and who, years later, conveys this testimony to an outside observer, the Englishman Robert Sutcliff who, in turn, records them in *Travels in Some Parts of North America* (1811). Delay and indirection, not to mention the accident of survival, all hint at the dangers in a language of communal threat.

The logic of further rebellion is inescapable in the slave's response. The hope for a black Washington and its corollary, the fear of a black Washington, flow from Locke's premises that slaves always exist *"in a State of War"* and that this state of war is especially acute in a culture dedicated to the protection of individual rights. The practical implications for America are present as early as Arthur Lee's "Address on Slavery" in 1767. Noting for the *Virginia Gazette* that the ancients were "brought to the very brink of ruin by the insurrections of their Slaves," Lee predicts "even more fatal consequences from the greater prevalence of Slavery among us." Lee is himself of a slave-owning family. "On us, or on our posterity," he warns, "the inevitable blow, must, one day, fall." And when it falls, no excuse can or should be given. The "Bondage of the Africans" supersedes every relative moral consideration. "There cannot be in nature, there is not in all history, an instance in which every right of men is more flagrantly violated."

The mutual appreciation in master and slave of intolerable ideological contradictions has a compound effect on African American commentaries. Foremost, the awareness of contradiction in the dominant culture bends an already virulent racism into a compulsion against every human entitlement for African Americans, including the most common rights of life, liberty, and property. This compulsion must be resisted by the African-American writer at all costs. At the same time, the inevitability of the logic of further rebellion makes the logic itself dangerous and, therefore, unacceptable as a form of expression – particularly as a form of African-American expression. For while the white citizen who employs that logic is merely silenced (the *Virginia Gazette* refuses to publish a sequel to Arthur Lee's essay), African Americans are destroyed (the insurrectionist of 1800 is immediately executed as he himself, "a willing sacrifice," foresees). The eighteenth-century African-American commentator who wishes to avoid this martyrdom must resist racist impositions without attempting any sustained narrative of final consequences. The result, at its best, is a disciplined language of subordinate intentions, one that vexes the surfaces of cultural repressions by moving just below them.

The typical eighteenth-century African-American text must question through its accommodations. The petitions to state legislatures against slavery by African Americans during the Revolution draw powerfully on the negative parallels between American enslavement and British tyranny, but they do so, as a petition from New Hampshire slaves on November 12, 1779, makes apparent, "in opposing the efforts of tyranny and oppression over the country in which we ourselves have been so long injuriously enslaved," and not to create a new dimension in rebellion. A similar petition from African Americans in Massachusetts on January 13, 1777, expresses "Astonishment that It has Never Bin Consirdered that Every Principle from which Amarica has Acted in the Cours of their unhappy Deficultes with Great Briton Pleads

Stronger than A thousand arguments in favowrs of your petioners," but, once again, the rhetorical emphasis is on a common effort within "the Lawdable Example of the Good People of these States." A justified "spirit to resent" is carefully circumscribed within the framework of supplicating petitioners.

Notably, these African American accommodations are not without their own flavor and bite. Contending with the usual Anglo-American assumption of cultural superiority over peoples of color, Caesar Sarter, an ex-slave writing for the *Essex Journal and Merrimack Packet* (August 17, 1774), boldly reverses the assumption for enslaved African Americans and, by insinuation, for slave cultures everywhere:

Though we are brought from a land of ignorance, it is as certain that we are brought from a land of comparative innocence – from a land that flows, as it were, with Milk and Honey – and the greater part of us carried, where we are, not only deprived of every comfort of life: But subjected to all the tortures that a most cruel inquisitor could invent, or a capricious tyrant execute and where we are likely, from the vicious examples before us, to become ten fold more the children of satan, than we should probably, have been in our native country.

In an ironic play upon the golden rule, Sarter inserts another reversal, that of master and slave, so that slaveowners may learn "to do to others, as you would, that they would do to you." The denouement of this section, couched in direct address that forces every reader into the role of slave, moves from uneasy feelings of conscience to the more substantial and direct sting of the body. Abduction, separation, enslavement, importation, sale and resale follow in misery after misery. "And after all this," entones Sarter, "you must be plied with that conclusive argument, that cat-o'nine tails to reduce you to what your inhuman masters would call Reason."

The key to successful assertion involves the use but not the uncritical acceptance of dominant cultural norms. Accordingly, although eighteenth-century African American commentaries and other early abolitionist texts tend to extol Christian training, they do not allow the blessings of conversion to obscure prior validations of African culture. Olaudah Equiano's *The Interesting Narrative of the Life of Olaudah Equiano or Gustavus Vassa, The African* (1789) and Broteer Furro's *A Narrative of the Life And Adventures of Venture, A Native Of Africa* (1798), along with the Quaker abolitionist Anthony Benezet's *Some Historical Account of Guinea* (1771), all insist upon the vitality, the prosperity, and general happiness of African communities before they are destroyed by slave traders. These adroit balances between African assertion and Christian acceptance represent a deliberate variation, or range of responses to racism – so much so that the balances themselves supply a gauge of literary creativity at work. As African assertion proclaims an original coherence and integrity of human identity, so Christian acceptance demon-

strates intellectual, emotional, and moral capacities of adjustment that establish a claim for equal treatment in Anglo-American culture.

The all but universal embrace of Christianity in slave narratives figures on
a variety of levels. Conversion not only proves capacity and gives equal access
to theological claims, it commandeers the religious voice, the first voice of
revolution in Anglo-American culture. Fully aware of the appropriation in
1774, Caesar Sarter's "Essay on Slavery" uses biblical lore to convey the
prospect of revolt that he dare not raise directly. "Only be pleased to recollect
the miserable end of Pharoah, in Consequences of his refusal to set those at
Liberty, whom he had unjustly reduced to cruel servitude," Sarter reminds
his real audience ("those who are advocates for holding the Africans in
Slavery").

In finer hands, the same device becomes a more sophisticated critique of
American slavery. Phillis Wheatley's letter to the Reverend Samson Occom
on February 11, 1774, draws a parallel between the ancient Hebrews and the
eighteenth-century African Americans who live and suffer under "Modern
Egyptians" and "the Exercise of oppressive Power" in the United States. In
the poet's account, printed widely in New England newspapers, civil and
religious liberty are inseparably united. Together, they stimulate a "Love of
Freedom" that is "impatient of Oppression and pants for Deliverance."
Wheatley surely speaks in part from personal experience; her manumission
takes place just months before her letter to Occom. But since this love of
freedom is a principle "implanted" directly by God, Wheatley can raise its
radical implications without the risk of counterattack. There is safety in
leaving the political details to God's separate and inscrutable agenda. As
Wheatley tells Occom, "God grants Deliverance in his own way and Time."

The mixture of urgency and resignation in Wheatley's letter is a source of
its power, and the combination captures something of the general precarious-
ness of African American life in the early Republic. Deliverance in her case
seems to have come through a six-week stay in England in the spring and
summer of 1773. "Since my return to America," she writes David Wooster
on October 18, 1773, "my Master, has at the desire of my friends in England
given me my freedom." The slave's dependence on external wishes and
protection is one message in this letter. She can speak with such phenomenal
yearning of her love of freedom precisely because freedom and life itself in
eighteenth-century culture remain so tentative for African Americans.
Though free, Phillis Wheatley will die in poverty at the age of thirty-one,
and the identity she carries to an unknown grave will still bespeak the
oppression that she pants against. Purchased "for a trifle" at the age of eight
in Boston Harbor, the future poet automatically takes the surname of her
masters, but John and Susanna Wheatley also mark the occasion, July 11,

1761, in a more specific manner. They name their newest possession after the *Phillis,* the slave schooner that brings her to America.

Somewhere in every slave account the scars of experience overwhelm the themes of success and acculturation. Success, after all, is the irresistible metaphor of the writer who has overcome prolonged illiteracy, and the typical slave narrative complements that triumph by accentuating the highest moments of assimilation (literacy, conversion, manumission, and marriage). Unavoidably, however, acculturation in slaves includes the domination of them. On the way to literacy, Olaudah Equiano is beaten until he will accept his Christian name Gustavus Vassa. James Gronniosaw, in *A Narrative of the Most Remarkable Particulars in the Life of James Albert Ukawsaw Gronniosaw* (1770), learns not to swear from a pious older slave who is then whipped by their master for presuming to convey the lesson. Christianity in both master and slave does not prevent flogging in *The Life, History, and Unparalleled Sufferings of John Jea, the African Preacher* (1811). Neither does manumission protect African Americans from the fixed cruelty and injustice of a racist culture. *A Brief Account of the Life, Experiences, Travels, and Gospel Labours of George White, an African* (1810) may recount another successful rise from slavery, in this instance to the vocation of Methodist minister, but the free and converted George White must still endure the regular obstruction of white Methodists, who tell him that "it was the devil who was pushing me to preach."

The starkest recognition of permanent injustice comes from Broteer Furro in his narrative as Venture Smith. Presented by his supporters and publisher as a Benjamin Franklin out of slavery, Venture Smith undercuts his own account of conversion, marriage, freedom, and material success with story after story about how white neighbors swindle him in business. These stories culminate in a New York courtroom where leading citizens cheat him and then amuse themselves by taunting their victim in his "unmerited misfortune." Not surprisingly, Venture Smith's account of this final incident has nothing to do with either the satisfaction or the reasonable tones of a Franklinian "way to wealth":

Such a proceeding as this committed on a defenceless stranger, almost worn out in the hard service of the world, without any foundation in reason or justice, whatever it may be called in a Christian land, would in my native country have been branded as a crime equal to highway robbery. But Captain Hart was a *white gentleman,* and I a *poor African,* therefore it was *all right, and good enough for the black dog.*

After sixty years and considerable success in America, Broteer as Venture remains "a defenceless stranger" in a foreign land. Racism leaves him upholding a homeland that is destroyed out from under him as a boy of seven.

Plainly, Venture is both acculturated and unacculturated as he finds himself consciously and unconsciously betwixt and between. The child who watches as his father is tortured to death by slavers in Africa is himself the father whose "lips are closed in silence and in grief" over the failures of his own children in America. Two separate standards join the traumatized child and angry man in their mutual questioning of "any foundation in reason or justice." The first standard is the sheer materiality of success. Venture, so named by a master who stamps his investment on the person of his slave, quickly accepts ownership as the primary social value. At one level, *A Narrative of the Life and Adventures of Venture* chronicles the material transformations from the first sale of Broteer for four gallons of rum and a piece of calico to the final accumulations of Venture ("more than one hundred acres of land, and three habitable dwelling houses"). Numbers and exchanges, fair and unfair, direct this narrative with bitter consequence. The rationale of the life in the value of property is vulnerable to the worst instrumentalisms of Enlightenment thought, not excluding slavery itself.

And yet a second and higher standard of success keeps Broteer and Venture together. The man from the child holds the fact of his liberty most dear. "My freedom is a privilege which nothing else can equal," concludes Venture on the last page of his narrative. Pride mixes with pain in this assessment. Personal freedom and physical accumulation form a traditional combination in America, but neither in life nor in language can Venture find rest within the combination. Nothing explains the alienation in the eighteenth-century African American text better than the way infringements on liberty and property have driven Venture Smith to reject his own success as a cultural identification. In the end, anger drives his narrative. For Venture, the sorrows of Solomon are more memorable than the joys of salvation. His last words are from Ecclesiastes: "Vanity of vanities, all is vanity."

Cognizance of the special crosscurrents, intentions, pressures, and disillusionments in eighteenth-century African American writings should aid interpretation of another work, perhaps the most misunderstood text of the entire period, Jupiter Hammon's essay to his fellow slaves in New York. *An Address to the Negroes in the State of New-York* (1787) shares many of the qualities already examined, and it, too, mirrors the dominant culture in a manner that sheds light upon its literary craft. In retrospect, we can appreciate many of the generic considerations that will dominate early African American discourse: the authenticating preface by white publishers, Hammon's occasional punning on his slave status ("I am, Gentlemen, Your Servant," he informs the African Society in the City of New York), his stress on education (most conspicuously on the capacity to read), and his resort to a double frame of reference in which "the poor, despised, and miserable state" of his auditors catches both the eternal spirit and the temporal body so as to condemn slavery within the safer condemnation of impiety.

Problems have occurred when twentieth-century readers misconstrue Jupiter Hammon's message of obedience to masters and his acceptance of slavery for himself. More attention should be given to the opening tones of the address; they are ones of overwhelming sorrow in the slave's fallen state, a sorrow that is "at times, almost too much for human nature to bear." With considerable finesse, Hammon's introduction also signifies that the price of addressing African Americans is white support. The same paragraph establishes, first, that "a number of the white people . . . thought [my writings] might do good among their servants" and, second, that the writings themselves should encourage greater solidarity among those servants. "I think you will be more likely to listen to what is said," Hammon observes, "when you know it comes from a negro, one [of] your own nation and colour, and therefore can have no interest in deceiving you, or in saying any thing to you, but what he really thinks is your interest and duty to comply with." The suggestion of a separate nation is arresting; so is the strong implication of insincerity in the dominant culture.

The prevalence of humble tones does not keep Hammon from asserting "that liberty is a great thing, and worth seeking for." The proof of the assertion lies not just in the slave's hopes but in "the conduct of the white-people, in the late war." Necessarily understated, the hypocrisy of the Revolution on slavery is nonetheless present in this essay. "I must say," notes Hammon, "that I have hoped that God would open their eyes, when they were so much engaged for liberty, to think of the state of the poor blacks, and to pity us." Interestingly, however, Hammon never relies on that pity. "If God designs to set us free," he writes late in the essay, "he will do it, in his own time, and way."

Christian humility is not without its edges. Most of the essay calls for reliance on the next world but with an immediate sociological significance. The next world, like this one, divides the free and the enslaved, but heaven and hell, an eternal division, will separate its peoples on the basis of merit rather than race. The democracy of Hammon's heaven is an impressive referent for future use. "There are some things very encouraging in God's word for such ignorant creatures as we are;" advises Hammon, "for God hath not chosen the rich of this world." Then, in an understated humor that reemphasizes the horror of the present, Hammon defines "the greatest fools" as those who become "miserable in this world, and in the world to come" by making themselves "slave here, and slaves forever." "What," he asks, at the age of seventy, "is forty, fifty, or sixty years, when compared to eternity?"

As the work of a slave, *An Address to the Negroes in the State of New-York* is doubly bound by the dictates of a consensual literature, and Jupiter Hammon's stress upon obedience to God's plan participates in a further complication of these conditions. Although he uses the scriptural injunction of St. Paul to the Ephesians (6:5–8) to remind his slave audience of the obedience of servant to master, the discussion allows a useful qualification. "Now whether it is right, and lawful, in the sight of God, for them to make slaves of us or not," Hammon reminds his slave audience, "it is our duty to obey our masters, in all their lawful commands." The matter of slavery is thus left in God's hands. Unfortunately, the overall strength of this argument has been lost because Jupiter Hammon writes out of a now forgotten shift in perspective. God's hands are tied in postrevolutionary politics in ways that they are not in the colonial period. Hammon's real energy belongs to an earlier era, when God is a more visible and active presence. When Hammon warns that God is "terrible beyond what you can think – that he keeps you in life every moment – and that he can send you to that awful Hell, that you laugh at, in an instant," his words reach back to Jonathan Edwards.

The nature of the divide is both subtle and vast. Arguably, the Revolution inflicts another disserve on the slave population of America by separating church and state with such rigor. To read the pamphlet literature of the period is to realize that the most dynamic opponents of slavery in eighteenth-century America are ministers. Moreover, the extraordinary eloquence of the clergy on the problems of slavery in the early 1770s has much to do with their political power. Preachers like Nathaniel Niles in Newburyport, Massachusetts, in 1774, Gad Hitchcock in Boston in the same year, and Levi Hart in Preston, Connecticut, in 1775 shake the foundations of the standing order because they represent communities-at-large and not just the spiritual keeping of their congregations.

Nathaniel Niles speaks for a generation of radical clergy in his masterpiece *Two Discourses on Liberty*. "God gave us liberty, and we have enslaved our fellow-men," Niles announces, putting the case as bluntly as possible. "May we not fear that the law of retaliation is about to be executed on us? What can we object against it?" The questions mount as Niles forces the contradiction on revolutionary America:

What excuse can we make for our conduct? What reason can we urge why our oppression shall not be repaid in kind? . . . Would we enjoy liberty? Then we must grant it to others. For shame, let us either cease to enslave our fellow-men, or else let us cease to complain of those that would enslave us. Let us either wash our hands from blood, or never hope to escape the avenger.

These words are close to and yet far from Thomas Jefferson's own cry over slavery in *Notes on the State of Virginia:* "I tremble for my country when I reflect that God is just: that his justice cannot sleep for ever."

One of several differences between Niles in 1774 and Jefferson in 1787 is the separation of church and state. Niles, like Phillis Wheatley and Jupiter Hammon, assumes that civil and spiritual liberty are inseparably united. "The former without the latter," he observes, "is but a body without a soul." The effect in politics of this juncture is to activate an angry God in the perception of civil injustice. Separation, the work of the Enlightenment, removes that anger from the political arena and replaces it with human reason. Jefferson sees the limits of reason in his indictment of slavery, but his comprehension does not lead to a coordination of divine and secular responses. His despairing gesture works, rather, to shift consideration of an impossible problem from human to divine hands. Even so, God remains a relatively distant figure. Sudden retribution does not shape Jefferson's rhetoric as it does the words of Niles or Hammon, and Jefferson's argument against slavery is correspondingly weaker and less convincing; gone from it is the religious voice that expects horrible and eternal punishment at any moment for the sin of slavery.

The oratorical shifts caused by the separation of church and state also protect slavery in another direction. When the clergy are removed from politics, a vital source of social protest goes with them. The peculiar right of ministers to address unpleasant and dangerous subjects in America has never extended to the other professions. (Certainly, no comparable unit replaces them in politics after 1776, and ministers have remained the most eloquent speakers in American civil rights to this day.) Benjamin Rush stumbles across the limitations imposed by this cultural truth when he writes "An Address to the Inhabitants of the British Settlements in America Upon Slave-Keeping" in 1773. "This publication . . . did me harm, by exciting the resentment of many slaveholders against me," Rush, a medical doctor, jots in his autobiography. "It injured me in another way, by giving rise to an opinion that I had meddled with a controversy that was foreign to my business." The moral issues in slavery are more intrinsic to preaching, and ministers never lose their right to comment, but their capacity to speak in politically effective forums dwindles in the early Republic, and their loss coincides with the rise of slavery. The answering rise of an effective abolitionism, thirty years later, will depend upon the reanimation of religious perspectives in the sectional debates over slavery.

These ramifications help to explain why the religious voice has been so intrinsic to African American narrratives. For more than two hundred years after the Revolution, religion has remained the surest, the safest, and the most vital source of minority protest. Psychologically, it also has allowed the expression of an anger that minimizes corrosion in the speaker. The persecuted Christian can both act and rest within God's wrath. Indeed, the

general importance of a contextualized anger cannot be sufficiently empha-
sized in analyzing the expanding dispensations in American life. Just as
reason is the irresistible tone of a national authority born of the Enlightenment, so anger becomes the inevitable voice of continuing change and response to that authority. Perceptive moments in early African-American
writings recognize the sign of reason as an enemy. Venture Smith, denying
any foundation in reason or justice, and Caesar Sarter, reifying reason in the
master's cat-o'nine tails, speak from experiences that are bitter beyond the
ability of ordinary emotion and language to express.

V

Anger is the necessary source of change among the disempowered because
postrevolutionary thought converts the original animus of rebellion into prospects of collective identity and manifest destiny. Nowhere is the cost of this
shift more evident than in the tonal controls placed on women's writing. The
emotion most frequently denied the educated eighteenth-century woman, or
"learned lady" as she is pejoratively termed, is anger in her own cause. Since
any strong assertion on her part runs the risk of that classification, gender
restrictions call for the most tractable tones in correct expression. Of course,
the more public the expression, the more exacting those restrictions become.

Only Tom Paine among revolutionary leaders addresses women's rights in
a sustained manner. *An Occasional Letter on the Female Sex,* written for the
Pennsylvania Magazine in 1775, summarizes the fact of injustice. "Man with
regard to [women], in all climates, and in all ages," writes Paine, "has been
either an insensible husband or an oppressor." His letter also details the
exclusion of women from the public sphere: "man, while he imposes duties
upon women, would deprive them of the sweets of public esteem, and in
exacting virtues from them, would make it a crime to aspire at honor."
Public virtues and honor are assigned to women rather than won by them,
and their general exclusion from activity in the public sphere, that unofficial
but powerful zone of influence between private discussion and formal governmental debate, sharply curtails their intellectual influence and range on every
issue.

Two factors, above others, detail the predicament of women who write in
the period. An explicit contradiction between the right of assertion and the
status of the lady — a contradiction that the eighteenth century assigns with
special weight to polite circles of literary production — traps women writers
within subordinating patterns of social and intellectual deference. Concur-
rently, the cultural fear of postrevolutionary America takes a gendered form
that effectively trivializes women when it does not charge them with danger-

ous behavior. Insofar as women occupy a positive space in republican ideology, it is in the figurative symbols of liberty and republican virtue, an iconography that underscores the expectation of their passivity in public forums. Liberty or virtue, often threatened in these renderings, refers to a purity of status or innocence of experience under masculine protection, categories that preclude independent female activity.

The conduct books and magazines of the period are filled with proscriptions relating to women. Virtually all spontaneous, energetic female behavior becomes suspect in them. Comparing the ideal woman to a delicate piece of porcelain in a typical treatment of the subject, *The Ladies' Pocket Library*, published in Philadelphia in 1792, argues that "greater delicacy evidently implies greater fragility; and this weakness, natural and moral, clearly points out the necessity of a superior degree of caution, retirement, and reserve." Since women "find their protection in their weakness, and their safety in their delicacy," it follows that "pretensions to that strength of intellect, which is requisite to penetrate into the abstruser walks of literature . . . they will readily relinquish." "Men, on the contrary, are formed for the more public exhibitions on the great theatre of human life" and "find their proper element" when they "appear terrible in arms, useful in commerce, shining in counsels."

The prevalence of this logic in early republican rhetoric is such that Judith Sargent Murray performs a rare act of intellectual and political courage in her total rejection of its implications. The "*apparent* superiority" of the male mind, she writes for *The Massachusetts Magazine* in "On the Equality of the Sexes" (1790), merely honors the circumstance that "the one is taught to aspire, and the other is early confined and limited." Weakness in the female is what to expect when "the sister must be wholly domesticated, while the brother is led by the hand through all the flowery paths of science." Sadly, the woman who overcomes these handicaps earns the unhappiness and maybe the scandal "of a *learned lady.*" Murray adds that the role of domesticity can never occupy an active mind; presumed failings in the female character – gossip, concern with fashion, idle visiting, lavish expenditure, and so on – actually reflect the frustration of exclusion from worthier forums.

Murray's last point deliberately touches a cultural nerve. Extravagance in the female figure is a lightning rod for paranoid fears in the early Republic. A vital simplicity, perceived to be everywhere on the wane in postrevolutionary America, suffers most from a spirit of luxury, and this vice frequently assumes female form in public discussion. The conventional synecdoche for luxury in early republican life is female dress. *A Treatise on Dress, Intended as a friendly and seasonable Warning to the Daughters of America* (1783) announces that "there is no one device, in which Satan is more successful, and by which he leads people captive to his will, and plunges them into hell, than he does by charming their minds, and setting them bewitched after gay, shining, and costly apparel." *Proverbs on the Pride of Women* (1787) deplores the vanity of women "going to church with the ribs of unrighteousness round their rumple; with a displayed banner of painted hypocrisy in their right hand, to guard their faces from the sun." Charges of this nature are habitual and intense in their specificity and in their prediction of terrible outcomes. "Many of those women," thunders *Proverbs,* "are more dangerous than the mouth of devouring cannons; though they appear as angels in the church, they are as serpents in the sheets, and as Beelzebub above the blankets."

Beneath the frequency and extremity of attack is an ingrained misogyny that eighteenth-century women have to accept when they enter political discourse, a price of admission that is almost incalculable. It is one thing for George Washington, writing to James Warren on October 7, 1785, to bring "luxury, effeminacy, and corruptions" together; quite another, for Abigail Adams to warn Mercy Otis Warren on May 14, 1787, that "luxury, with ten thousand evils in her train, exiled the humble virtues" in America after the Revolution; and still another, for Warren herself to conclude her *History of the Rise, Progress, and Termination of the American Revolution* (1805) with the fear that America will someday be "effeminated by luxury." Lost somewhere in the process of gender accommodation is the capacity to meet political conflict collectively in the public sphere as gentlemen of letters frequently do. Could any circle of women writers have taken a decisive political position together in the 1780s without raising overwhelming cries of unnatural opposition and effeminacy? On politics, women write in isolation if at all. It is not until 1932 that scholars discover that Mercy Otis Warren writes *Observations on the New Constitution, And on the Federal and State Conventions* (1788), one of the most effective essays in anti-Federalist protest.

The reflexive defensiveness that women writers must bring to the subject of their own sex is just one measure of a definitive vulnerability in address. When Esther de Berdt Reed, wife of the president of Pennsylvania, organizes a Ladies Association in support of the Revolution, she must first try to exculpate women who take an active role. "Who knows if persons disposed to censure, and sometimes too severely with regard to us," asks Reed, "may not disapprove our appearing acquainted even with the actions of which our sex boasts?" Her broadside, *The Sentiments of an American Woman* (1780), lingers over the heroines of antiquity and glories "in all that which my sex has done great and commendable," but it also quietly accepts as it laments the relative limitations placed upon the modern woman: "if the weakness of our Constitution, if opinion and manners did not forbid us to march to glory by the same path as the Men, we should at least equal and sometimes surpass them in our love for the public good."

Even a formidable intellectual like Abigail Adams eschews anger when she is attacked along gender lines. Responding on February 3, 1814, to Judge F. A. Vanderkemp's complaint against "learned ladies," Adams casts her antagonist into the third person where she heaps ironies upon him: "And in the first place, to put him perfectly at his ease, I assure him that I make not any pretensions to the character of a learned lady, and therefore, according to his creed, I am entitled to his benevolence." She drolly traces "the true cause" of Vanderkemp's accusation to his fear of a rival, but the underlying tone of her letter is one of regret that softens irony and assertion. "There are so few women who may be really called learned," she ponders, "that I do not wonder they are considered as black swans." This language gently resists what it must admit. Pressing against dominant assumptions, it clarifies otherwise obscure ideological boundaries. The black swan is a blight not to itself but in the eye of the beholder — a faulty male beholder who fixes on a false incongruity between education and capacity.

Abigail Adams both welcomes and denies the power of blackness. The innate grace of the simile retains all sense of earned capacity, even as the circumstance suggests sharp limits on the progress of the Enlightenment and maybe on the very nature of the Enlightenment. What can be the importance of learning in a world where "learned" has become a pejorative term? Adams insists upon the capacity under challenge. "It is very certain," she observes, "that a well-informed woman, conscious of her nature and dignity, is more capable of performing the relative duties of life, and of engaging and retaining the affections of a man of understanding, than one whose intellectual endowments rise not above the common level." The instrumental acknowledgment of functionalism in marriage — approved by her male antagonist — marches hand in hand with the separate ideal of knowing one's own nature and dignity.

For women who live more on the margins of republican culture, the cost of suppressing and internalizing their anger is noticeably higher. The "aged matron" of *The Female Advocate,* an anonymous pamphlet printed in New Haven in 1801, "belongs to a class, whose weakness is become quite proverbial among the self sufficient lords of this lower world." She expects reproach "if she should attempt to say any thing, on behalf of her own sex, or a single word on the long exploded subject of female merit." This speaker has been "so wounded" by the "contempt" and "self distant superiority" of patriarchal structures that she must struggle to hush her thoughts on the ingratitude and reproaches of others. Fearing to give offense but bitterly "cumbered with much serving," the female advocate asks only for the merit to which she is entitled, a share in literary concerns. "I contend indeed for the honor of intellectual worth," she declares. Her aspirations and tensions are joined in this statement. Using both, the author produces the single most compelling American pamphlet on women's rights for a decade in either direction.

Many themes percolate through *The Female Advocate*, including the need for equality between the sexes for there to be real friendship, the goal of women's education to secure that equality, the type for equality in the Christian religion, the active danger of ignorance for women left alone in an unfriendly world, the arbitrary rule of "all arrogating man," the double standard in seduction, the unfair opprobrium reserved for "masculine" or active women, and the unacceptable narrowness of a life confined to domestic cares ("shall women . . . never expand an idea beyond the walls of her house?"). But every theme is informed and driven by an initial, stunned, and stunning recognition: namely, that the Enlightenment, as defined by men, utterly excludes women from its purview. If the Enlightenment signifies the capacity to know and the spread of knowledge, what can it mean, asks the female advocate, when "the arrogant assumers of male merit" believe that "our sex arrived at its zenith of improvement, at the age of twenty-one"? Is it possible, she wonders, that she has not improved since that age? "If so, what a pitiable misfortune to me, that I was born a woman!" The rest of the pamphlet is a triumphant reversal of these connotations. The "sincere Advocate for the Merits of her Sex" explains her situation through the knowledge of experience. She is the living image of the Kantian imperative "dare to know."

The anonymity of the female advocate is a reminder that every assertive woman in early republican culture needs some disguise for protection and control. For Deborah Sampson that mask is the literal one of cross dressing. Hired out as a farm employee from the age of ten, Sampson adopts men's clothing and joins the revolutionary army as Robert Shurtleff when she completes her indenture at twenty-one. It is, she decides, the one way that an impoverished but vigorous woman can satisfy her curiosity to see the world, or, in the words of her eighteenth-century biographer, "she determined to burst the bands which, it must be confessed, have too often held her sex in awe." Deborah Sampson serves for three years undetected (1781–4), sees heavy fighting at White Plains, Tarrytown, and Yorktown, and receives serious wounds before her real identity is finally discovered in Philadelphia. Passing is as much a question of performance as appearance. "Her countenance and voice were feminine; but she conversed with such ease on the subject of theology, on political subjects, and military tactics, that her manner would seem to be masculine."

This cross-gendered voice, now regrettably lost, gives way to a biography of the female soldier with more conventional purposes in mind. Herman Mann's *The Female Review; Or, Memoirs of an American Young Lady* (1797) reclaims the propriety undermined by Sampson's disguise, rejects "Female Enterprise," and extols the unblemished purity and retiring modesty of the maiden ideal. According to Mann, men and women should read Deborah Sampson's story with their separate spheres in mind. The woman soldier's "irregular" heroism, "while it deserves the applause of every patriot and veteran, must chill the blood of the tender and sensible female." Women must learn to rechannel the example of Sampson's energy back into their proper, domestic sphere. Throughout, the soldier's accomplishments remain "a great presumption in a female, on account of the inadequateness of her nature." The biography both reveres and resists the revolutionary heroism of its subject. In a unique ambivalence for the times on this theme, one that vividly confirms the exclusiveness of connection between patriotism and patriarchy in the early Republic, *The Female Review* reveals itself in reversals. Deborah Sampson may stand for patriotic heroism, but Herman Mann — the very name of the male author redoubles his theme — writes to raise the alarm of eighteenth-century men; he seeks to expose the disguise of the assertive woman.

The disguise of Eliza Lucas Pinckney (1723–93) is harder to penetrate because more conventional. A surviving letterbook shows how it worked. Scientist, farmer, businesswoman, and matriarch of the leading family in South Carolina, Pinckney masks herself in a life of service. The young Eliza Lucas is mistress of three plantations by the age of seventeen; her responsibilities include the cultivation of five thousand acres of land, commercial arrangements and correspondence in the sale and shipping of products, the direct supervision of twenty slaves and of the overseers of two other plantations, the education of a younger sister, and the management of family interests in Charleston society. "I shall begin to think my self an old woman before I am well a young one having these weighty affairs upon my hands," she wryly observes at nineteen. Her every enterprise, in the constant refrain of her letters, is the work of an "obedient and ever devoted daughter," one who mollifies the demands of an anxious and complaining absent father, George Lucas, a British army officer and the lieutenant governor in Antigua.

The school of obedience serves Eliza well in 1744 when, at twenty-one, she marries Charles Pinckney, a widower twenty-four years her senior. She resolves "next to my God, to make it my Study to please him," and when Pinckney dies suddenly in 1758, she automatically transfers all sense of service to familial honor and her three surviving children. Few accomplish as much as Eliza Lucas Pinckney in the midst of self-abnegation. Her experimentations in indigo and crop rotation earn her a name in the history of agricultural science, her letterbook of correspondence encapsulates colonial Charleston from 1738–1762, and her adroit management of economic and social assets raises the Pinckney name over all others in South Carolina.

Self-deprecation always accompanies the accomplishments of Eliza Lucas Pinckney; the device shrouds the enormous energy and intelligence that might otherwise have upset the community around her. The young girl evades an early marriage proposal by disarming the wishes of her father with self-disparaging humor. When her future husband sees "a fertile brain at schemeing" and "the little Visionary" in her agricultural experiments, she confirms his opinions without changing her course. The language of deference is her shield. "Your reasoning is convincing and unanswerable," she tells him on one occasion, "and your reproof more obliging than the highest compliment you could have made me." Typically, her reading of Richardson's *Pamela, or Virtue Rewarded* (1740–1) finds fault with the heroine for "that disgusting liberty of praising herself." Eliza Pinckney, by way of contrast, deflects attention by minimizing her role. The wealthy and cultivated young widow will avoid envy and suspicion in 1762 by mocking herself, "an old woman in the Wilds of America." Tenaciously protecting the Pinckney holdings amidst the war and devastation of 1779, she will minimize loss by telling her children "I cant want but little, nor that little long." Meanwhile, her creditors receive a careful account of extensive properties to offset the embarrassment of temporary financial inconvenience.

The rewards in these strategies coexist with a concession. The matriarch succeeds partly by muting all sense of a political voice. Eliza Pinckney can be supremely effective in negotiating for the care and release of her captured son Major Thomas Pinckney in 1780. On the other hand, the success of those negotiations has something to do with her decision to speak and write in nonpartisan terms. Fully committed to the Revolution, this mother of two army officers does not seem to have engaged in public commentary on the conflict itself; her apparent restraint, even in extant family correspondence, is part of her discipline in dealing with patriarchal authority. And the accommodation is not an unusual one. Martha Ballard, a New England midwife, supplies a parallel example in very different circumstances when she keeps a diary between 1785 and 1812 in Hallowell, Maine. A leading figure in her community, Ballard also maintains herself by avoiding political engagement and local controversy. For the successful woman of the period, political articulation on major issues is rarely part of an independent engagement in communal affairs.

The hallmarks of Pinckney's thought are piety and reason. As the first quality insures humility and sacrifice, so the second avoids enthusiasm and imbalance with all of these combinations geared toward successful endeavor. These virtues are ones to expect in the accomplished figure of neoclassical lore, but they grow into rigid prerequisites for the lady who would lead. "Consider what you owe to your self, your Country and family," Eliza Pinckney counsels a grandson in 1782. For herself and the women around her, these priorities are exactly reversed: family, then country, then self. The primary virtue of disinterestedness leads toward public service and recognition for the early republican man; toward self-effacement and the hope of private acknowledgment in the accomplished republican woman. Pinckney's achievements are all the greater for their necessary indirections, but they must also be understood in the context of fixed and sharp gender restriction.

There is no place for transforming anger to enter Eliza Lucas Pinckney's frame of reference or, for that matter, for it to legitimate the role of any other American woman as a public figure in eighteenth-century life – one reason, perhaps, why the new and still suspect form of the novel will situate anger so strongly as pathos in writings such as Susanna Rowson's *Charlotte Temple* (1791) and Hannah Foster's *The Coquette* (1797). The more covert strategies of fiction not only welcome anonymity when needed, they also establish an ideal forum for mixing private and public events and understandings.

Anger is transformative, however, when it partakes of the enabling wrath of the Revolution. By the same token, to be without it in early republican culture is to be disenfranchised. For if the Revolution comes alive in the spirit of declaration, women must still ask for their rights. It may be that Thomas Paine, as the angriest revolutionary, comes closest among men to writing out the plight of women in the revolutionary period, but he also robs them of all access to his most vital emotion. Women, unlike men, do not seize their rights in Paine's writings. They remain the supplicants of a masculine world, and they ask for the minimal justice of recognition.

" 'Be not our tyrants in all,' " runs Paine's imagined version of this supplicating voice in *An Occasional Letter on the Female Sex*. " 'Permit our names to be sometimes pronounced beyond the narrow circle in which we live. . . . deny us not that public esteem which, after the esteem of one's self, is the sweetest reward of well doing.' " The ability of the female voice to *demand* its rights, instead of pleading for them, will take centuries rather than years to develop, and central to that slow realization will be its difficulty in coming to grips with an ugly fact. Self-esteem in American culture depends upon the capacity to express public anger in a righteous cause.

VI

The dilemma of the disempowered can be read in their inability to wield that emotion within the workings of the new nation, and a number of variables are at work in the limitation. In part, the shift from participation in the

Revolution to contemplation of it forces corresponding changes in the understanding and expression of originating angers. In part, the widely perceived fragility of early republican culture qualifies all further disruptive exercises of revolutionary spirit. In part, too, the success of revolutionary anger leads away from the solidarity of facing external enemies and toward the fragmentary and divisive practice of finding enemies within.

All of these variables work against Americans with limited access to the public sphere. Indeed, the same tendencies, raised in certain ways and applied in given situations, channel cultural resentments directly against the disenfranchised. The hope for cohesion in republican society is a dangerous perception for those left outside. The Native American as logical opponent, the slave as feared rebel, and the woman as a symbol of luxury are only the easiest targets of early republican rage. Many other categories, essentially any group not identifiable as successfully republican, have been occasional candidates and sometime victims.

The loose displacement of originating communal angers appears in a striking detail, the official seal of the Commonwealth of Massachusetts from 1780. In formal description, the seal shows "an Indian, dressed in his Shirt, Maggosins, belted proper, in his right hand a Bow, TOPAZ, in his left an Arrow, its point towards the Base." A crest, just above this representation, depicts "On a Wreath a Dexter Arm clothed and ruffled proper, grasping a Broad Sword, the Pummel and Hilt, TOPAZ, with this Motto: *Ense Petit Placidam Sub Libertate Quietem* [by the sword, he seeks peace under liberty]." The inscription, taken from Algernon Sidney, martyr to English liberty and author of the influential *Discourses Concerning Goverment* (1698), signals the need for willed acts of violence in the name of liberty, but the overall representation gives that meaning an additional turn, and the extent of the turn appears in a basic shift in iconography. The original seal of the Massachusetts Bay Colony in 1675 also presents a Native American, though one who clearly symbolizes peaceful agrarian purposes and who formally salutes English settlers to "come over and help us." With this salutation dropped, the added configuration of elements in 1780 is quite different in meaning.

The entirety of the new seal portrays the right arm of authority (the gentleman's arm, shirt, and sword) raised in threatening posture over an oblivious Native American. And the immediacy of this image is strengthened by historical context. The seal of 1780 is conceived within three years of the murder of Jane McCrea, a tragedy in which the worst fears of New Englanders are fanned into wartime frenzy when the daughter of a Presbyterian minister is scalped and further mutilated by Native Americans as part of the British advance from Canada under General Burgoyne. The design also follows by just a year the military expedition that systematically devastates

Iroquois civilization in the western part of the northern states. Obviously, and for many republicans in 1780, more than symbolism is involved in their coat of arms; the sword of Massachusetts is poised for righteous and repeated descent.

Postrevolutionary Americans refocus the anger of their beginnings without quite recognizing the shift. Remembrance includes a mode of forgetting. Tom Paine, writing *To the People of England on the Invasion of England,* tries in 1804 to revive the original moment by reminding everyone that "the American Revolution began on untried ground" and that "some bold exertion was necessary to shock [benumbed reasoning faculties] into reflection." Not coincidentally, these views bespeak the radical side of the Enlightenment: rejection of the past with trust in the awakening power of reason. But Paine, as always, is asking for too much. No culture can long sustain itself on untried ground or bold exertions, and reason alone cannot control communal uncertainties. Republicans want to curb their fear of the unknown. Familiar ground, not untried, is what they seek, and they expect the completed success of the Revolution to provide it for them.

It is not easy, in consequence, to determine how long or in what sense the Republic remains a revolutionary culture. What is plain is how quickly the achievements of the Enlightenment (the spread of knowledge) and of the Revolution (victory) overshadow the processes of Enlightenment thought (daring to know) and distort the practices of revolutionary action (galvanizing anger in the name of liberty). Tired of years of strife and eager to create a uniform foundation out of the Revolution, early republicans want most of all to secure their achievement in time and place. They need the standard that a spirit of achievement and an appropriate sense of story can give them, and their search for heroes is the most prominent manifestation of that need.

A function of narrative expectations as well as cultural aspirations, the revolutionary hero literalizes anger by sealing it off in postrevolutionary discourse. The wrath of a Patrick Henry or of a George Washington now belongs to the highest order. A figure of this sort becomes a simulacrum of angers completed or at least stilled. Cast together in the role of founding fathers, these figures acquire the status of achievers almost before they are fully recognized as rebels. Soon enough in the popular imagination, the expectation of high-mindedness in the hero replaces the acrimony of actual wartime participation. By 1826, antebellum orators like Daniel Webster will have turned these founders into fixed and eternal constellations that guide America with "the united blaze of a thousand lights." And although it is simplicity itself to attach these motionless and mythologized figures to the victory of the Revolution, it becomes increasingly difficult to apply them with any force to the animus of further action.

The cult of the hero as a symbol system explains a great deal about early republican ideology, and the first histories of the Revolution show what is really at stake in the phenomenon. David Ramsay in *The History of the American Revolution* (1789) and Mercy Otis Warren in *History of the Rise, Progress and Termination of the American Revolution* (1805) are Federalist against anti-Federalist in politics, southerner against northerner in regional identity, male against female in domestic character, and parvenu against social pillar in society, but they agree on three things as historians: the Revolution is the struggle of American virtue against European avarice, the American historian rightly extols that virtue in a narrative of events, and, finally, virtue itself declines dangerously in the aftermath of the Revolution. All three premises dictate vigorous commemoration of the revolutionary hero, where heroism magnifies and celebrates disinterested, patriotic action. Although the conspicuous type for this figure is always George Washington, recognition of every hero helps republicans, in Ramsay's words, to "cultivate justice both public and private." The presentation of patriotic action, correctly comprehended, sustains the revolutionary victory of public interest over private feeling.

For both Ramsay and Warren, there is every reason for urgency in the personification of public virtue. Ramsay's history deplores the aftermath, "the languid years of peace, when selfishness usurped the place of public spirit." Warren begins her own work warning that principles "have been nearly annihilated. . . . the causes which involved the thirteen colonies in confusion and blood are scarcely known, amidst the rage of accumulation and the taste for expensive pleasures that have since prevailed." If the exaltation of virtuous leaders seems to have been shrill in these histories, it is because both writers think that virtue unaided will not restrain vice. The battle of good over evil, foreordained in religious discourse, unfolds with extreme uncertainty in these secular histories. "It is an unpleasing part of history," Warren concludes, "when 'corruption begins to prevail, when degeneracy marks the manners of the people, and weakens the sinews of the state.' " Ramsay, for his part, ends with the hope of progressive happiness, but he fears in the same breath that republicans will "degenerate into savages."

Employment of the revolutionary figure in patterns of emulation responds to these anxieties, but it also subverts ideological impetuses for further change. When David Ramsay writes that the victory at Yorktown produces "a social triumph and exultation, which no private prosperity is ever able to fully inspire," he locks Americans into a worthier past. The disempowered, in particular, are frozen in time when the fixed achievements of the Revolution replace all sense of a radical awareness in the people. The eighteenth-century pantheon of heroes contains no models for newer and different kinds of Americans to emulate in their struggle for equal representation. Neither does it suffice for the unrepresented to add their own heroes as eighteenth-century women writers like Esther de Berdt Reed and "the Female Advocate" of New Haven try to do.

The problems in emulation go well beyond representation. Recognition of the hero or heroine – however inspiring and however indicative of capacity – runs counter to the technical articulation and procedural protection of human rights. The timeless achievement of the one cuts across the timely process in the other. The celebration of detached or dispassionate service can easily deflect new quests for entitlement as petitioners turn into factions or interest groups under the critical gaze of those who can afford a disinterested mien. Inevitably, the retrospective tendencies in emulation resist the safeguards of formal complaint and proper redress.

Of course, the Revolution simultaneously encourages the exercise of inalienable rights, protects the right of petition, maintains the legality of formal complaint, and allows for redress. It is both radical possibility and reified monolith in early republican ideology. David Ramsay, whose Federalist leanings produce a conservative vision in 1789, can also discern and celebrate the effect of change. The Revolution brings "a vast expansion of the human mind." "It seemed," he adds, "as if the war not only required but created talents. Men . . . spoke, wrote, and acted, with an energy far surpassing all expectations which could be reasonably founded on their previous acquirements." As the conservative Ramsay is able to extol the expansive energy in expectations, so the more radical Mercy Otis Warren can worry about the "truly alarming" disturbances that threaten "civil convulsions" in the 1780s.

Closely examined, the Revolution is always both triumph and troubling event. It figures in both a radical frame and a conservative continuum, and it can be either one in Warren's insistence that it appear "the pole-star of the statesman, respected by the rising generation." At issue in the conflict of impulses is the variable and volatile revolutionary understanding of republicans caught up in constant and stressful cultural change. Then, as now, claims of a guiding uprightness, assertions of patriotic well-being, and assumptions about a place in human history are the elements of a successful public American voice. The main difference in the early Republic is that each element revolves obsessively around the suddenly colossal past.

Who will own the Revolution and to what end? The voices of postrevolutionary discourse are explosive and timid, hopeful and despairing, angry and complacent – often in the same moment – in a battleground of conflicted and conflicting voices over the meaning of the Revolution. To what extent does the disappearing past animate a claim about the future? Should revolutionary triumphs be conserved or their spirit extended? The perceptive critic can find these cautionary and expansive voices and tendencies in just about every major intellectual figure and must gauge which elements dominate and for what reasons.

Compounding these questions is a final element in postrevolutionary American expression that is so ubiquitous as frequently to be missed altogether. The universally acclaimed success of the Revolution enters into an equally omnipresent possibility of pervading loss. These tones reach an apotheosis of sorts in Abraham Lincoln's First Inaugural Address (1861), where "the mystic chords of memory" stretch back to touch "the better angels of our nature," but they exist throughout the public literature of the early Republic and antebellum culture.

Everywhere the recognition of rapid change vies with the desire to appear in control of it, and over everything looms a vague nostalgia about what is passing or missing. Loss is the elusive variable in determining voice in early republican literature. Speaker after speaker points to the fragility of what has been gained in the fact or likelihood of breakage, and in these perceptions the anger of the Revolution competes with something that comes very close to a communal sense of mourning. The American Enlightenment begins in the time of Samuel Davies's refrain over the death of George II in 1760: "George is no more!" It ends in 1826 with Daniel Webster entoning "Adams and Jefferson are no more!" How and where increasingly democratic voices place themselves within this ever-moving sense of regret is, in large measure, the story of American literature.

BIBLIOGRAPHY

This bibliography includes only immediately relevant book-length studies that have been especially influential or significant in the field. It excludes dissertations, articles, studies of individual authors, and primary works, with the exception, in the last case, of presentations of collections of materials that have been generally unknown or inaccessible to students and scholars. The goal, within considerations of length, has been to represent every subject of scope with a range of sources that will lead the general reader toward deeper inquiry.

At the same time, the decisions behind a limited bibliography of this kind create omissions of note for the committed scholar, and it is in symbolic recognition of all such exclusions that I acknowledge a leading essay from the article literature in this headnote. All contemporary literary understandings of the intellectual texts of the formative era begin with William Hedges, "The Myth of the Republic and the Theory of American Literature," *Prospects: An Annual of American Cultural Studies* 4 (1979), 101–120.

Ackerman, Bruce. *We the People: Foundations*. Cambridge, Mass.: Harvard University Press, 1991.

Adair, Douglass. *Fame and the Founding Fathers: Essays*. Edited by Trevor Colbourn. New York: Norton, 1974.

Ahlstrom, Sydney E. *A Religious History of the American People*. New Haven, Conn.: Yale University Press, 1972.

Aldridge, Alfred Owen, ed. *The Ibero-American Enlightenment*. Urbana: University of Illinois Press, 1971.

Anderson, Benedict. *Imagined Communities: Reflections on the Origin and Spread of Nationalism*. London: Verso, 1983.

Andrews, William L., ed. *Journeys in New Worlds: Early American Women's Narratives*. Madison: University of Wisconsin Press, 1990.

Appleby, Joyce. *Capitalism and a New Social Order: The Republican Vision of the 1790s*. New York: New York University Press, 1984.

Appleby, Joyce, Lynn Hunt, and Margaret Jacob. *Telling the Truth about History*. New York: Norton, 1994.

Arendt, Hannah. *On Revolution*. New York: Viking Press, 1963.

Axtell, James. *The Invasion Within: The Contest of Cultures in Colonial North America*. New York: Oxford University Press, 1987.

Bailyn, Bernard. *Education in the Forming of American Society*. Chapel Hill: University of North Carolina Press, 1960.

———. *The Ideological Origins of the American Revolution*. 1967. Enl. ed., Cambridge, Mass.: Harvard University Press, 1992.

———, ed. *Pamphlets of the American Revolution*. Cambridge, Mass.: Harvard University Press, 1965.

Bailyn, Bernard, and John B. Hench, eds. *The Press and the American Revolution*. Worcester, Mass.: American Antiquarian Society, 1980.

Banning, Lance. *The Jeffersonian Persuasion: Evolution of a Party Ideology*. Ithaca, N.Y.: Cornell University Press, 1978.

Becker, Carl L. *The Declaration of Independence: A Study of the History of Political Ideas*. New York: Alfred A. Knopf, 1922.

Berger, Raoul. *Federalism: The Founders' Design*. Norman: University of Oklahoma Press, 1987.

Beeman, Richard R. *The Old Dominion and the New Nation, 1788–1801*. Lexington: University Press of Kentucky, 1972.

Beeman, Richard R., Stephen Botein, and Edward D. Carter II, eds. *Beyond Confederation: Origins of the Constitution and American National Identity*. Chapel Hill: University of North Carolina Press, 1987.

Bercovitch, Sacvan. *The American Jeremiad*. Madison: University of Wisconsin Press, 1978.

———. *The Puritan Origins of the American Self*. New Haven, Conn.: Yale Univerity Press, 1975.

Berens, John F. *Providence and Patriotism in Early America, 1640–1815*. Charlottesville: University Press of Virginia, 1978.

Berlin, Ira, and Ronald Hoffman, eds. *Slavery and Freedom in the Age of the American Revolution*. Urbana: University of Illinois Press, 1986.

Bloch, Ruth H. *Visionary Republic: Millennial Themes in American Thought, 1756–1800*. Cambridge, England: Cambridge University Press, 1985.

Bonomi, Patricia U. *Under the Cope of Heaven: Religion, Society, and Politics in Colonial America*. New York: Oxford University Press, 1985.

Boorstin, Daniel J. *The Americans: The Colonial Experience*. New York: Random House, 1958.

———. *The Americans: The National Experience*. New York, Random House, 1965.

———. *The Lost World of Thomas Jefferson*. New York: Henry Holt, 1948.

Breen, Timothy H. *Puritans and Adventurers: Change and Persistence in Early America*. New York: Oxford University Press, 1980.

Breitwieser, Mitchell Robert. *Cotton Mather and Benjamin Franklin: The Price of Representative Personality*. Cambridge, England: Cambridge University Press, 1984.

Bridenbaugh, Carl. *Mitre and Sceptre: Transatlantic Faiths, Ideas, Personalities, and Politics, 1689–1775*. Oxford: Oxford University Press, 1962.

———. *Myths and Realities: Societies of the Colonial South*. Baton Rouge: Louisiana State University Press, 1952.

Brown, Richard D. *Modernization: The Transformation of American Life, 1600–1865*. New York: Hill & Wang, 1976.

Brumm, Ursula. *American Thought and Religious Typology.* Translated by John Hooglund. New Brunswick, N.J.: Rutgers University Press, 1970.

Bruns, Roger, ed. *Am I Not a Man and a Brother: The Antislavery Crusade of Revolutionary America, 1688–1788.* New York: Chelsea House, 1977.

Buel, Richard, Jr. *Securing the Revolution: Ideology in American Politics, 1789–1815.* Ithaca, N.Y.: Cornell University Press, 1972.

Buell, Lawrence. *New England Literary Culture: From Revolution through Renaissance.* Cambridge, England: Cambridge University Press, 1986.

Cady, Edwin Harrison. *The Gentleman in America: A Literary Study in American Culture.* Syracuse: Syracuse University Press, 1949.

Calhoon, Robert M. *Dominion and Liberty: Ideology in the Anglo-American World, 1660–1801.* Arlington Heights, Ill.: Harlan Davidson, 1994.

Canetti, Elias. *Crowds and Power.* Translated by Carol Stewart. New York: Viking Press, 1962.

Carafiol, Peter C. *The American Ideal: Literary History as a Worldly Activity.* New York: Oxford University Press, 1991.

Carroll, Peter N. *Religion and the Coming of the American Revolution.* Waltham, Mass.: Ginn-Blaisdell, 1970.

Cassirer, Ernst. *The Philosophy of the Enlightenment.* Translated by Fritz C. A. Koelln and James Pettegrove. Princeton, N.J.: Princeton University Press, 1951.

Charlton, Donald Geoffrey. *New Images of the Natural in France: A Study of European Cultural History, 1750–1800.* Cambridge, England: Cambridge University Press, 1984.

Charvat, William. *The Profession of Authorship in America, 1800–1870.* Edited by Matthew Bruccoli. Columbus: Ohio State University Press, 1966.

Cherry, Conrad, ed. *God's New Israel: Religious Interpretations of American Destiny.* Englewood Cliffs, N.J.: Prentice-Hall, Inc., 1975.

Cheyfitz, Eric. *The Poetics of Imperialism: Translation and Colonization from "The Tempest" to "Tarzan."* New York: Oxford University Press, 1991.

Clark, Harry Hayden, ed. *Transitions in American Literary History.* New York: Octagon, 1975.

Clark, J. C. D. *The Language of Liberty, 1660–1832: Political Discourse and Social Dynamics in the Anglo-American World.* Cambridge, England: Cambridge University Press, 1994.

Cohen, Lester H. *The Revolutionary Histories: Contemporary Narratives of the American Revolution.* Ithaca, N.Y.: Cornell University Press, 1980.

Cott, Nancy. *The Bonds of Womanhood: "Woman's Sphere" in New England: 1780–1835.* New Haven, Conn.: Yale University Press, 1977.

Countryman, Edward. *Americans: A Collision of Histories.* New York: Hill and Wang, 1996.

Cronon, William. *Changes in the Land: Indians, Colonists, and the Ecology of New England.* New York: Hill & Wang, 1983.

Cunliffe, Marcus. *The Nation Takes Shape, 1789–1837.* Chicago: University of Chicago Press, 1959.

Dangerfield, George. *The Era of Good Feelings.* New York: Harcourt, Brace and Company, 1952.

Dann, John C., ed. *The Revolution Remembered: Eyewitness Accounts of the War for Independence.* Chicago: University of Chicago Press, 1980.

Davidson, Cathy. *Revolution and the Word: The Rise of the Novel in America.* New York: Oxford University Press, 1986.

Davidson, James West. *The Logic of Millennial Thought.* New Haven, Conn.: Yale University Press, 1977.

Davis, Richard Beale. *Intellectual Life in the Colonial South, 1585–1763.* 3 vols. Knoxville: University of Tennessee Press, 1978.

Derry, John. *English Politics and the American Revolution.* London: J. M. Dent & Sons, 1976.

Egnal, Marc. *A Mighty Empire: The Origins of the American Revolution.* Ithaca, N.Y.: Cornell University Press, 1988.

Elkins, Stanley, and Eric McKitrick. *The Age of Federalism.* Oxford: Oxford University Press, 1993.

Elliott, Emory. *Revolutionary Writers: Literature and Authority in the New Republic.* New York: Oxford University Press, 1982.

Ellis, Joseph J. *After the Revolution: Profiles of Early American Culture.* New York: Norton, 1979.

Ellis, Richard E. *The Jeffersonian Crisis: Courts and Politics in the Young Republic.* New York: Oxford University Press, 1971.

Emerson, Everett H., ed. *American Literature, 1764–1789: The Revolutionary Years.* Madison: The University of Wisconsin Press, 1977.

———, ed. *Major Writers of Early American Literature.* Madison: University of Wisconsin Press, 1972.

Epstein, David F. *The Political Theory of the Federalist.* Chicago: University of Chicago Press, 1984.

Faust, Langdon Lynne. *American Women Writers: A Critical Reference Guide from Colonial Times to the Present.* 4 vols. New York: Ungar, 1979–1982.

Faÿ, Bernard. *The Revolutionary Spirit in France and America: A Study of Moral and Intellectual Relations between France and the United States at the End of the Eighteenth Century.* Translated by Ramon Guthrie. New York: Cooper Square Publishers, Inc., 1966.

Fender, Stephen. *American Literature in Context, I: 1620–1830.* London: Methuen and Company, 1983.

Ferguson, Robert A. *Law and Letters in American Culture.* Cambridge, Mass.: Harvard University Press, 1984.

Fischer, David Hackett. *The Revolution of American Conservatism: The Federalist Party in the Era of Jeffersonian Democracy.* New York: Harper & Row, 1965.

Fliegelman, Jay. *Declaring Independence: Jefferson, Natural Language, and the Culture of Performance.* Stanford: Stanford University Press, 1993.

———. *Prodigals and Pilgrims: The American Revolution against Patriarchal Authority, 1750–1800.* Cambridge, England: Cambridge University Press, 1982.

Friedman, Lawrence J. *Inventors of the Promised Land.* New York: Alfred A. Knopf, 1975.

Furtwangler, Albert. *American Silhouettes: Rhetorical Identities of the Founders.* New Haven, Conn.: Yale University Press, 1987.

————. *The Authority of Publius: A Reading of the Federalist Papers.* Ithaca, N.Y.: Cornell University Press, 1984.

Gaustad, Edwin S. *Faith of Our Fathers: Religion and the New Nation.* New York: Harper & Row, 1987.

————. *A Religious History of America.* Rev. ed. New York: Harper & Row, 1990.

Gay, Peter. *The Enlightenment: An Interpretation.* 2 vols. New York: Alfred A. Knopf, 1966–1969.

Gilbert, Bil. *God Gave Us This Country: Tekamthi and the First American Civil War.* New York: Atheneum Press, 1989.

Gilmore, Michael T., ed. *Early American Literature: A Collection of Critical Essays.* Englewood Cliffs, N.J.: Prentice Hall, 1980.

Gilmore, William J. *Reading Becomes a Necessity of Life: Material and Cultural Life in Rural New England, 1780–1835.* Knoxville: University of Tennessee Press, 1989.

Granger, Bruce I. *American Essay Serials from Franklin to Irving.* Knoxville: University of Tennessee Press, 1978.

————. *Political Satire in the American Revolution, 1763–1783.* Ithaca, N.Y.: Cornell University Press, 1960.

Greene, Jack P., ed. *The American Revolution: Its Character and Limits.* New York: New York University Press, 1987.

————, ed. *The Reinterpretation of the American Revolution, 1763–1789.* New York: Harper & Row, 1968.

Greven, Philip J. *The Protestant Temperament: Patterns of Child-Rearing, Religious Experience, and the Self in Early America.* New York: Alfred A. Knopf, 1977.

Gummere, Richard M. *The American Colonial Mind and the Classical Tradition: Essays in Comparative Culture.* Cambridge, Mass.: Harvard University Press, 1963.

Gustafson, Thomas. *Representative Words: Politics, Literature, and the American Language, 1776–1865.* Cambridge, England: Cambridge University Press, 1992.

Habermas, Jürgen. *The Structural Transformation of the Public Sphere: An Inquiry into a Category of Bourgeois Society.* Translated by Thomas Burger with the assistance of Frederick Lawrence. Cambridge, Mass.: MIT Press, 1989.

Hatch, Nathan O. *The Democratization of American Christianity.* New Haven: Yale University Press, 1989.

————. *The Sacred Cause of Liberty: Republican Thought and the Millennium in Revolutionary New England.* New Haven, Conn.: Yale University Press, 1977.

Havard, William C., and Joseph L. Bernd, eds. *Two Hundred Years of the Republic in Retrospect.* Charlottesville: University Press of Virginia, 1976.

Heimert, Alan. *Religion and the American Mind: From the Great Awakening to the Revolution.* Cambridge, Mass.: Harvard University Press, 1966.

Heimert, Alan, and Perry Miller, eds. *The Great Awakening: Documents Illustrating the Crisis and Its Consequences.* Indianapolis: Bobbs-Merrill, 1967.

Henretta, James A., and Gregory H. Nobles. *Evolution and Revolution: American Society, 1600–1820.* Lexington, Mass.: Heath, 1987.

Hickey, Donald R. *The War of 1812: A Forgotten Conflict.* Urbana: University of Illinois Press, 1989.

Higonnet, Patrice. *Sister Republics: The Origins of French and American Republicanism.* Cambridge, Mass.: Harvard University Press, 1988.

Hill, Christopher. *Reformation to Industrial Revolution: A Social and Economic History of Britain, 1530–1780.* London: Weidenfeld and Nicolson, 1967.

Hobsbawm, E. J. *Nations and Nationalism since 1780: Programme, Myth, Reality.* Cambridge, England: Cambridge University Press, 1990.

Hoffman, Ronald, and Peter J. Albert, eds. *Women in the Age of the American Revolution.* Charlottesville: University Press of Virginia, 1989.

Horkheimer, Max, and Theodor Adorno. *Dialectic of Enlightenment.* Translated by John Cumming. New York: Continuum, 1972.

Hulme, Peter. *Colonial Encounters: Europe and the Native Caribbean, 1492–1797.* London: Methuen, 1986.

Hyneman, Charles S., and Donald Lutz, eds. *American Political Writing during the Founding Era, 1760–1805.* 2 vols. Indianapolis: Liberty Press, 1983.

Jackson, Blyden. *A History of Afro-American Literature.* Vol. I, *The Long Beginning, 1746–1895.* Baton Rouge: Louisiana State University Press, 1989.

Jacobs, Wilbur R. *Dispossessing the American Indian: Indians and Whites on the Coloniel Frontier.* 1972. Reprinted. Norman: University of Oklahoma Press, 1985.

Jehlen, Myra. *American Incarnation: The Individual, the Nation, and the Continent.* Cambridge, Mass.: Harvard University Press, 1986.

Jennings, Francis. *The Invasion of America: Indians, Colonialism, and the Cant of Conquest.* Chapel Hill: University of North Carolina Press, 1975.

Jensen, Merrill. *The Founding of a Nation: A History of the American Revolution, 1763–1776.* New York: Oxford University Press, 1968.

Johansen, Bruce E. *Forgotten Founders: Benjamin Franklin, the Iroquois, and the Rationale for the American Revolution.* Ispwich, Mass.: Gambit, Inc., 1982.

Jones, Howard Mumford. *O Strange New World: American Culture—The Formative Years.* New York: Viking Press, 1964.

Jordan, Winthrop. *White over Black: American Attitudes toward the Negro, 1550–1812.* Chapel Hill: University of North Carolina Press, 1968.

Joyce, William L., David D. Hall, Richard D. Brown, and John B. Hench, eds. *Printing and Society in Early America.* Worcester, Mass.: American Antiquarian Society, 1983.

Kammen, Michael. *Mystic Chords of Memory: The Transformation of Tradition in American Culture.* New York: Alfred A. Knopf, 1991.

———. *People of Paradox: An Inquiry Concerning the Origins of American Civilization.* New York: Alfred A. Knopf, 1972.

———. *A Season of Youth: The American Revolution and the Historical Imagination.* New York: Alfred A. Knopf, 1978.

Kant, Immanuel. *Political Writings.* Translated by N. H. Nisbet. Edited by Hans Reiss. Cambridge, England: Cambridge University Press, 1970.

Karsten, Peter. *Patriot-Heroes in England and America: Political Symbolism and Changing Values over Three Centuries.* Madison: University of Wisconsin Press, 1978.

Kerber, Linda K. *Federalists in Dissent: Imagery and Ideology in Jeffersonian America.* Ithaca, N.Y.: Cornell University Press, 1970.

————. *Women of the Republic: Intellect and Ideology in Revolutionary America*. Chapel Hill: University of North Carolina Press, 1980.

Koch, Adrienne, ed. *The American Enlightenment: The Shaping of the American Experience and a Free Society*. New York: Braziller, 1965.

Kolodny, Annette. *The Lay of the Land: Metaphor as Experience and History in American Life and Letters*. Chapel Hill: University of North Carolina Press, 1975.

Krupat, Arnold. *The Voice in the Margin: Native American Literature and the Canon*. Berkeley and Los Angeles: University of California Press, 1989.

————, ed. *Native American Autobiography: An Anthology*. Madison: University of Wisconsin Press, 1994.

Kupperman, Karen Ordhal. *Settling with the Indians: The Meeting of English and Indian Cultures*. Totowa, N.J.: Rowman and Littlefield, 1980.

Kurland, Philip B., and Ralph Lerner, eds. *The Founders' Constitution*. 5 vols. Chicago: University of Chicago Press, 1987.

Lancaster, Bruce. *The American Revolution*. New York: American Heritage, 1971.

Lawson-Peebles, Robert. *Landscape and Written Expression in Revolutionary America: The World Turned Upside Down*. Cambridge, England: Cambridge University Press, 1988.

Leary, Lewis. *Soundings: Some Early American Writers*. Athens: University of Georgia Press, 1975.

Lemay, J. A. Leo. *Men of Letters in Colonial Maryland*. Knoxville: University of Tennessee Press, 1972.

Lerner, Ralph. *Revolutions Revisited: Two Faces of the Politics of Enlightenment*. Chapel Hill: University of North Carolina Press, 1994.

————. *The Thinking Revolutionary: Principle and Practice in the New Republic*. Ithaca, N.Y.: Cornell University Press, 1987.

Levernier, James, and Douglas Wilmes, eds. *American Writers before 1800: A Biographical and Critical Dictionary*. 3 vols. Westport, Conn.: Greenwood Press, 1983.

Levin, David. *Forms of Uncertainty: Essays in Historical Criticism*. Charlottesville: University Press of Virginia, 1992.

————. *In Defense of Historical Literature: Essays on American History, Autobiography, Drama, and Fiction*. New York: Hill & Wang, 1967.

Levine, Lawrence W. *Highbrow/Lowbrow: The Emergence of Cultural Hierarchy in America*. Cambridge, Mass.: Harvard University Press, 1988.

Lipset, Seymour Martin. *The First New Nation: The United States in Historical and Comparative Perspective*. New York: Basic Books, 1963.

Looby, Christopher. *Voicing America: Language, Literary Form, and the Origins of the United States*. Chicago: University of Chicago Press, 1995.

Lovejoy, Arthur O. *Essays in the History of Ideas*. Baltimore: Johns Hopkins Press, 1948.

————. *The Great Chain of Being: A Study of the History of an Idea*. Cambridge, Mass.: Harvard University Press, 1936.

Lowance, Mason I. *The Language of Canaan: Metaphor and Symbol in New England from the Puritans to the Transcendentalists*. Cambridge, Mass.: Harvard University Press, 1980.

Lowance, Mason I., and Georgia B. Bumgardner, eds. *Broadsides of the American Revolution*. Amherst: University of Massachusetts Press, 1976.

Lutz, Donald. *The Origins of American Constitutionalism*. Baton Rouge: Louisiana State University Press, 1988.

Maier, Pauline. *The Old Revolutionaries: Political Lives in the Age of Samuel Adams*. New York: Alfred A. Knopf, 1980.

Main, Jackson Turner. *The Anti-Federalists: Critics of the Constitution, 1781–1788*. Chapel Hill: University of North Carolina Press, 1961.

———. *The Social Structure of Revolutionary America*. Princeton, N.J.: Princeton University Press, 1965.

Marsak, Leonard M., ed. *The Enlightenment*. New York: John Wiley & Sons, Inc., 1972.

Martin, Calvin, ed. *The American Indian and the Problem of History*. New York: Oxford University Press, 1987.

Martin, Terence. *The Instructed Vision: Scottish Common Sense Philosophy and the Origins of American Fiction*. Bloomington: Indiana University Press, 1961.

May, Henry. *The Enlightenment in America*. New York: Oxford University Press, 1976.

McDonald, Forrest. *Novus Ordo Seclorum: The Intellectual Origins of the Constitution*. Lawrence: University Press of Kansas, 1985.

McGiffert, Michael, ed. *In Search of Early America: The William & Mary Quarterly, 1943–1993*. Richmond: William Byrd Press, 1993.

Meinig, D. W. *The Shaping of America: A Geographical Perspective on Five Hundred Years of History*. Vol. I. *Atlantic America, 1492–1800*. New Haven, Conn.: Yale University Press, 1986.

Merrell, James H. *The Indians' New World: Catawbas and Their Neighbors from European Contact through the Era of Removal*. Chapel Hill: University of North Carolina Press, 1989.

Miller, Lillian B. *Patrons and Patriotism: The Encouragement of the Fine Arts in the United States, 1790–1860*. Chicago: University of Chicago Press, 1966.

Miller, Perry. *The Life of the Mind in America from the Revolution to the Civil War*. New York: Harcourt, Brace and World, 1965.

———, ed. *The Legal Mind in America from Independence to the Civil War*. Garden City, N.Y.: Doubleday, 1962.

Morgan, Edmund S. *American Slavery, American Freedom: The Ordeal of Colonial Virginia*. New York: Norton, 1975.

———. *The Birth of the Republic, 1763—1789*. Rev. ed. Chicago: University of Chicago Press, 1977.

———. *Inventing the People: The Rise of Popular Sovereignty in England and America*. New York: Norton, 1988.

———. *The Meaning of Independence: John Adams, George Washington, Thomas Jefferson*. Charlottesville: University Press of Virginia, 1976.

Morgan, Lewis Henry. *League of the Iroquois*. 1851. Reprinted. New York: Corinth Books, 1962.

Morris, Richard B. *The Forging of the Union, 1781–1789*. New York: Harper & Row, 1987.

Mott, Frank Luther. *A History of American Magazines*. 5 vols. Cambridge, Mass.: Harvard University Press, 1930–1968.

Murray, David. *Forked Tongues: Speech, Writing, and Representation in North American Indian Texts.* Bloomington: Indiana University Press, 1991.

Nash, Gary B. *Race and Revolution.* Madison: Madison House, 1990.

Nelson, Dana D. *The Word in Black and White: Reading "Race" in American Literature, 1638–1867.* New York: Oxford University Press, 1992.

Norton, Mary Beth. *Founding Mothers and Fathers: Gendered Power and the Forming of American Society.* New York: Alfred A. Knopf, 1996.

———. *Liberty's Daughters: The Revolutionary Experience of American Women, 1750–1800.* Boston: Little, Brown, 1980.

Nye, Russel Blaine. *American Literary History: 1607–1830.* New York: Alfred A. Knopf, 1970.

———. *The Cultural Life of the New Nation, 1776–1830.* New York: Harper & Row, 1960.

Pagden, Anthony. *European Encounters with the New World: From Renaissance to Romanticism.* New Haven, Conn.: Yale University Press, 1993.

———. *The Fall of Natural Man: The American Indian and the Origins of Comparative Ethnology.* Cambridge, England: Cambridge University Press, 1982.

Pearce, Roy Harvey. *Savagism and Civilization: A Study of the Indian and the American Mind.* Berkeley and Los Angeles: University of California Press, 1988. (First published as *The Savages of America,* 1953.)

Persons, Stow. *The Decline of American Gentility.* New York: Columbia University Press, 1973.

Peterson, Merrill D. *The Jeffersonian Image in the American Mind.* New York: Oxford University Press, 1960.

Philbrick, Francis S. *The Rise of the West, 1754–1830.* New York: Harper & Row, 1965.

Plumstead, A. W., ed. *The Wall and the Garden: Selected Massachusetts Election Sermons, 1670–1775.* Minneapolis: University of Minnesota Press, 1968.

Pocock, J. G. A. *The Machiavellian Moment: Florentine Political Thought and the Atlantic Republican Tradition.* Princeton, N.J.: Princeton University Press, 1975.

———. *Politics, Language, and Time: Essays on Political Thought and History.* 1971. Reprinted. Chicago: University of Chicago Press, 1989.

———. *Virtue, Commerce, and History: Essays on Political Thought and History, Chiefly in the Eighteenth Century.* Cambridge, England: Cambridge University Press, 1985.

Potter, Janice. *The Liberty We Seek: Loyalist Ideology in Colonial New York and Massachusetts.* Cambridge, Mass.: Harvard University Press, 1983.

Premo, Terri L. *Winter Friends: Women Growing Old in the New Republic, 1785–1835.* Urbana: University of Illinois Press, 1990.

Presser, Stephen B. *The Original Misunderstanding: The English, the Americans, and the Dialectic of Federalist Jurisprudence.* Durham, N.C.: Carolina Academic Press, 1991.

Prucha, Francis Paul. *American Indian Policy in the Formative Years: The Indian Trade and Intercourse Acts, 1790–1834.* Cambridge, Mass.: Harvard University Press, 1962.

Rabinowitz, Richard. *The Spiritual Self in Everyday Life: The Transformation of Personal Religious Experience in Nineteenth-Century New England.* Boston: Northeastern University Press, 1989.

Rakove, Jack N. *The Beginnings of National Politics: An Interpretive History of the Conti-nental Congress.* New York: Alfred A. Knopf, 1979.

————. *Original Meanings: Politics and Ideas in the Making of the Constitution.* New York: Alfred A. Knopf, 1996.

Reid, John Phillip. *The Concept of Liberty in the Age of the American Revolution.* Chicago: University of Chicago Press, 1988.

————. *Constitutional History of the American Revolution.* Madison: University of Wis-consin Press, 1986.

Reinhold, Meyer. *Classica Americana: The Greek and Roman Heritage in the United States.* Detroit: Wayne State University Press, 1984.

————, ed. *The Classick Pages: Classical Reading of Eighteenth-Century Americans.* University Park, Pa.: American Philological Association, 1975.

Richardson, Lyon. *A History of Early American Magazines, 1741–1850.* New York: Nelson, 1931.

Rodgers, Daniel T. *Contested Truths: Keywords in American Politics since Independence.* New York: Basic Books, 1987.

Rossiter, Clinton. *Seedtime of the Republic: The Origins of the American Tradition of Political Liberty.* New York: Harcourt, Brace, 1953.

————. *Seventeen Eighty-Seven: The Grand Convention.* New York: Macmillan, 1966.

Rubin, Louis D. *A Bibliographical Guide to the Study of Southern Literature.* Baton Rouge: Louisiana State University Press, 1969.

Ruether, Rosemary Radford, and Rosemary Skinner Keller, eds. *Women and Religion in America: The Colonial and Revolutionary Periods.* San Francisco: Harper & Row, 1981–1986.

Rutland, Robert Allen. *The Birth of the Bill of Rights, 1776–1791.* Rev. ed. Boston: Northeastern University Press, 1983.

Sandoz, Ellis. *A Government of Laws: Political Theory, Religion, and the American Founding.* Baton Rouge: Louisiana State University Press, 1990.

————, ed. *Political Sermons of the American Founding Era.* Indianapolis: Liberty Press, 1991.

Scheer, George F., and Hugh F. Rankin, eds. *Rebels and Redcoats: The American Revolution through the Eyes of Those Who Fought and Lived It.* New York: World Publishing Co., 1957.

Seelye, John. *Prophetic Waters: The River in Early American Life and Literature.* New York: Oxford University Press, 1977.

Sennett, Richard. *The Fall of Public Man.* New York: Alfred A. Knopf, 1977.

Shaw, Peter. *American Patriots and the Rituals of Revolution.* Cambridge, Mass.: Harvard University Press, 1981.

Shea, Daniel B., Jr. *Spiritual Autobiography in Early America.* Princeton, N.J.: Princeton University Press, 1968.

Shields, David S. *Oracles of Empire: Poetry, Politics, and Commerce in British America, 1690–1750.* Chicago: University of Chicago Press, 1990.

Silverman, Kenneth. *A Cultural History of the American Revolution.* New York: Thomas Y. Crowell, 1976.

Simmons, R. C. *The American Colonies from Settlement to Independence.* London: Longman Group, Ltd., 1976.

Simpson, David. *The Politics of American English, 1776–1850.* New York: Oxford University Press, 1986.

Simpson, Lewis P. *The Brazen Face of History: Studies in the Literary Consciousness in America.* Baton Rouge: Louisiana State University Press, 1980.

————. *The Dispossessed Garden: Pastoral and History in Southern Literature.* Athens: University of Georgia Press, 1975.

————. *The Man of Letters in New England and the South.* Baton Rouge: Louisiana State University Press, 1962.

————, ed. *The Federalist Literary Mind.* Baton Rouge: Louisiana State University Press, 1962.

Sisson, Daniel. *The American Revolution of 1800.* New York: Alfred A. Knopf, 1974.

Sloan, Douglas. *The Scottish Enlightenment and the American College Ideal.* New York: Teachers College Press, 1971.

Slotkin, Richard. *Regeneration through Violence: The Mythology of the American Frontier, 1600–1860.* Middletown, Conn.: Wesleyan University Press, 1974.

Smith, Henry Nash. *Virgin Land: The American West as Symbol and Myth.* Rev. ed. Cambridge, Mass.: Harvard University Press, 1978.

Smith, James Morton. *Freedom's Fetters: The Alien and Sedition Laws and American Civil Liberties.* Ithaca, N.Y.: Cornell University Press, 1956.

Somkin, Fred. *Unquiet Eagle: Memory and Desire in the Idea of American Freedom, 1815–1860.* Ithaca, N.Y.: Cornell University Press, 1967.

Spencer, Benjamin T. *The Quest for Nationality: An American Literary Campaign.* Syracuse, N.Y.: Syracuse University Press, 1957.

Spengemann, William C. *A Mirror for Americanists: Reflections on the Idea of American Literature.* Hanover, N.H.: University Press of New England, 1989.

————. *A New World of Words: Redefining Early American Literature.* New Haven, Conn.: Yale University Press, 1994.

Spiller, Robert E., Willard Thorp, Thomas H. Johnson, and Henry Seidel Canby, eds. *Literary History of the United States.* 1953. 4th ed. Revised. 2 vols. New York: Macmillan, 1974.

Stedman, Raymond William. *Shadows of the Indian: Stereotypes in American Culture.* Norman: University of Oklahoma Press, 1982.

Stewart, Donald H. *The Opposition Press of the Federalist Period.* Albany: State University of New York Press, 1969.

Storing, Herbert J., ed. *The Complete Anti-Federalist.* 7 vols. Chicago: University of Chicago Press, 1981.

Stout, Harry S. *The New England Soul: Preaching and Religious Culture in Colonial New England.* New York: Oxford University Press, 1986.

Swann, Brian, and Arnold Krupat, eds. *Recovering the Word: Essays on Native American Literature.* Berkeley and Los Angeles: University of California Press, 1987.

Takaki, Ronald. *Iron Cages: Race and Culture in Nineteenth-Century America.* 1979. Reprinted. New York: Oxford University Press, 1990.

Tebbel, John. *A History of Book Publishing in the United States.* Vol. I. *The Creation of an Industry, 1630–1865.* New York: Bowker, 1972.

Thomas, Isaiah. *The History of Printing in America, with a Biography of Printers and an Account of Newspapers.* Edited by Marcus A. McCorison. New York: Weathervane, 1970.

Tichi, Cecilia. *New World, New Earth: Environmental Reform in American Literature from the Puritans to Whitman.* New Haven, Conn.: Yale University Press, 1979.

Tolles, Frederick B. *Meeting House and Counting House: The Quaker Merchants of Colonial Philadelphia, 1682–1783.* Chapel Hill: University of North Carolina Press, 1948.

Toulouse, Teresa. *The Art of Prophesying: New England Sermons and the Shaping of Belief.* Athens: University of Georgia Press, 1987.

Tuveson, Ernest. *The Redeemer Nation: The Idea of America's Millennial Role* Chicago: University of Chicago Press, 1968.

Tyler, Moses Coit. *The Literary History of the American Revolution, 1785–1812.* 2 vols. New York: Putnam, 1898.

Ulrich, Laurel Thatcher. *Good Wives: Image and Reality in the Lives of Women in Northern New England: 1650–1750.* New York: Alfred A. Knopf, 1982.

Veit, Hellen E., Kenneth R. Bowling, and Charlene Bangs Bickford, eds. *Creating the Bill of Rights: The Documentary Record from the First Federal Congress.* Baltimore: Johns Hopkins University Press, 1991.

Ver Steeg, Clarence L. *The Formative Years, 1607–1763.* New York: Hill & Wang, 1964.

Voegelin, Eric. *From Enlightenment to Revolution.* Edited by John H. Hallowell. Durham: Duke University Press, 1975.

Wald, Priscilla. *Constituting Americans: Cultural Anxiety and Narrative Form.* Durham, N.C.: Duke University Press, 1995.

Wall, Helena. *Fierce Communion: Family and Community in Early America.* Cambridge, Mass.: Harvard University Press, 1990.

Wallace, Anthony F. C. *The Death and Rebirth of the Seneca.* New York: Random House, 1969.

Warner, Michael. *The Letters of the Republic: Publication and the Public Sphere in Eighteenth-Century America.* Cambridge, Mass.: Harvard University Press, 1990.

Washburn, Wilcomb E. *The Indian in America.* New York: Harper & Row, 1975.

Watts, Steven. *The Republic Reborn: War and the Making of Liberal America, 1790–1820.* Baltimore: Johns Hopkins University Press, 1987.

Weber, Donald. *Rhetoric and History in Revolutionary New England.* New York: Oxford University Press, 1988.

Webking, Robert H. *The American Revolution and the Politics of Liberty.* Baton Rouge: Louisiana State University Press, 1988.

White, G. Edward. *The Marshall Court and Cultural Change, 1815–1835.* New York: Macmillan, 1988.

White, Morton. *The Philosophy of the American Revolution.* New York: Oxford University Press, 1978.

———. *Philosophy, the Federalist, and the Constitution.* New York Oxford University Press, 1987.

Wiebe, Robert H. *The Opening of American Society From the Adoption of the Constitution to the Eve of Disunion.* New York: Alfred A. Knopf, 1984.

Willey, Basil. *The Eighteenth-Century Background: Studies on the Idea of Nature in the Thought of the Period.* London: Chatto and Windus, Ltd., 1940.

Wills, Garry. *Cincinnatus: George Washington and the Enlightenment.* New York: Doubleday & Co., 1984.

———. *Explaining America: The Federalist.* New York: Doubleday & Co., 1981.

———. *Inventing America: Jefferson's Declaration of Independence.* New York: Doubleday & Co., 1978.

Woloch, Isser. *Eighteenth-Century Europe: Tradition and Progress, 1715–1789.* New York: Norton, 1982.

Wood, Gordon. *The Creation of the American Republic.* Chapel Hill: University of North Carolina Press, 1969.

———. *The Radicalism of the American Revolution.* New York: Alfred A. Knopf, 1992.

Wright, Louis B. *The Cultural Life of the American Colonies, 1607–1763.* New York: Harper & Row, 1957.

———. *Tradition and the Founding Fathers.* Charlottesville: University Press of Virginia, 1975.

York, Neil Longley. *Mechanical Metamorphosis: Technological Change in Revolutionary America.* Westport, Conn.: Greenwood Press, 1985.

Youngs, J. William T. *God's Messengers: Religious Leadership in Colonial New England, 1700–1750.* Baltimore: Johns Hopkins University Press, 1976.

Ziff, Larzer. *Writing in the New Nation: Prose, Print, and Politics in the Early United States.* New Haven, Conn.: Yale University Press, 1991.

Zuckerman, Michael. *Peaceable Kingdoms: New England Towns in the Eighteenth Century.* New York: Alfred A. Knopf, 1970.

INDEX

abolition, abolitionists, 151; and religion, 172, 178

Adams, Abigail, 181; on women, 152–153, 182

Adams, John, 4, 7, 21, 23, 38, 70, 77, 95, 103, 105, 126, 152–153; on the American Revolution, 1–4, 6, 8–9, 80; on the Constitutional Convention, 149; on constitutions, 144–145; on Continental Congress, 17; death of, 191; on the Declaration of Independence 18–19, 126–127; on discontent, 158, 160; on Enlightenment, 29, 118; European influences on, 35; and fast days, 78; language of, 42, 120; and Massachusetts Convention (1780), 119, 136; on Paine, 117–119; on property, 155, 158; on recording history, 1–2; on religion, 42, 45, 47, 73–74, 76; and slavery, 151, 158

Adams, John, *works*: autobiography, 118–119; *Defence of the Constitutions*, 29–30, 32, 42, 136, 144–145; *Dissertation on the Canon and Feudal Law*, 88–89; *Thoughts on Government*, 117–118

Adams, John Quincy, 151

Adams, Samuel, 2

Adams, Zabdiel, 42, 70–71

Address to the Public . . . on the Present Political State of the American Republicks, 121

aesthetics, aesthetic value: of consensual literature, 6, 8, 164; and men of letters, 141; of political control, 132, 135; in revolutionary writings, 3

Africa, Africans, 172; and slave trade, 151, 156, 172, 175

African Americans, 151–153, 172; and democracy, 176; and freedom, 173–174; and law, 161–162; literature of, 170–179; and property, 158. *See also* slaves, slavery

agriculture, 46, 70, 152; literary representations of, 16, 87, 97–103

Albany Plan of Union, 132

ambiguity, 65; in literature of public documents, 128, 130–134

America, Americans, 40, 110, 121; Biblical images of, 59, 70, 77, 112 (*see also* Bible); character of, 149; communal identity of, 2, 6, 11–12, 24, 26, 38, 42, 53, 68, 79, 90, 93, 95, 106, 109, 115–116, 125, 136, 145, 170; constitutionalism in, 120, 124–125, 144–145; Edwards on, 51–52; vs. England, 7–8, 25, 48, 94, 97, 107, 109–112; vs. Europe, 88–89, 103, 108–109; in founding documents, 5, 15; futurity in, 29–30, 35, 39–40, 53, 136; and history, 22, 26, 32, 37, 42, 191; internal conflicts of, 14; law in, 106–107, 111, 118; mind of, 6, 21, 33; mob uprisings in, 112, 114; oppositional language in, 7–8, 67–68, 95; Paine's view of, 111–115; pamphleteering in, 95–97, 100, 116; political representation in, 140; and progress, 22; and property, 60, 157; as pure, 48, 66, 110, 121, 189; religion in, 21, 45, 55, 73, 78–79; Revolutionary writings in, 1–5; secularization in, 72, 77; symbology of, 9–11, 25–29, 109; in Whig mythology, 129; women in, 160, 179–186; and writing, 5, 124, 148

American Philosophical Society, 104, 108–110

Anglican Church, 57; clergy of, 47; in Parson's Cause, 90

Annual Register, 96, 129

anonymity (in writing), 92, 119, 121, 140, 182–183, 186

antebellum culture, 191

anti-catholicism, 10–11, 73

anti-episcopacy, 47

anti-Federalism, anti-Federalists, 122, 181, 189; on Constitution, 142

anti-institutionalism, 46

antinomianism, 56

Apocalypse, 47–48, 154

Articles of Confederation, 130–132, 136, 142